THE ABOLITION OF WAR

The 'Peace Movement' in Britain, 1914-1919.

THE ABOLITION OF WAR
The 'Peace Movement' in Britain, 1914-1919

KEITH ROBBINS

Professor of History
University College of North Wales
Bangor

CARDIFF
UNIVERSITY OF WALES PRESS
1976

First published 1976
© Keith Robbins
ISBN 0 7083 0622 5

Printed by The Faith Press Ltd., Leighton Buzzard, Beds. LU7 7NQ

Contents

TO

J. R. AVERY
now Headmaster, Bristol Grammar School

C. P. HILL
now Senior Lecturer in Education, The University of Exeter

M. L. R. ISAAC
now Headmaster, Latymer Upper School

for 'History' at Bristol Grammar School, 1955–1958

ACKNOWLEDGEMENTS

The author wishes to thank the following holders of copyright who kindly gave him permission to publish correspondence and apologizes if any other holders of copyright have been inadvertently overlooked: Lady Allen of Hurtwood, Miss Felicity Ashbee, Ball State University at Muncie, Indiana, Mrs. Evamaria Brailsford, the British Library Board, Miss Eglantyne Buxton, Dr. T. J. Cadoux, Cumbria County Council, The Dowager Viscountess Davidson, Lord Dickinson of Painswick, Mrs. Pauline Dower, Mr. Palme Dutt, the Fellowship of Reconciliation, Lord Henderson of Enfield, The President and Fellows of King's College, Cambridge, Professor A. K. S. Lambton, Mr. C. J. C. Lloyd of Warren Murton & Co., the London School of Economics and Political Science, the London Yearly Meeting of the Society of Friends, Rt. Hon. Malcolm MacDonald, Mr. Alexander Murray, The Warden and Fellows of New College, Oxford, Newcastle-upon Tyne University, Lord Ponsonby of Shulbrede, Res-Lib Ltd. (Bertrand Russell Ms), Mr. L. P. Scott, the Union of Democratic Control.

The author also wishes to thank the following who either granted him interviews, made relevant documentary material available or allowed him to read their unpublished theses: the late Sir Norman Angell, Miss Vera Brittain, the late Dame Kathleen Courtney, Dr. S. Kernek, Dr. R. I. McKibbin, Professor David Martin, the late Mr. Kingsley Martin, Dr. C. M. Mason, Mrs. Lucy Middleton, Edward H. Milligan, Sir Dennis Proctor, Dr. John Rae, the late Mary, Lady Trevelyan.

Professor Agnes Headlam-Morley supervised my Oxford D.Phil. thesis. Professor F. H. Hinsley and Professor James Joll encouraged me to transform it into a book. I am grateful to them all.

CHAPTER ONE

The Anatomy of the Peace Movement

War and peace seem to stand in stark contrast. War involves fighting and famine, death and destruction, darkness and despair. Peace describes a state of harmony and order. At a deeper level, however, there is a dialectical relationship between apparent opposites: without some knowledge of war the nature of peace cannot be fully appreciated. In any case, it might be argued, the line between war and peace is blurred and uncertain. States very often exist in a world which is neither at war nor at peace. In many cultures, over many centuries, skill in warfare has been a mark of distinction and a necessary condition of survival. Devotion to peace as an ideal is a relatively recent and fragile development. The 'Peace Movement' in Britain during the First World War inherited a concern for peace which was, in organized form, scarcely a century old.

It was in the aftermath of the Napoleonic Wars that the question of stimulating public interest in peace arose. About this time, many previously acceptable aspects of human behaviour were questioned by Evangelicals and Enlightened alike. Why was it not possible to 'eliminate' war together with slavery, insobriety, cruelty to children and animals and many other human vices? The British Peace Society, founded in 1816, had just such a task. Its leaders, many of them Quakers, saw themselves as directing the 'Peace Movement'. They began to establish contacts with like-minded people in France, Switzerland and the United States. Some twenty years later, their activities received fresh stimulus from the campaign for Free Trade. Cobden and Bright encouraged the idea that the surest way to prevent war was to remove trade barriers between the nations. It was, they believed, the public which would enable them to defeat the martial propensities of governments. In

7

their eyes, war was an aristocratic anachronism for in order to thrive capitalism needed lasting peace. At a time when so much was being 'improved', it was surely possible to improve on war. However, the heights scaled by Cobden and Bright were not exactly commanding and the popularity of Palmerston's foreign policy grieved the Peace Society. The Crimean War demonstrated that the power of the peacemakers was very limited. Public opinion seemed more willing to rejoice with Tennyson that the long, long canker of peace was over than to weep with Bright. The series of international peace congresses held in the eighteen-forties had seemed impressive but their results were disappointing. It took some time for the optimism they had engendered to revive.

For nearly forty years, the dominating figure in the Peace Society was Henry Richard. He was tireless in preaching the cause of peace. It was, however, only one of his interests. As an M.P. for Merthyr Tydfil after 1868 he was a powerful spokesman for Welsh Liberalism. As a Congregational minister, he was a strong Liberationist, crusading for Disestablishment. It is not therefore surprising that a number of peace advocates felt that the Peace Society was too closely identified with Nonconformist pressure groups. In the seventies and eighties a number of new societies were founded which approached the problem of preserving the peace in a different way. An influential International Law Association, American by origin but with British members, devoted itself to furthering the cause of arbitration among lawyers and politicians. Appealing to a different constituency, chiefly of Radical artisans, was the Workmen's Peace Association founded in 1871 by Randal Cremer. Cremer, who later changed the name of his group to the International Arbitration League, had extensive trade union contacts both in Britain and on the continent. After his election to parliament in 1885 he became one of the best known peace workers in the country. He also made extensive trips abroad, particularly to the United States, and was the inspiration behind the foundation of the Inter-Parliamentary Union in 1889. His idea was that regular meetings between parliamentarians from as many countries as possible would encourage mutual understanding amongst those with the power to make important political decisions. He constantly urged peace societies to pass resolutions in favour of arbitration. They had little difficulty in complying with his requests. There was also a further body, the International Arbitration and Peace Association of Great Britain and Ireland, founded in 1880 by a retired Indian Civil Servant, Hodgson Pratt. This association was avowedly secular in its emphasis, avoiding an appeal to Christian morality and concentrating on working out the best arbitration procedures.

The leaders of these groups succeeded in gaining impressive lists of signatures endorsing their favourite projects. It is clear, however, reading between the lines of their reports at annual meetings, that there were periods of personal depression, financial insecurity and political inactivity. Radicals like Richard and Cremer had assumed that 'the masses' would take their side against 'the interests'. It was both unpleasant and surprising that the masses seemed in large measure unmoved by the wickedness of war. Sir Wilfrid Lawson, the Liberal M.P. and Temperance advocate was not the only one to lament at the end of the century that what he called the Fighting interest, the Liquor interest, the Aristocratic interest, and the Ecclesiastical interest 'could none of them have been safer in the hands of a restricted franchise than they have been in the hands of the enfranchised masses.' While some recent research attempts to contest the extent of British working class enthusiasm for Empire, the peace advocates were saddened by the support for the Boer War which they observed. Some Liberal M.P.'s were indeed sharply critical of Government policy, but attempts to commit the whole party to an 'anti-war' position did not succeed. While some areas of the country, such as Wales, may possibly have been more critical than others, the results of the 1900 General Election confirmed that the electorate, as then constituted, gave strong support to the war policy. Cremer, for example, just managed to keep his seat, but his chief aide, Maddison, was defeated in a Sheffield constituency heavily dependent on armaments manufacture. With rare exceptions, the Church of England clergy supported the war. The Nonconformist churches were divided and those ministers who were 'pro-Boer' were likely to have disgruntled congregations. On the Labour side, Keir Hardie condemned the war, but I.L.P. candidates had disappointing results. Many Fabians, however, lacked any enthusiasm for farming republics and preferred the efficient tidiness of Empire. The Government did come under severe criticism as the Boer War progressed—or failed to—but public opinion as a whole did not swing round and demand a compromise peace without victory.

At the turn of the century, therefore, the British Peace Movement was in a puzzling condition. Comparable groups on the continent were enjoying a fresh lease of life, a growth only partly to be explained by the fact that some governments suddenly found that peace propaganda had the great merit of being anti-British. For the first time, it seemed, war on war, to take the title of the journalist W. T. Stead's book, evoked responses right across Europe. In 1897 the Nobel Peace Prize was instituted. The first The Hague conference on disarmament was called on the initiative of the Tsar. In Austria-Hungary, Baroness von Suttner's book *Die*

Waffen Nieder enjoyed unexpectedly wide circulation. Helpful schemes for organizing the future were constantly appearing in the United States. This growing interest in the preservation of peace needs to be stressed when so much has been written about the militarization of European opinion in these years. The Boer War did not in fact bring the contacts of British peace workers to an end. They were determined, in a new century, to inaugurate a new series of international congresses which would demonstrate the existence of a growing solidarity between peoples. It was at the Glasgow congress of 1901 that the word 'Pacifist' was first coined—by a Frenchman, Emile Arnaud, President of the International League of Peace and Liberty. The British, it seems, tried unavailingly, to insist on 'Pacificist'. It was agreed that a pacifist was anyone who, in a general sense, was working to create or perpetuate peace. The more optimistic believed that a century of peace would be an accurate description of the twentieth century.

It may be, however, that it was the existence of a war climate that stimulated this peace activity. Recent events in Britain made it difficult to suppose that there was something inevitable about the steady march of peace. The Liberal intellectuals who wrote for the *Manchester Guardian,* for example, saw little evidence of inexorable advance towards a harmonious order; indeed, they thought they were confronted by a powerful reaction against the principles of peace. J. A. Hobson, the economist, recognized the shallowness of contemporary peace sentiments. He resurrected Cobden, the 'International Man', exposed the psychology of Jingoism and analysed the nature of Imperialism—all in an attempt to remedy the situation. L. T. Hobhouse, too, admitted that the old cry of peace, retrenchment and reform was dead. The workers no longer rallied to it because they were within sight of earthly paradise. The great middle class now favoured the established order since it had too much to lose from its overthrow. Intellectual developments as well as social phenomena also worried Hobson and Hobhouse. They disliked Social Darwinism which, in its varying forms, popularized the notion of an inevitable struggle for survival. Nor was contemporary Oxford Idealist philosophy to their taste. Its interest in the problems of the State seemed dangerously non-liberal. In the popular journalism of the time, too, pacifist writers could find ample evidence that the virtues of war were being frequently extolled.

In view of these trends, the sweeping Liberal victory of 1906 came as rather a surprise to some pacifists. Naturally, they preferred a Liberal government, but they did not find it easy to extend their support wholeheartedly to any government. While they could perhaps rely on the sympathy of the large number of radical and Nonconformist members, could they trust a Cabinet which contained Grey, Asquith and Haldane in prominent positions? In this new political situation, Cremer gained great satisfaction from organizing a huge assembly of the Inter-Parliamentary Union in London in 1906. The Prime Minister, in his speech of welcome, referred to the ruinous competition in armaments. It was the task of statesmanship to reduce this burden on mankind and the new government would rise to the challenge. After a reception at Windsor, many delegates proceeded (apparently unconscious of any incongruity) to view Portsmouth dockyard. Cremer, now an old man, was at the height of his fame. He received a knighthood and the Nobel Peace Prize in 1907, but died the following year. The purpose of these official occasions was to keep the Liberal Government publicly committed to the pursuit of disarmament. All the peace groups ardently supported the calling of a second conference at The Hague. When it met, in 1907, they looked to the British Foreign Secretary to achieve a lasting agreement with Germany. The conference was a disappointment. Some, like W. T. Stead, began to make public their disenchantment with the policies of the Goverment. It was alleged that Grey was dominated by his permanent officials who refused to countenance any reduction in arms. The conscience of the Liberal Party was being restricted by the reactionary views of the Foreign Office and the Admiralty.

The peace societies, on the whole, were more restrained than Stead in their comments. The reason is not difficult to find. A Liberal Government might be disappointing, but a Conservative would be disastrous. Besides, in trying to work through the political establishment, the peace groups hoped to achieve more by permeation than they would by public criticism. They tried, however, to please everybody. The Peace Congress held in London in July 1908 offers a neat illustration. The British delegation was drawn from all the existing peace societies. They were honoured at Windsor by the King—a Peacemaker himself, of course—and were commended by the new Prime Minister, Asquith. Lloyd George, who also spoke, added a populist touch to the occasion. Was it true, he asked his audience, that the people of the world hated each other? Not surprisingly, he received a negative reply. Thus fortified, the congress then resolved that all the nations should settle their disputes through the Court of Arbitration at The Hague. There was one other significant feature. As an adjunct to the congress, the T.U.C. and the I.L.P. held a rally against war in Trafalgar Square. Before Ramsay MacDonald spoke, the London Socialist Sunday School Union Choir of Girls, dressed in appropriate white, sang 'Angel of Peace'. Thus, perfect exponent of the arbitration it advocated, the Seventeenth Universal Peace Congress made the right gestures to the established order and the working class.

After this congress, the British National Peace Council, which had been formed four years earlier, was put on a more efficient basis. It was henceforth supposed to co-ordinate the activities of the religious, radical and socialist sections of the Peace Movement. The intention was to give some coherence to a movement which, whatever its pretensions, was inchoate and disunited. It was decreed that an annual national congress should be held. There was also to be a vigorous publishing programme. In these ways it was hoped that the Council would provide a much needed forum for pacifist activity. From 1910 until 1919, the organizing secretary was Carl Heath, an ardent pacifist who had joined the Society of Friends. Despite his efforts, Heath found that the member societies took particular pleasure in stressing their distinctive rather than their common features. It was apparent to many observers that if the Peace Movement was advancing, some of its leaders were conspicuously out of step with each other.

It is not surprising that the attempt to create a vigorous National Peace Council made slow headway. In the half dozen years before 1914, complicated changes were taking place within many of the groups. New ideas were developing and new men appeared in order to propagate them. The elderly societies and their officials did not always welcome these intrusions. They had often owed their impetus to one man and after his departure found it difficult to continue his work. The International Arbitration League, for example, survived Cremer's death, but it was rather moribund. Its journal, *The Arbitrator* appeared irregularly. The ethos of the League was that of the eighteen seventies, of Liberal working men active in such bodies as the Reform League. Eminent survivals from that era still graced the list of vice-presidents, but their day was passing. The President, Thomas Burt, the veteran Northumberland Miners' M.P. was respected by all but was hardly the man to initiate any striking new policies. Younger men looked elsewhere if they were interested in the peace question. It is essential to be aware of these tensions and difficulties. Otherwise, an attempt to describe the various elements in the Peace Movement in the years just before the First World War would give a misleading impression of strength.

Conscious of its antiquity, the Peace Society still gave the impression that other associations had never been necessary. Its secretary at this juncture, the Rev. Dr. Evans Darby, was in the true line of succession, being Welsh, Congregationalist and Liberal. Its membership was still predominantly Nonconformist. There was no elaborate theological framework for its convictions: simply a reiteration that Christians held out the hand to all men of goodwill. Its speakers rarely went further than stressing the incongruity of followers of the Prince of Peace preparing vigorously for war. The absurdity of the situation was supposed to be self-evident. In addition, the Peace Society made occasional references to the waste and expense of fighting. The *Herald of Peace* therefore denounced war as both immoral and unnecessary; addresses, sermons and pamphlets all rammed the point home. They stressed that arbitration was the method of the future—Italy, for example, should have gone to The Hague with her complaints against Turkey before going to war in 1912. Yet, although arbitration was the ideal means, the incident made it clear that the vital task was to persuade men that they had a moral obligation to use it. 'We believe' said the Society's journal 'it is our business to teach and urge the *vital* factor is the moral and religious, and, that omitted, the movement lacks the great dynamic which alone will carry it to its goal.'[1] There was nothing novel about this contention and it seemingly had little effect. There were members who thought that the Society had degenerated into an established institution for the purveying of pious and worthless pronouncements. 'We are too eager for accommodation and imitation' admitted the journal. 'Pacifists are not thorough-going enough.' Too many members of the Peace Society declared that they were not 'Peace-at-any-price' men. It seemed likely that such men were hardly 'Peace-at-any-price-at-all'.[2] As in the case of the Nonconformist churches generally, it was becoming clear that the defiant ideology of dissent inherited from the past was separating from its social base. Woe unto the Peace Society when all men spoke well of it.

While the Peace Society tried to resist the encroachments of approval, it also had to make up its mind about the new trends in pacifist thinking. Other groups were talking more about the futility of war and less about its immorality. An editorial in the *Herald of Peace* welcomed the new voices, so long as they did not suppose that they invalidated the old. The fact was, however, that among 'neo-pacifists' the use of religious arguments and appeals was strongly resented. Darby protested. 'It comes to this' he wrote 'that if for a single day those who believe in God were to live as if their belief was true, the result of that one day . . . would make war impossible and armaments unnecessary.'[3] The Peace Society was also sceptical about too much stress being placed on disarmament, since reduction might leave the relative strength of nations unimpaired. States with smaller forces might be tempted to fight more often because the consequences would be less devastating. 'We believe in this Peace Society' said an editorial in

June 1914 'that if we are unable to settle our differences by negotiation we should resort to international arbitration.' Furthermore,
the Society did not want arbitration to be enforced by sanctions.
Its objection was twofold. At one level, there was no international
sovereignty behind the court which possessed the power to enforce
its decisions. More fundamentally, to attempt to enforce sanctions
against sovereign states would be not only of the nature of war, but
would be war.

Such general views did not produce any substantial adhesion
of strength to the Peace Society. Faced with this stagnation, it
decided to lend support to a campaign against the threat of
'militarism'. The most serious danger, it believed, was the agitation
to introduce some form of conscription. There was indeed considerable official alarm about the organization and recruitment of
the British Army. Lord Roberts had resigned from the Committee
of Imperial Defence in 1905 in order to be free to support compulsory military service. He deplored the decline of patriotism and
what he considered to be the neglect of the country's defences. The
National Service League was formed under his presidency, with
a membership which reached thirty-five thousand in 1909 and
which continued to rise. 'My country right or wrong' was regarded
by Roberts as the sentiment 'most treasured in the breast of anyone
worthy of the name of man.' Other public figures also thought
that the times required greater preparation for war rather than
less. 'There are encroaching opinions' Lord Rosebery told the boys
of Wellington School 'which threaten patriotism, menace our love
of country, and imply the relaxation, if not the destruction, of all
the bonds which hold our Empire together.'⁴ Support for such
sentiments came from such diverse figures as Lord Milner,
Rudyard Kipling and Robert Blatchford.

The Peace Society regarded this agitation as 'adverse to the
development of peace.' It supported a group of Liberal M.P.'s
in their 'implacable campaign' of resistance. It opened its doors to
Philip Snowden who pledged working class support for the
organizers. Meetings were held up and down the country protest-
ing against the increasing power of 'militarism'. Compulsory
military service was held to constitute a menace to British liberty
and was entirely contrary to the national interest. The campaign
had a positive as well as negative aspect. Pacifists wanted the
educational system to be reformed so that the young would not be
brought up to admire the military type. The *Herald of Peace*
regularly printed exposés of the evils of 'Scouting for Boys' and
attacked the uniformed Boys' Brigade. Pacifists liked to believe
that their campaign against conscription was successful. Their
agitation, however, was not the main reason why compulsory

military service was not introduced in peacetime. Its leading supporters were, politically, maverick figures. They were also divided
among themselves as to whether conscription was to be solely for
home defence or was to involve service overseas. The Admiralty
saw the attempt to train a mass army as something of a threat
to its position. By and large, the Army was itself not convinced
of the merits of the proposals. Pacifist protest was, therefore, a
minor element. Nevertheless, participation in the anti-conscription
campaign restored some of the Peace Society's morale; something
which it badly needed.

When the old Peace Movement talked about 'neo-pacifism', what
it chiefly had in mind was the Norman Angell campaign. Many
intelligent young men, indifferent to religion but dedicated to peace,
wanted a new approach to the entire problem. Norman Angell met
it. He swept to international and national fame with the publication
of his book *The Great Illusion* in 1910. In its various editions, it
sold over a million copies and was translated into some twenty-five
languages. Not quite forty at the time, Angell was not cast in the
conventional pacifist mould. He had been sent by his father, a
Lincolnshire businessman turned country gentleman, to school in
France and to university in Geneva. Then came a surprising turn:
he set out for the United States and spent most of the eighteen-
nineties as a cowboy, taking cattle to and fro across the Mexican
border. At the same time, he became interested in the press, and
it was as a journalist that he was sent to Paris by several American
newspapers in 1898. Later, he had his own English daily paper in
Paris before becoming, in 1905, editor of the continental edition
of Northcliffe's *Daily Mail*. From this vantage point, he became
fascinated by the way in which international news was reported
and, at times, distorted. Angell set out to clear away the myths
which stood in the way of international understanding.

At his own expense, he published in 1909, *Europe's Optical
Illusion* but it received little attention from reviewers. However,
it came to the notice of Lord Esher, confidant of kings, generals
and politicians. The Foreign Secretary referred to Angell's thesis
in a speech at Guildhall. With a new title, it became a bestseller
and provoked widespread controversy. The book studied the
relation of military power in nations to their economic and social
advantage. Hitherto, peace advocates had often been compelled to
admit that war might be in the interest, though the immoral
interest, of the victorious party. Their plea that nations had no
right to take possessions by force had not hitherto met with much
success. Instead, Angell put forward a new set of ideas. Firstly,
he argued, in the contemporary world, it was impossible for states
permanently or for any considerable period to destroy or greatly

damage the trade of others by military conquest. Trade depended on the existence of natural wealth and a population capable of working it. Secondly, even if an invasion by Germany did involve the total collapse of the British Empire he contended that 'German capital would, because of the internationalisation and delicate inter-dependence of our credit-built finance and industry, also disappear in large part.' Thirdly, for similar reasons, 'the exaction of tribute from a conquered people has become an economic impossibility. . . .' Fourthly, 'no nation could benefit by the conquest of British colonies, and Britain could not suffer material disadvantage by their loss, however much such loss would be regretted on sentimental grounds.' The crux of Angell's argument was that 'international hostilities are largely based on the notion of collective responsibility in each of the various states against which our hostility is directed, which does not, in fact, exist.' He was certain that 'if the Germans are convinced they will obtain no benefit by our conquest, they will not attempt that conquest.' He was prepared to admit that until the Germans were so convinced then aggression would have to be met by force. It was clear, however, that no leagues, ententes or understandings would avail 'if the great illusion on which the whole armament competition is based, remains undisturbed.'[5]

Angell was an ambitious man, and the success of his book gave him great scope. He was in heavy demand as a speaker all over Britain. His ideas were taken up by Lord Esher and by Sir Richard Garton, an industrialist who set up a foundation to assist him. Since Angell was determined not to be thought the leader of a pacifist sect, he accepted invitations to address the Royal United Service Institution and the Institute of Bankers. He wanted to influence men in power, not form a pressure group on traditional lines. Nevertheless, *Norman Angell* or *International Polity* clubs sprang up in the universities to spread his ideas. A new journal, *War and Peace* first appeared in October 1913. It admitted that only a real difference of outlook could justify a further pacifist publication. However, 'Norman Angellism' did get to the root of the problem in a realistic manner. It was no good calling for disarmament without removing the misconception on which armaments rested. Pacifists of the old school remained somewhat sceptical. The press and politicians who gave such praise to his ideas would desert in the time of jingo fever. Angell, however, was adamant that there was nothing sordid in using 'the common facts of the world.' He received support from J. W. Graham, a prominent Quaker, who saw no need for 'any throwing of stones by officials in the two camps.' Angell himself equally saw no grounds for a quarrel. Morality, he contended in a lecture before the South Place Ethical Society, was a statement of the interest of the community and it therefore followed that when talking of communities, interest and morality had to coincide.

Whatever may be thought of this prosposition, Angell found it difficult to be acceptable both to those who stressed interest and those who stressed morality. His personal fame grew as academics across Europe and America were converted to his views. Yet he did not want mere academic approval. He wanted to convert the mass public and when Andrew Carnegie set up a huge endowment for peace work in 1910, Angell regretted that university men like Nicholas Murray Butler were so prominently involved. He subsequently recalled that he tried to persuade Carnegie that the establishment of the facts was inadequate unless such enquiry was accompanied by penetrating propaganda. The real enemy, he considered, was the confusion in the public mind. Belief in the necessity of understanding the processes of communication led Angell to entertain a commission from Northcliffe to visit Germany. As he informed a sceptical Ramsay MacDonald, 'I do not care tuppence what his motives are, so long as the result of his motives is to put certain facts before a very stupid section of the English public, who are at present unaware of them.'[6] In pursuit of such objectives, Angell might have done better, as he subsequently confessed, to keep his movement in strict separation from the Society of Friends or the Peace Society. However, at the time, he did not allow intellectual disagreement to destroy practical collaboration. The result was that despite the ardent support of many bright young men, particularly economists from Cambridge, 'Norman Angellism' was regarded with some suspicion from all sides. The Peace Society could not understand Angell's relations with Northcliffe and soldiers. Sensible rationalists disliked his willingness to consort with Christians. Nevertheless, 'That Pacifism is on the upgrade' wrote *War and Peace* in November 1913, 'few will care to deny.' If this statement is correct, the achievement was Norman Angell's.

If the Peace Movement, as it manifested itself in the activities of these individuals and groups, was to have any influence over the course of events, it needed to penetrate larger segments of opinion, like the churches and the Labour Movement. It also needed effective spokesmen in Parliament. In some moods, pacifists were optimistic about the support they could expect from these sources.

In the years before the war, the churches, both Anglican and Nonconformist, began to interest themselves in the peace question in a new way. Some clergy and laymen, conscious of the disparity between the ideal of the Church International and the reality of churches imprisoned within national frontiers, decided to set up a specific organization to promote Anglo-German reconciliation through the churches. The prime movers of this British Council of Associated Churches for fostering Friendly Relations between the British and German peoples were two Liberal M.P.s, J. Allen Baker, a Quaker, and Willoughby H. Dickinson, an Anglican. They both looked for the day when, in Baker's words 'some great leader may arise who, with commanding eloquence and force will advocate a Christian method of settling international disputes.'[7] They both worked hard to gain contacts on the continent. Dickinson raised funds to set up a new journal, *The Peacemaker*. Its editorial proclaimed that 'No one who realises, even for a passing moment, the physical horror, the economic waste, the irreparable disaster to Christendom of a collision between the two great Teutonic peoples . . .'[8] could doubt that it ought, at all costs, to be prevented. Another anxiety drove the churchmen on. Failure to prevent war would be 'a disastrous revelation of the powerlessness of the Churches.' An Anglo-German Understanding Conference was held in October 1912 and condemned both dangerous economic competition and the hysteria of the press. Churchmen in both countries claimed to detect 'the signs of advancing cordiality in the relations of the two great peoples.' Bishop Boyd Carpenter declared the Kaiser to be 'a lover of peace, earnestly desirous of promoting the welfare of mankind; they knew him to have a simple trust in Divine guidance.' So successful were these exchanges that by June 1914 the British Council found it 'almost difficult to realise that there are still unsolved problems affecting the relations of the two countries.'[9]

In 1914, the British membership of this body was just over ten thousand. The *Peacemaker* achieved a circulation of sixty seven thousand in the same year.[10] Therefore, although drawn from the chief denominations, the British Council could not really claim to speak for the millions of ordinary church members. Historically, neither the Church of England nor the main Nonconformist churches were 'peace-at-any-price'. As the established Church, the Church of England was in a specially difficult position. Nevertheless, there was a specific Peace League for Anglicans. Canon W. L. Grane wrote *The Passing of War* in 1912 and it was well-received in other sections of the Peace Movement. At the assemblies and meetings of the main Nonconformist churches there was also a growing concern with peace. The Social Gospel, then so prevalent among Protestants, stressed the duty of Christians to participate in politics and social affairs. The preservation of peace was a vital task. Yet, for all the sermons on the subject, it was difficult to tell precisely what this commitment involved, particularly if a 'just war' should appear. In such circumstances, the only

Christian body which might be resolute was the Society of Friends.

Quakers were identified in a special way with the Peace Movement. Since the seventeenth century they had maintained their own peace testimony in difficult and dangerous circumstances. However, within the Society there was greater disagreement about its implications than outsiders believed. The peace testimony was one of a number of issues which had caused dissension in the nineteenth century. For a time, characteristic tenets and insights of Quakerism seemed likely to dissolve into general Evangelical Christianity. Many of the distinctive customs of dress and speech were abandoned. There were even Friends who held that the special task of the Society was over. By the end of the nineteenth century, however, this attitude had been held in check. Quakers rediscovered their roots and placed fresh stress on the doctrine of the 'Inner Light', specially relevant when the authority of both bible and church were being questioned. While many Victorian Friends, John Bright among them, had not held rigidly to absolute pacifism, the renewal movement stressed its vital importance. To talk about circumstances in which war was the lesser of two evils was to compromise. Nevertheless, the Quaker stress upon the individual conscience, guided by the light within, meant that it was difficult to formulate a corporate statement. The original radical doctrine had been forged in circumstances very different from those in which most Friends found themselves in the early twentieth century. For the time being, however, disagreements did not become serious. The Society had an important Peace Committee and individual Friends were active in other peace societies. The Peace Committee kept a close watch on the international situation but it did not favour extravagant proposals for the preservation of peace. A General Strike as a measure for the maintenance of peace was 'not advisable'. On the other hand, the Committee was prepared to advocate arbitration, realistically suggesting that it was better to start by securing a wide treaty between Britain and the United States as a beginning rather than offering such an agreement to every country in the world. The idea of restricting loans to foreign countries to those who were prepared to use them for peaceful purposes was also considered, but no one quite knew how this could be guaranteed.[11]

The support for the Peace Movement from the churches was therefore important, but it was wishful thinking to suppose that it could provide the basis for a powerful peace party. Christians were so divided, both politically and ecclesiastically, that a united front of the churches against war was an unlikely prospect. If the peace societies were to command political influence they would have to rely on support from elsewhere.

The aim of the Peace Movement, as so far considered, was to persuade and convince public opinion. The societies gave no thought to campaigns of civil disobedience or disruption. They accepted the existing political structure and wished simply to work within it effectively. What pressure they could exert, they would exert through parliament. They looked hopefully to those M.P.'s who wrote for their journals, addressed their meetings and sat on their committees. The Liberal Party had been the traditional home of peacemakers in the past, yet by 1911 the links had become strained. The Moroccan crisis of that year created many fears of war. Liberal journalists, almost to a man, pressed the Foreign Secretary for more information about the extent of Britain's continental commitments. Criticism of Grey's action and methods was not confined to the back benches. On this occasion, he was attacked in the Cabinet by veteran 'Little Englanders' like Lords Morley and Loreburn. There was widespread anxiety that Britain would be drawn into war by France. The critics stressed that Britain should remain on good terms with France and Germany. In the event, Sir Edward rode out the immediate storm, but discontent with his policy remained. The agreement with Russia was widely attacked by radicals because it made the independence of Persia a mockery, confirmed the domestic tyranny of the Tsar and gave the Germans just cause to feel encircled.

No one directly accused the Foreign Secretary of desiring war. The complaint was rather that he was prepared to go to the 'razor-edge of strife' when British interests were at stake. This discontent led to the formation of a parliamentary Liberal Foreign Affairs Committee in 1912. The President, Lord Courtney of Penwith, represented the old-guard while the real driving force came from two new M.P.'s, both in their early forties, Noel Buxton and Arthur Ponsonby. Buxton was a member of the well-known philanthropic family. His younger brother, Charles, would have been also active on the committee if he had not had the misfortune of losing his seat at the General Election in December 1910. The military preparations in the autumn of 1911 had so alarmed Buxton that he went to Berlin to test opinions for himself. He wanted to remove the mischievous impression prevailing in Germany that Britain was somehow hostile. He concluded that however badly governments might behave the man in the street was 'beginning to see, with Mr. Norman Angell, that any war, however successful, would be ruinous.'[12] Noel Buxton and his associates felt there was room for Germany in the Cabinet of Nations and some colonies could surely be made available as a sign of goodwill. Everything could be sorted out sensibly if the Foreign Office refrained from adding fuel to the fire of hatred and rivalry which the Yellow Press of the two countries seemed so zealously to be keeping alight. Ponsonby had an even greater distrust of the Foreign Office. Born in the shadow of the royal purple—his father was Queen Victoria's private secretary—he had himself been bound for diplomacy but had been bored and disgusted by the inane social life of the embassy where he found himself sent. He returned to the Foreign Office in London but displeased his superiors by bothering them with suggestions for reform. He then left the service and took to politics, becoming Campbell-Bannerman's private secretary. On the Prime Minister's death in 1908, Ponsonby inherited his parliamentary seat. Fame then came when his criticism of the Anglo-Russian agreement caused him to be struck off the list of guests for a royal garden party.

The two major themes of the Foreign Affairs Committee were distrust of the 'Balance of Power' and dislike of 'Secret Diplomacy'. In *Democracy and the Control of Foreign Affairs,* Ponsonby expressed alarm because one individual, with sole control over foreign relations, was under great stress yet was unwilling to tolerate outside advice. The policy of a close friendly association with another power might conceivably be right, but it was worrying that the people had no say in the matter at all. The framework of secrecy was no longer tolerable. It was the duty of Liberals and lovers of peace to devise a new method of conducting foreign affairs. The peoples of the world were on the side of peace; ambitious statesmen, jealous politicians and interested financiers caused war. Therefore, Ponsonby believed 'the more the guidance of foreign policy ceases to be bureaucratic, oligarchic and aristocratic, the greater the security and the less the risk.'[13]

Ponsonby and Buxton succeeded in getting a group of some 80–100 M.P.'s to give general support to their campaign. As a group there is nothing specially distinctive about them. They included men like W. H. Dickinson and J. Allen Baker who were already active in other peace societies and J. C. Wedgwood, A. Sherwell, P. Alden who were not so involved. Philip Morrell, husband of the exotic Lady Ottoline, succeeded Buxton as Chairman, to be followed by Ponsonby in 1914. How effective the Committee was is not easy to decide. It was a mixed body of ambitious young men and solid Nonconformists. The Government made a number of changes which could be interpreted as a response to the agitation of the Committee. A Cabinet Committee on Foreign Affairs was established, though it only had a short life. Although Grey did not bend his policy deliberately to meet his critics, he was not anxious to exaggerate the strength of the link with France for his own reasons. Dissent over foreign policy did not disappear, but just before the war it was less strident than it had been in 1911-12. Neither Ponsonby nor Buxton, for all their qualities, were men of sufficient weight in the party as a whole to mount a successful campaign against the leadership. It was in a moment of irritation at Buxton's meddling in Balkan politics that the Prime Minister described him as a 'nincompoop' but, nonetheless, the remark is revealing.[14] There was only one man with sufficient personal magnetism, experience and following who could have made the 'Peace Party' a reality. But it was Lloyd George, to the dismay of those who considered him a pacifist, who had behaved so 'provocatively' at the height of the Moroccan crisis. Time alone would tell whether this speech was an aberration or whether it represented the real Lloyd George.

The belief in 'the people' led the parliamentary radicals to show sympathy for the Labour movement. The struggle for peace and the struggle for social reform were intimately connected. 'Armaments and war are a vested interest' Ponsonby told the National Peace Congress in 1912, 'Social Reform is not. As long as you have a selfish appeal against a social appeal the selfish appeal is likely to prevail.'[15] War could be made impossible if society was reconstructed. It was therefore increasingly to Labour that pacifists looked. 'Anti-war' men, both Liberal and Labour, had been accustomed to sharing the same platform since the days of the Boer War. Many I.L.P. members couched their pacifism in the rhetoric of their Nonconformist upbringing. In sentiment there was little to distinguish them from their Liberal partners. Keir Hardie sat, symbolically, for Henry Richard's old constituency of Merthyr Tydfil. Arthur Henderson sent a message to the National Peace Congress at Cardiff in 1909 deploring the clamour for increased expenditure on armaments. The demand was influenced by feelings of suspicion and mistrust of the German nation—'feelings which are not justified by either the naval policy or the real intentions of that country.' There was nothing specifically Socialist about insights of this kind.

Nevertheless, there was an attempt to develop a distinct Labour approach to the peace question. A special conference was held at Leicester in 1911 to consider how Labour could prevent war. A resolution was passed expressing dismay at the burden of armaments and urging that international disputes should be settled 'by reason and arbitration'. Nothing distinguished the contents of this statement from many others passed at Liberal and Nonconformist assemblies. Keir Hardie's amendment calling for co-operation with European Trade Unions in a General Strike against war was lost by a narrow margin. Although this idea divided the party, most I.L.P. members agreed that the party's peace strategy should rest on the action of the international proletariat. Ramsay MacDonald had led a Labour delegation to Germany in 1908, though he was rather dismayed to find that it had been sponsored by anti-Socialist politicians. Kautsky, Ledebour and Bernstein subsequently returned the visit. The party monthly, the *Socialist Review*, was convinced that war would pass away for 'with the moral, the economic, the political justification of militarism shattered, and its literary and artistic glorification gone, the task of raising armies and popularising war politics will be too hard for governments to attempt.'[16] The only real danger was the threat of conscription, for the emancipation of the working-class would be harder if the men were disciplined outside as well as inside the factories. The I.L.P. mounted a special campaign in which Snowden was prominent. He had to confess that the working class seemed indifferent to the danger, but claimed to have no doubt about their eventual attitude.

While the Labour movement was prepared to co-operate with other pacifists, it was also in a competitive party situation. Some of its leaders were worried by the new peace theories. Norman Angell had written a special book *War and the Workers* appealing to men in factories and mines to emerge from their apathy. On its money side, the whole problem of poverty could be solved 'by the diversion into the social field of our annual expenditure upon war preparations.' Public opinion could bring about this decisive change. However, he firmly placed the responsibility for maintaining peace on all sections of the community. War was not a capitalist plot. The truth of the matter was that 'the forces, both economic and psychological making for war cut clean athwart class division.'[17] This was not good enough for Bruce Glasier. He had no wish to enter into controversy with Angell, but it was strange that he did not speak of 'our international Socialist and Trade Union movement at all—the greatest and surest of all the forces "working against war".' Socialists should not hesitate to convert pacifists to their views for, however well-intentioned, radical Liberals were wrong.[18] As Chairman of the I.L.P., Ramsay MacDonald did not dispute this contention, but he tempered his zeal with realism. There was, he claimed, no jingoism among the workers—at least, not when they were in their 'normal frame of mind'. Nevertheless it was essential to build up a sense of international solidarity indirectly. Labour, he admitted, had been misled in the past and the future task was to prevent the workers from siding with 'the war-making minorities which have always been responsible for the disruption of peace between civilised countries.'[19] As always, MacDonald saw the problem as essentially one of educating the people. He distrusted notions of a General Strike against war as much as he did violence in pursuit of domestic aims. Labour could be a great force for peace, but the workers had first to be taught to stay sane. There were a number of writers and journalists prepared to see this task as their vocation.

The most distinguished 'pacifist' writer was the economist J. A. Hobson, now in his mid-fifties. Although sympathetic to the Labour movement, he did not regard himself as a Socialist. After the publication of his classic study of Imperialism in 1902, he became a prominent speaker on peace platforms and continued his contributions to the radical press. A devotee of the South Place Ethical Society, Hobson disliked Christianity and sentimental pacifism. The idea that there might not be a rational explanation for war disturbed him. Imperialism, he believed, was 'far more rational than at first sight appears. Irrational from the standpoint of the whole nation, it is rational enough from the standpoint of certain classes in the nation.' There was too much surplus revenue to spare and it was idle for pacifists 'to attack Imperialism or Militarism as political expedients or policies unless the axe is laid at the economic root of the tree.' Popular government was vital, otherwise military imperialism and international conflict would remain. The 'deep, true, underlying harmonies of interest between peoples' were simply waiting to surface. Pacifists should not deceive themselves into supposing that their task was easy. Conservatives would use every art of menace, cajolery, corruption and misrepresentation which their control of a party machinery, landlordism, 'the trade', finance, the press, the church, 'Society', 'sport', the 'Services' made possible.[20] The sentiment beneath the sophistication was very old. 'Man' as Tom Paine put it 'is not the enemy of man, but through the medium of a false system of government.'

Although often seen in 'progressive' company, Hobson's critical disposition always made it difficult for him to be at home in either the Peace or Labour Movements. Henry Noel Brailsford, a younger man, also possessed a fluent pen, and he had the added advantage of enjoying commitment to causes. Son of a Wesleyan minister and educated at Glasgow University, his first adventures had been Byronlike in support of the Greeks in their war against Ottoman Turkey in 1897. However, the sight of a dead Turk on a battlefield in Thessaly turned him from a romantic nationalist into a pacifist. Thereafter his chief mission was to bring balm to the Balkans. At home, he was an ardent supporter of social reform and the vote for women. Unlike most other journalists who wrote for *The Nation* and other radical periodicals, he had already joined the I.L.P. In 1914, he published his celebrated book *The War of Steel and Gold*, arguing that the days of Britain's splendid isolation were over. She was 'in the full sense of the word' a European Power, closely involved with two partners in the rivalries of the continent. Pacifists should not be too gravely concerned by this development since, in Europe, the era of conquest was over. Save perhaps in the Balkans and on the fringes of the Austrian and Russian Empires, the frontiers of the modern national states were 'finally drawn'. This did not mean that all was well. The peace of Europe was secured at the expense of satellite states like Persia or Morocco where European Powers exercised control. Brailsford was closer to Hobson in his analysis than he was to Angell. While war was folly from the national standpoint, it was perfectly rational from that of a small but powerful governing class. The survival of armies and navies was due to something more rational and more permanent than the prevalence of fallacious thinking and the persistence of barbaric sentiments. Nevetheless, he was firm in his belief that 'there will be no more war among the six Great Powers.' [21]

Brailsford's optimism in 1914 was, on the whole, shared by all the groups and parties interested in the preservation of peace. Pacifists all recognized the dangers of the international situation but felt that these had been as acute in the past. There was no special danger, only the usual struggle against naval competition. The annual conferences of the I.L.P. and the peace societies all passed resolutions in 1913 against the 'ever-worsening burden of armaments.' They urged the British government to reach agreement with Germany and to this end, to abandon the right to capture private property at sea. The announcement by Churchill in November 1913 that there would be large increases in the estimates triggered off protest meetings throughout the country. Forty Liberal M.P.'s claiming to represent another sixty, saw the Prime Minister and protested at the danger to peace. A National Committee for the Reduction of Armaments was formed. Pacifists of all shades took part in the protests. There was nothing very unusual about these moves. What was significant, however, was that the opposition in the Cabinet to the First Lord's proposals was greater than normal. Some of his colleagues felt that Churchill's enthusiasm for naval matters had become too extreme. It was time for him to return to the Tory fold where such sentiments were better appreciated. To the delight of pacifists, on New Year's Day 1914, Lloyd George made a public statement deploring the proposed increase. Balfour felt that the Chancellor was hankering for an election cry which would rally what remained of the Radical Nonconformist Party, the new semi-Socialist-Radical and the Labour Party. The crisis rumbled on for some weeks. Runciman, Beauchamp, Hobhouse, McKenna and Simon warned Asquith that a large defection from the party would occur if Churchill got his way entirely. In the middle of February, Churchill agreed to accept a compromise, though it gave him substantially what he had asked for.

Pacifists were despondent at the increased estimates, yet at the same time were conscious of a changing mood in their favour. They kept up their campaign against armaments in the belief that, another time, Churchill could be stopped. G. H. Perris, a pacifist journalist, published an 'exposure' of *The War Traders* which was typical of the propaganda of the period. The task of pacifists was to break the connexion between political power and the private trade in arms. No party or government had dared tackle the problem, but recent events had made it clear that if British Democracy did not find a way of destroying 'this hydra', it would itself be destroyed. The I.L.P. took these arguments a stage further. There was no room for argument. The War Traders had to be shackled to prevent disaster. It was time to realize, Snowden told the House of Commons in March 1914, that a beautiful school was a grander sight than a battleship. He assured members that the workers of the world had no animosities, no jealousies, no divergent interests. Now was the time for them to trust each other.

The summer of 1914, therefore, found this ramshackle 'Peace Movement' in a paradoxical position. A year earlier, the President of the Peace Society had told delegates that 'never in the history of this country were we in better relations with other nations than we are today.' The feeling of strain in Anglo-German relationships had 'passed away'.[22] Nothing had occurred in the interval to cause most pacifists to change this assessment. There seemed to be grounds for supposing that the armaments race had reached a peak and would then decline. There was even, *mirabile dictu,* a Royal Commission to investigate the structure of the Foreign Office, the Diplomatic Service and the Consular Service. Critics like Ponsonby and F. W. Hirst, the editor of *The Economist,* were able to suggest changes which would weaken the position of wealth and influence, promote publicity, and enlarge contacts with the political and commercial world. The last months of peace also disclose a curious situation elsewhere. Looking back, the Chairman of Nobel Industries Ltd. described the state of the armaments firms in 1914 as one of 'the most appalling unpreparedness.' In the same year the Financial Director of Vickers dismissed French fears of a German invasion as ridiculous. The British armaments industry accepted the pacifist view that war between the major Powers would be irrational and unlikely.[23] Equally, for all their public dislike of large fleets, many pacifists found private consolation in the fact that their sheer destructive power made it unlikely that they would be used. If in no other respects united, 'War Traders' and pacifists were alike surprised when war actually did occur.

CHAPTER TWO

The Impact of the War

The relationship between public opinion and policy making is enigmatic. On a number of occasions, both publicly and privately, British Foreign Secretaries had expressed the view that public opinion limited the scope of their actions. If it did so, however, it was not in any obvious fashion. Sir Edward Grey reacted to the July crisis of 1914 as he had reacted in the past. Doubtless aware of division in the Cabinet and the country, he kept his thoughts to himself. Although prepared to resign if he could not persuade his colleagues to go to war. Grey made no attempt to whip up popular support for his views. He had never taken the public into his confidence and it was a little late to start. When the situation was so critical, it was not the time to begin a national debate on the question of relations with Europe. There was no attempt to restrict the free expression of opinion, but equally Grey did not regard the views of the press as constituting that opinion. In a fluid situation, the politicians had to make their own estimates of the state of national feeling.

When the full gravity of the summer crisis of 1914 became apparent, the Peace Movement did its best to persuade the government that it represented public opinion. At one level, sympathetic M.P.'s tried to persuade Cabinet Ministers to stand out against war; at another, there were meetings and demonstrations. The campaign against entry was hasty and improvised, and could have been more successful if events in Europe had turned out differently. The agitation was not specifically against all war as such. The emphasis was on British 'neutrality' in the dispute, and although the committees were chiefly composed of Liberal and Labour supporters, they were not necessarily pacifists in a strict sense. Lord Rosebery, for example, not normally regarded as a hero by pacifists, was among those who felt grave doubts about the wisdom of British involvement. Although Grey was his former disciple, he regarded the

Foreign Secretary's alignment with France as quite mistaken. The argument that Britain should keep out was therefore adopted both by those who favoured a more judicious intervention later and by those who never wanted to fight at all. An agreed end masked very different reasoning.

Many neutralists also contended that it was premature for the nation to be forced to a decision on the question of war or peace. What happened on the continent concerned the continent. Britain was not part of Europe and only if the war spread and invasion threatened would a choice have to be made. The existence of the English Channel meant that the country could wait to be attacked. If an invasion was mounted then the aggressor would be clearly revealed and the country would rally in self-defence. There was, again, nothing specifically pacifist about this view; strong convictions about British detachment from Europe were not the prerogative of any one political party and could lead as easily to support for a powerful navy as to pacifism. Nor were Balance of Power arguments altogether despised. Shall we fight for a Russian Europe, was the question asked in the manifesto of the Neutrality League. Once Germany was defeated—and it was generally assumed that this would be the case—Russia would dominate Europe. It was a horrifying prospect to be subordinate to a state with such a huge population, only partly civilized and governed by a military autocracy largely hostile to western ideas of political and religious freedom. Germany, on the other hand, was highly civilized, racially akin, and with similar moral ideals. The last war Britain had fought had been to check Russia and it was absurd to contemplate an intervention which could only promote her expansion. Britain should stand aside and, as a neutral, exercise pressure on both combatants. It was an attractive argument both to Liberals who feared Russian power in Europe and Tories who feared it in Asia. Again, non-intervention had no necessary connexion with pacifism.

For a short time, neutrality did not seem a hopeless cause. The leading Liberal newspapers, the *Daily News*, the *Daily Chronicle* and the *Manchester Guardian* were all against intervention. Half a million critical pamphlets were speedily printed. Three hundred sandwich men patrolled most of the main streets of London. The Liberal intelligentsia—Gilbert Murray, L. T. Hobhouse, Bertrand Russell, G. Lowes Dickinson, J. A. Hobson, Graham Wallas among them—were mobilized in support of the campaign. It was supposed that at least half the population—measured by resolutions and statements from churches, constituency parties, trade unions and newspapers—felt that a sufficient case for war had not been made.

Since being neutral meant carrying on as before, they argued that there was much to be said for doing just that.

This display of public opinion would have to be matched by pressure in the House of Commons if it was to be effective. Several years earlier, Ponsonby had warned Lloyd George that the peace group in parliament might not seem very influential but it did represent a depth of feeling in the country.[1] Now was the time for the House to appreciate this fact. There seemed to be a promising base of dissent since, by some calculations, there were two hundred M.P.'s who were against the war—enough to prevent a Liberal government carrying on without Tory support. Eighty Irish Nationalists were apparently to be joined by a similar number of dissident Liberals, with forty Labour men making up the total. This figure of two hundred, however, was rather notional. The three groups did not act in a concerted fashion. If the Irish voted against intervention it might cause some wavering English Liberals to support their party. In political terms, therefore, the threat of a massive vote for peace was a possibility, though not a probability. For the moment, Ponsonby, as Chairman of the Foreign Affairs Committee of Liberal M.P.'s, became an important figure.

At a meeting on 29 July, a dozen Liberals instructed him to write to the Foreign Secretary expressing the view that in 'no conceivable circumstances' should Britain depart from a position of 'strict neutrality'. In a covering letter to Sir Edward, Ponsonby explained that the danger of war was assumed to come from France and Russia. If these two Powers were informed that 'on no account' would Britain be drawn in, 'it would have a moderating effect on their policy.' He also sought an interview with Grey, which was granted. When they met, the Foreign Secretary argued that it would be wrong to make an open statement that Britain would stay out of the war. Uncertainty as to the country's intentions helped his diplomacy. He hoped that Ponsonby's group would not embarrass him. Could they delay making a public statement for at least a few more days? Ponsonby reported this conversation to a gathering of over twenty Liberal M.P.'s on the following day, 30 July. They instructed him to write to the Prime Minister that they had considered demanding a party meeting, but had decided against publicity on the grounds that it might disturb Grey's diplomacy. Nevertheless, they stressed their 'strongest possible convictions' that Britain should not fight a war in which 'neither treaty obligations, British interests, British honour or even sentiments of friendship are at present in the remotest degree involved. . . .' Ponsonby added that he might not be able to speak for more than thirty members but they were 'representative men and in my opinion nine-tenths of the party are behind us.'[2]

The Prime Minister no doubt discounted the latter claim, though he appreciated the strength of feeling which did exist. As things stood, however, the Cabinet itself was not committed to intervention 'at present'. 'Our actions must depend upon the course of events,' Asquith wrote 'including the Belgian question and the direction of public opinion here.'[3] Despite previous suspicion of him, most of the group were prepared to admit that Grey was doing 'his hardest and doing his utmost to prevent a general war' as T. E. Harvey, Liberal M.P. and Quaker wrote to his father. The great majority of the Cabinet, he believed, wanted to keep Britain out, but a minority did not—'one dreads the influence of Churchill.'[4] The following day, however, Churchill wrote to assure Ponsonby that so long as no treaty obligation or true British interest was involved, he shared the desire for neutrality. Balkan quarrels were no vital concern of Britain. He warned, however, that the march of events was sinister and the extension of the conflict 'by a German attack upon France or Belgium would raise other issues than those which now exist and it would be wrong at this moment to pronounce finally one way or the other as to our duty or our interests.'[5] Despite their claims to great influence, Ponsonby's group was in fact trapped. By agreeing to keep silent, they had forfeited their chance of linking up effectively with public disquiet. Like everybody else, they had to watch events and leave the final decision to the Cabinet.

The story of the waverings in the Cabinet during these critical days has been told in great detail elsewhere and there is no call to repeat it. Neutralists were, of course, right to suppose that there was opposition at the highest level to going to war. Morley, Burns, Lloyd George, Harcourt, Beauchamp, Simon, Pease, Samuel and McKinnon Wood were all in varying degrees unhappy. Some did not like Serbia, some objected to war on behalf of France and Russia and some felt that everything hinged upon the treatment of Belgium. Lloyd George was best equipped to lead a public campaign against intervention but, despite prompting from C. P. Scott of the *Manchester Guardian* and others, he refused to be drawn. His reasoning in these anxious days can only be a matter of conjecture. The invasion of Belgium decided the other waverers, or at least gave them a convenient excuse for stifling their doubts. In the end, despite earlier rumours, there were only two resignations from the Cabinet: Lord Morley and John Burns. Grey's speech to the House of Commons on 3 August completed the defeat of the neutralists. The remaining dissentients passed a resolution that '. . . no sufficient reason exists in present circumstances for Great Britain intervening in the war and most strongly urges His Majesty's Government to continue our negotiations with

Germany with a view to maintaining our neutrality.'[6] Their request had no chance of success.

However much Ministers may have purported to have listened to public opinion, the decision to go to war had been taken by a small group of men. C. P. Scott, writing on 5 August, found it 'a monstrous thing that the country should find itself at war to all intents and purposes without being consulted.'[7] It was a galling situation for the Peace Movement. When the crisis came, its pretensions were exposed; the congresses, conferences, resolutions, sermons and good intentions counted for very little. A group of leading British churchmen, on their way to a conference at Constance to discuss international questions with their continental counterparts, had hastily to return. Their governments did not require their services at this juncture. Norman Angell, too, had just finished what he regarded as a highly successful International Polity Summer School. The delegates went away on 24 July convinced that public opinion was moving in their direction. Angell and his associates had just reiterated that if Germany were beaten, 'German competition would go on just as before.' The new pacifism needed only to be understood 'by no more than quite a small number of people' to be effective. They thought this was happening. As the international crisis developed, the Angellite journal, *War and Peace,* told its readers that as regards the dispute between Austria and Serbia, 'whatever view we may take of the merits of the quarrel, it is not our affair.' The prime obligation was to see that 'Great Britain shall have no part or lot in the conflict.'[8] The coming of war showed, however, that Angell had not converted either 'the mass mind' or the 'influential few'.

If the new pacifism failed, so did the old. The Peace Society's conduct during the crisis was somewhat handicapped by the fact that its President, J. A. Pease, was a member of the Cabinet. He wavered, but in the end did not resign. To many, his conduct was an example of the Society's ineffectiveness. It could not protest vigorously because many of the long-established 'peace' families, like the Peases, were not in fact strong opponents of intervention. It seemed that all the Peace Society could do was to issue a statement on 5 August declaring, unexceptionably, that the war would never have broken out if its principles had been followed.

The hopes that the various churches would not support the war were also disappointed. 'Even the foremost pacifist leaders of the Churches have surrendered', lamented the *Herald of Peace.* 'Up to a certain point they were firm. At that point their Christianity failed them, and they had to leave it, as unworkable.'[9] It would, indeed, have been surprising if the hierarchy of the Church of England had opposed intervention. Yet, although some Bishops may have committed themselves to phrases which they later regretted, the public statements and private sentiments of most Bishops were of regret and anguish. Nevertheless, the war was just. The 'surrender' was also conspicuous among Free Churchmen. Shortly before the invasion of Belgium, Sir William Robertson Nicoll, editor of the influential *British Weekly* had informed Lloyd George that Nonconformists would not fight. In the event, however, they fell into line, using the treatment of Belgium as the reason or excuse for their conversion. The fact that the veteran Baptist pro-Boer, Dr. John Clifford, supported the war probably swayed many in their decision. For him the issue was plain: Kaiser or Christ. In a further sermon he declared that the war was one 'of principles, central and fundamental to man's existence, development, progress and well-being in all the coming ages.' The struggle was 'for the rights of the human soul to freedom, independence and self-control against an arrogant, autocratic, swaggering and cruel military caste.'[10] He did not deny that Britain had herself sustained the false doctrine of the Balance of Power. Nevertheless, there could never be future improvement unless Germany was defeated. It would then be the time to destroy for ever the fallacy that the way to peace was to prepare for war. Similar sentiments can be found in innumerable sermons at this time. It is significant that it was at the City Temple in London that Lloyd George made one of his early speeches on the war. Its minister, the Rev. R. J. Campbell had frequently appeared on peace platforms before the war. The occasion set the seal on Nonconformist support.

The Society of Friends was in a different category from the other Nonconformist bodies. It issued a general statement on 8 August. Friends described the conditions which caused the war as 'unchristian' and urged that conflict should not prevent love and charity being shown to all men. Even at this early juncture, they urged that consideration be given to the situation which would arise at the end of the war. Finally, they expressed the hope that it would not be conducted in any harsh vindictive spirit. Notwithstanding this statement, Quakers were split by the .fighting. Many Friends agreed with the action the government had taken, and younger members rushed to enlist. Probably many of these were 'birthright' Friends who were members of the Society by family tradition rather than personal conviction. Leading Quaker writers were extremely critical of their actions. Edward Grubb, for example, attacked those who felt that the testimony that all war was anti-Christian could be 'put into cold storage until times were more favourable for bringing it out.' It was imperative for the Society to stick to its conviction that the 'true way of life' was possible for nations as well as for individuals, and that international harmony depended upon acceptance of this way.[11] Despite Grubb's strictures, Friends continued to enlist. It is impossible to give an accurate figure, but it is likely that by 1917 between a third and a quarter of the total number of eligible Friends had enlisted.[12]

Disappointed by the churches, pacifists looked hopefully to the Labour Movement. Here, as elsewhere, the right noises seemed to be heard. The Labour M.P.'s published a manifesto on 30 July declaring their support for Grey in his attempts to preserve peace, but suggesting that the country should on no account be dragged into the European conflict in which it had 'no direct or indirect interest'. It called upon all Labour organisations to oppose, in the most effective way possible, any action which might involve Britain in war. This stand seemed resolute. On 1 August, the manifesto of the British Section of the International Socialist Bureau was issued under the signatures of Keir Hardie and Arthur Henderson. 'Hold vast demonstrations against war in every industrial centre' workers were urged. 'Compel those of the governing class and their press who are eager to commit you to co-operate with Russian despotism to keep silence and respect the decision of the overwhelming majority of the people. . . . Down with class rule. Down with the rule of brute force. Down with war. Up with the peaceful rule of the people.'[13]

On 2 August, a large protest meeting was held in Trafalgar Square. Keir Hardie, Arthur Henderson, Mary Macarthur, Margaret Bondfield, Will Thorne, George Lansbury and others all spoke against the war. Once again, resolutions were passed with acclamation declaring opposition to any steps to support Russia, either directly or in consequence of an undertaking to France. Such a step would be disastrous to Europe and offensive to the political traditions of Britain. The invasion of Belgium, however, shattered this show of unity. While Hardie, Lansbury and others did not change their minds, the prospect of leading a mass movement against the war disappeared. Henderson however, in a strong position as Secretary of the National Executive Committee of the party, did change his mind. Reluctantly, he supported the action the government had taken. The views of the Chairman of the Parliamentary Party, MacDonald, were enigmatic. He did not appear on the Trafalgar Square platform. Some believed that he did not want to commit himself to a public statement; others, that he had stayed at home preparing a speech which would sweep the House of Commons against the war. He did indeed speak in the debate on 3 August, declaring that if Grey had come before the House and said that the country was in danger, 'I do not care what party he appealed to, or to what class he appealed, we would be with him

C

and behind him.' However, MacDonald claimed that no such case had been made and he was not persuaded that war was justified. Such a statement clearly implied that there were circumstances in which he would support war. As he stated in an article in the *Socialist Review,* non-resistance was 'emerging from the moral evolution of the world.' He waited for it 'like Simeon on the temple steps' but such doctrines had to be 'embodied before they can be followed.'[14] The division in the parliamentary party between supporters and opponents of the war led him to resign the Chairmanship. Whether he was compelled to resign it is another matter. Personal relations between Hardie, Snowden, Henderson had been poor. For several years the Labour Party had made little electoral progress and its leadership was divided on the question of its relationship to the Liberal Party. It is as likely that MacDonald used the occasion of the war to step down from an office which had become distasteful as that he was driven out for his pacifist convictions. He continued to retain his post as Treasurer on Labour's National Executive Committee throughout the war. The I.L.P. statement that MacDonald resigned because of 'his desire to preserve a free hand in criticism, to be free to state the case against British diplomacy' underestimates the complexity of the situation.[15]

Further to the left, not even the British Socialist Party was immune from the 'virus of chauvinism'. For years the question of war had divided its members. Hyndman, its veteran leader, held to the view that nations had a right of self-defence. In 1913 the elections to the party's executive had resulted in success for more orthodox Marxists. Nevertheless, when war broke out, the entire executive signed a manifesto which recognized that the workers of Europe had no quarrel with one another and that the war was the product of the struggle for the domination of the world market, but which also recognized that the national freedom and independence were threatened by Prussian militarism. The party therefore desired 'to see the prosecution of the war to a successful issue.' Members volunteered for military service; some even became army recruiting agents. In Scotland, John Maclean was rather isolated in his refusal to accept this 'abdication'. For him the issue of aggression was quite irrelevant. 'Let the propertied class go out, old and young alike,' he urged 'and defend their blessed property. When they have been disposed of, we of the working class will have something to defend, and we shall do it.' He had some support on Clydeside, but not enough to carry the whole party—at least for the time being.[16]

It was, therefore, apparent that not only had the Peace Movement failed to stop the war, but it was itself in a parlous condition. All over the country there must have been many who wrote of the outbreak of the war that 'from the internal point of view a war may do good by cleansing public life of its present excrescences. . . . Ponsonby, Byles, Keir Hardie and the like, by bringing every one up with a round turn to the realities of life.'[17] The reality of life for pacifists was that the international acquaintanceship cultivated by a conference-going elite of Christians and Socialists had crumbled. The great majority of the British people saw the war in straightforward national terms. It was also clear that even many who had taken part in the activities of the Peace Movement had deserted to the front. Now a new set of questions had to be answered. In this changed situation, when the very existence of the nation was in danger, what did it mean to be a pacifist? It seemed ludicrous to describe people as pacifists when they had joined up or were in other respects actively supporting the war. But did this mean that the only true pacifist was one who tried to stop the conflict by actively disrupting the war effort, or was it sufficient to oppose the war passively? In the context of 1914 did pacifism imply opposition in principle to all wars whatsoever or simply to the particular war which had started? The pre-war Peace Movement had not probed these issues too deeply for fear of revealing disunity. Now they could no longer be avoided.

The fact that, initially, the war was fought by volunteers meant that, for a time, a sharp confrontation with the authority of the state was unnecessary. While all sorts of social and moral pressures existed, men were not legally compelled to join up. However, in view of their pre-war struggles against conscription, pacifists did not believe that this situation would last for very long. They also feared that there would be other restrictions on freedom, to such a degree that British society might fall the victim of 'militarism'. Did this mean that the pacifist should not simply oppose 'fighting', narrowly defined, but also this wider 'militarism'? And if conscription was introduced, should the pacifist refuse to enlist? If so, to what lengths should he carry his refusal? These questions raised formidable issues in political philosophy, carrying the Peace Movement far away from its pre-war discussions on arbitration.

Equally perplexing, and equally divisive, was the extent to which pacifists should discuss the nature of the peace which would follow the ending of hostilities. Was it their duty to prepare plans and documents while the war was still in progress, and if so, were these plans to be kept private or to form the basis of public discussion? Further, was it right to advocate 'peace by negotiation' and to do so in and out of season regardless of whether defeat or victory threatened? Was it right to publish and circulate critical interpretations of the causes of the war with the intention of showing that France and Russia, even Britain, were not free of responsibility?

The issues of conscientious objection, 'peace by negotiation', and planning for the future peace were all inter-related. Many individuals were simultaneously concerned with all of them throughout the war. Others, however, devoted themselves largely to one aspect to avoid frittering away their energies. Some even disapproved of one kind of concern while devoting themselves to another. The problems were, of course, not equally important at the same time. The aim of subsequent chapters is both to isolate the distinctive issues and to show how the individuals and groups which concerned themselves with them were related to each other. All the time, the scope of their activities and their chances of success depended on factors largely beyond their control; the progress of the war itself and the political behaviour of the nation.

The immediate problem in the first few months of the war was whether any kind of Peace Movement would survive at all. It soon became clear that neither of the two Cabinet Ministers who had resigned intended to place themselves at the head of an active opposition to the war. At seventy-five Morley was content to disappear into his library. He refused to make public speeches or write articles on the war and correspondents who asked for his views received laconic postcards. He only emerged to have the occasional dinner with his contemporaries like Lords Bryce and Courtney of Penwith. It was unlikely that he would stop the war. John Burns was similarly reticent. No one was quite clear why he had resigned. In his diary for 27 July, however, he held that, quite apart from the merits of the case it was his 'especial duty' to dissociate himself and the principles he held and the 'trusteeship for the working classes' which he carried, from such a universal crime as the contemplated war would be. He received applause from admiring Liberal M.P.'s like T. E. Harvey, J. King, P. A. Molteno, A. Williams and others, but he was not inclined to follow the advice contained in the letter from Emily Hobhouse that he should 'join the ranks of Labour, the only party likely to save us now.' [18]

It was a different story with the other member of the government to resign, Charles Trevelyan, who had been a junior minister at the Board of Education since 1908. Son of the historian and Liberal politician Sir George Otto Trevelyan, he had been M.P. for Elland since 1899. At that stage he had not been 'pro-Boer' and wrote to his fellow Northumbrian and Cambridge contemporary, Walter Runciman suggesting that they should employ all their efforts 'to showing that if R(osebery) A(squith) and G(rey) were to take the lead, they would have at their call . . . a set of vigorous young politicians such as are not to be found in the other sections of the party.'[19] Trevelyan's views subsequently changed, though, as

Ponsonby remarked in September 1914, as a member of the government he had not been closely associated with those who during the previous half dozen years had been continually fighting against armaments, the Balance of Power and secrecy.[20] However, his actions in August 1914 were not greatly inhibited by this membership. He helped Graham Wallas organize a Neutrality Committee on 1 August and, in fact, financed its operations. He kept in close contact with his friends in the Cabinet, particularly Runciman and Samuel, urging them to distinguish between German policy in temporarily violating Belgian soil and a specific intention to destroy its independence. Only the latter, in his view, could justify going to war. A memorandum from young Philip Baker (son of J. Allen Baker) fortified him in this contention.[21] Trevelyan's views made little impression. After hearing Grey's speech on 3 August he was bitterly depressed. 'The Entente was an alliance after all' he wrote to Runciman 'no less real in Grey's mind because it was not written. That whole policy I believe to have been wrong. . . .'[22] In his opposition to the war he was at variance with his younger brother, the historian G. M. Trevelyan, an initial supporter of the Neutrality League but a convert to war after the invasion of Belgium.

Trevelyan, at forty-four, belonged to a different generation from either Morley or Burns. Although some of his admirers felt that he had sacrificed his political career by his action, he had in fact not made as much ministerial progress as he expected. He was therefore prepared to take a risk. Desiring immediate action, he sketched out a plan for a British Democratic League or a British League for uniting the democracies of Europe. The objective would be to secure peace at the earliest possible moment, to press for a complete change in the character of British diplomacy, to establish close links at the end of the war with democratic parties in Europe and to combat the doctrine that armaments promoted peace.[23] His first move was to write to E. D. Morel to ask whether he would act as secretary of the new body. It would consist of 'Liberal members united for common action on the war question trying to establish connection with the Labour Party.' He mentioned the names of Ponsonby, Morrell and Rowntree as likely to be associated.[24]

Morel expressed interest in the proposal. He had known Trevelyan for several years. They had corresponded on the subject of Britain's links with France. Trevelyan had become convinced, after a visit to Berlin in 1913, that it was the belief that Britain was obliged to send an army to support France 'and absolutely that alone, which keeps the Germans from the best relations with us.'[25] He considered that the events of 1914 justified all his earlier anxieties. Morel shared these fears and resolved to devote all his formidable energies to the new project. Of Anglo-French parentage, he had made his reputation as organizer of the Congo Reform Association a decade earlier. His work for that cause turned him into a fierce critic of the entente with France, the Foreign Office and the Foreign Secretary. As an agitator he was very successful, being both self-confident and self-righteous. He was also very ambitious, having been prospective Liberal candidate for Birkenhead for several years before 1914. If he entered the House he saw himself as a potential Foreign Secretary. In a book, *Morocco in Diplomacy,* published in 1912, he made it clear that in his view Germany was not being fairly treated. He felt Englishmen were misinformed about the real sentiments of the supposedly peace-loving, laborious, thrifty masses of the French nation. This became something of an obsession and it is tempting to find an explanation for his Francophobia in his personal circumstances. The events of 1914 confirmed him in his views.

Contact was then made with MacDonald and Angell. The four men already knew each other. Trevelyan and MacDonald had previously collaborated—not altogether successfully—in the running of an advanced Liberal journal the *Progressive Review* in the late eighteen nineties. The quartet soon agreed to distribute a private circular which expressed deep dissatisfaction with the general course of pre-war policy. They believed that a turning point in national history had arrived. The democracy should assert itself and prevent a repetition of the disaster of war. Three steps would be necessary to achieve this goal: the end of secret diplomacy and its replacement by parliamentary control, the creation of international understanding based on popular parties rather than on governments, and the establishment of a peace settlement that neither humiliated the defeated nation nor artificially rearranged frontiers in such a way as to cause future conflicts.

There was little novelty about such sentiments. The problem, however, was to relate them to the immediate situation of the war. Trevelyan's own original first point, 'to assist in securing peace at the earliest moment', had disappeared from the circular, but had it disappeared from his mind? Was the Union of Democratic Control (U.D.C.)—as the group called itself shortly afterwards—a 'stop the war' body? Could it include both those who supported the war, however reluctantly, while endorsing the long-term objectives, and those who opposed the war? Was it to be a high-powered discussion-group or a pressure group with political ambitions? It was the ambiguity upon these central issues which troubled many of those who were approached for support. A clear division soon appeared between the former neutralists—naturally they were approached first—who opposed public discussion and those pacifists who wished to see even issues like the responsibility for the war debated in public. Trevelyan began to find himself confronted with the choice between a body which would have the approval of respected and influential public figures and one which would be somewhat disreputable. It could either rely on the contacts of men like C. P. Scott, Lord Bryce and Lord Loreburn or it could take a leap in the dark in the hope, ultimately, of creating a new political force. Trevelyan's brother George, fresh from his biography of John Bright and mindful of the Crimean War, advised 'You will be more effective for peace when the time comes if you show patriotism now and don't make yourselves wildly unpopular.'[26]

Some of those who might have been expected to lend assistance ruled themselves out from the beginning. Many previous critics of government policy would have agreed with Barbara Hammond when she wrote to Lady Mary Murray: 'I wish Ramsay Mac-Donald wouldn't argue that because we have sinned about Finland and Persia we must also sin about Belgium. . . .'[27] There would also be agreement with L. T. Hobhouse when he wrote to John Burns: 'We cannot continue criticism of the policy which has led to this war as we did in the case of South Africa, for our safety is at stake. We can none of us now think of anything but this one object.'[28] Trevelyan tried to counter these anxieties when he assured Graham Wallas that it was their intention to prepare, but not to publish, relevant literature, so as to be ready to serve the public when it wanted to think again. Wallas was not happy and refused to join. His reservations were well-founded. Morel and MacDonald saw no reason to hold their fire, believing that there was little hope of gaining a good cross-section of support anyway. MacDonald published an outspoken attack on Grey's foreign policy. Morel drew up a draft in which he argued that the military superiority of the Franco-Russian alliance had forced Germany to march through Belgium.[29] In order to keep the balance, Trevelyan tried to persuade Bryce to join. There was, he stressed, 'an enormous underlying opinion, at present obscured by the anxieties of the situation, craving for reasonable explanation and discussion, and utterly dissatisfied with the pleas of the Government and the patriotism of the Press.' Bryce was afraid that the group would be led astray and campaign prematurely for a negotiated peace.[30] When he met Morel, Trevelyan and MacDonald, C. P. Scott was disturbed to find that what he termed the 'Watching Committee' was fast developing into an acting committee 'part of whose function was to expose the diplomatic errors which had involved us in the war.'[31] He took exception to this change of policy and, in response, the publication of Morel's critical pamphlet was postponed for the time being.

When the original private circular was published in the *Morning Post* on 10 September, another crisis developed. Morel's constituency association informed him that it was 'against you publishing this document at a time of national crisis'.[32] Morel denied that he had published it: the newspaper had got hold of a copy. As a result of this disclosure, however, a week later Trevelyan, MacDonald, Angell and Morel wrote an open letter to the press. They had no alternative if they were to rebut charges of secret pro-German activity. Unless they stood firm, Trevelyan wrote to Ponsonby, they would be depriving public opinion of the eventual opportunity to insist on democratic diplomacy and would end 'by being classed with those who approve the war.'[33] C. P. Scott took the contrary view. In the face of patriotic enthusiasm, it would be sensible for the U.D.C. to restrict its activities.[34] Trevelyan saw no need to tread carefully. He considered that the tide of war had turned and England no longer stood in any sort of danger—'Our troops are victorious.' There was, therefore an immediate need to think about peace terms.[35] The contents of the letter were sensible. It was reasonable to urge a plebiscite before territory was transferred from one state to another. It was desirable to urge that parliament should give its sanction to any treaty signed by a British government. Democratic control of foreign policy, the abolition of the Balance of Power, and the drastic reduction of armaments and control of their manufacture, were also necessary steps. Scott thought the campaign injudicious and informed Morel that he was 'better out of it'.[36]

Other prominent Liberals who had taken part in the preliminary stages also dropped out at this point. Arnold Rowntree, Quaker Liberal M.P. for York, who had told the House of Commons on 3 August that he would have nothing to do with the war, now made it clear that he would have nothing to do with peace either. Everybody was in some way to blame for the international catastrophe, he told Morel, and while the government had such tremendous burdens to carry he was prepared to 'err on the side of reticence'.[37] Philip Morrell, too, had protested against the tone of Morel's writing, particularly his assault on Grey's foreign policy, which amounted to a personal attack on the Foreign Secretary. That was not the way to attract support from Liberals.[38] Even Trevelyan was a little embarrassed, no doubt recalling that as late as January 1905, he talked of the essential stupidity 'of the present gang' and singled out Asquith and Grey as 'alone fit to lead.'[39] Morel's attacks on Grey repelled others too. MacDonald had tried to persuade Professor Gilbert Murray, a former neutralist, to join the Union, arguing that it would be 'one of the biggest things that we have seen in our time.' He detected the working of the war spirit and feared that 'the country would demand the complete humiliation of Germany.'[40] At this juncture Murray did not find this such a disturbing prospect. 'When I see that 20,000 Germans have been killed in such-and-such an engagement' he wrote in the *Hibbert Journal* in October 1914, 'and next day that it was only 2000, I am sorry.' He did not want to crush Germany, but England was fighting not just for her own survival but 'for the liberty of western Europe, for the possibility of peace and friendship between nations; for something which we would die rather than lose. And lose it we shall unless we can beat the Germans.'[41] He did not join the U.D.C.

Despite such rebuffs, the U.D.C. pressed on. From the outset, Morel started to establish local branches, usually building on existing peace contacts. Above them stood a General Council and an Executive. The Executive consisted of the original founders, together with such as they co-opted. At the first meeting of the General Council on 17 November, Morel outlined the history of the Union, reported a balance in the bank of nearly £1,500 and a steadily increasing membership. A General Committee of eighteen was announced, which, by including Labour men like Henderson, Anderson and Jowett, and Liberals like R. D. Denman, M. Philips Price and H. B. Lees Smith, brought together players and gentlemen. Other prominent members were Brailsford, Hobson and Bertrand Russell.

Despite this apparent vigour, it remained difficult for outsiders to understand exactly what the Union stood for, especially in regard to the war. The letter which had been sent to the press on 17 September stated that there was 'no question of this association embodying a "stop-the-war" movement of any kind, not a suggestion even has been made as to the stage in the military operations at which peace should be urged. The whole emphasis of our effort is laid upon indicating clearly the fundamental principles which must mark the final terms of peace. . . .'[42] This seemed to be clear enough, yet the U.D.C. also stated that it did plan to take any opportunity offered by public dissatisfaction to urge a negotiated peace. In letters to Bryce and others, Trevelyan made it plain that they wanted to be able to harness the discontent among thinking people which he thought he detected. If there was no rallying point, 'when the moment comes', the country might be swept into another year of war. The government would, he feared, be forced into an irreconcilable line and it was his firm conviction that 'we are in for a war *à outrance* unless English opinion can be made to change.'[43] The ambiguity can perhaps best be expressed by saying that if the U.D.C. was not 'Stop the War' it was equally not 'Fight for Victory'.

The ambivalence of the Union naturally sprang from the contrasting attitudes and personalities of the leading members. It was inevitably confusing to have a body supported both by Henderson and MacDonald when they were popularly supposed to represent strongly diverging attitudes towards the war. MacDonald's personal position was indeed baffling. In September, information about the military situation led him suddenly to feel that everybody in the country would be driven into the hands of the recruiting officers to meet the danger that threatened.[44] At Leicester, his own constituency, he made a strange appeal for volunteers to go and fight. A couple of weeks later, he was writing to Gilbert Murray that he found himself being brought up against the Tolstoian position in a way he never had before. 'I am afraid' he added 'I have to accuse myself of inconsistency, taking part of my creed from Tolstoi and the remainder from Tolstoi's opponents. The result is a very workable amalgam which I daresay if I knew more about Pragmatism I might find had some sort of philosophical unity. . . .'[45] Others had less polite descriptions of this 'workable amalgam'. At one moment Henderson must have felt that the great divide which was supposed to exist between them was a wafer-thin crack; at another, a yawning chasm. MacDonald was also somewhat out of step with Ponsonby and Trevelyan on the more technical question of parliamentary control of foreign policy. It was his experience which had taught him that no mere mechanical changes could be effective. 'Given Sir Edward Grey and the two or three present heads of the Foreign Office in control of our Foreign Policy' he told Morel 'and I do not care whether the House of Commons ratified treaties or a Committee of the House of Commons were instructed to appear to look after foreign business, we would probably have been in this war. . . .' It was public opinion and the personality of statesmen that had to be 'got at'.[46] Quite apart from these differences of approach and emphasis, both Morel and MacDonald were highly strung, sensitive to slights and quick to misunderstand. Keeping the peace among the leading pacifists was not always easy, particularly when Philip Snowden returned to the fraternity from his trip to Australia which had coincided with the outbreak of war.

The position of Norman Angell was also somewhat ambiguous. He resisted many calls upon his time on the grounds of ill-health —which perhaps explains his survival till the age of ninety-four. He did not consider himself a politician, and his pre-war fame had been built up quite independently of party. Many of those who admired his writings regretted his association with Trevelyan and MacDonald. While not abandoning their belief in Angell's theories, many of his associates joined up. Neither Esher nor Northcliffe liked the stand Angell had taken and, after a few months, the

Garton Foundation withdrew its support. Angell himself was depressed and dispirited, talking of going into the country and working as an agricultural labourer. His reputation was to some extent shattered by the outbreak of the war.[47] Despite his own statements to the contrary, he was popularly supposed to have said that war would be impossible. Since he had apparently been proved wrong, his prophetic status was diminished. A. D. Lindsay submitted his arguments to rigorous examination in the *Political Quarterly*. He suggested that the lesson of the crisis was that Angell was wrong to suppose that the nation state was of diminishing importance. It had only, to an extent, been ignored because its existence had been taken for granted. Let its survival be threatened and all other interests would be subordinated in its defence. Angell had seriously underestimated the strength of national ideals. Far from merging all societies into one, 'the monotonous effects of industrialism have already called out in reaction a cult of nationalism, a revival of national games and dances, of national language and poetry.' As the case of Ulster illustrated, men could enter into close economic and commercial relations with each other without developing any real political purpose in common. In short, Lindsay argued, 'Recognition that men are interdependent is thus not enough to prevent them from fighting so long as their interests are not absolutely identical, which they are never likely to be.'[48] In November, Morel warned Trevelyan of an effort on foot among Angell's immediate entourage to separate him from the U.D.C.[49] Angell himself was looking out for an honourable way of escape from an awkward situation.

The founders of the Union regarded their new organisation as *the* successor to the pre-war Peace Movement. They hoped to permeate both the world of Labour and the pacifist societies. 'Democracy may arise stronger out of this terrible refining fire' Trevelyan suggested to Lansbury. 'Let us not insist too furiously on our own formulae, land tax, socialism, what not. For it is the right *spirit* that gives life, as now it is the wrong spirit that killeth.'[50] Lansbury occupied a position all his own. He had left the I.L.P. because of its attitude to female suffrage and general annoyance with its parliamentary behaviour. His opposition to the war was partly religious—he had just returned to the Church of England after a spell with an Ethical Society—and partly socialist. He had no organization behind him, but he did have a small group of contributors who, between them, made the *Herald* a lively journal of dissent. In its view, the only war worth fighting for was the war for 'the destruction of competitive capitalism, exploitation and anti-social selfishness' and the only settlement worth aiming at was one which would destroy the spirit which had animated the governing classes of all time, 'the spirit which breeds mutual distrust and hatred.'[51] To achieve this end, Lansbury was prepared to collaborate, up to a point, with his fellow Socialists. As a leading member of the I.L.P., Dr. Alfred Salter, suggested to him, 'out of this war and out of the strange readjustments and reshapings that are taking place, it may be that we may yet evolve a united Socialist party. . . .'[52]

The I.L.P., however, was in an intransigent mood. It was proud of the fact that alone 'of all the organisations affiliated to the Labour Party' it had withstood the onrush of war passion. It had refused to identify itself and Socialist and Labour principles with the foreign policy that led the country into the war. Its statement on the war concluded with a note of prophetic doom. In forcing such an appalling crime upon the nations, it was the rulers, the diplomats and the militarists who had sealed their doom. In tears and blood and bitterness, the greater democracy would be born. However, as in the individual instance of MacDonald, it is not possible to state very clearly the grounds on which the I.L.P. based its pacifism. Explanations and emphases varied very considerably. Some, like Jowett, were satisfied with a verbal assault on the evils of capitalism. It was as if they opposed war because they opposed capitalism. Behind the secret cabals and international intrigues, he wrote, was 'the sinister figure of Capitalism, concession-hunting, armament building, risking the lives of men, women and children and the fate of nations for profit.'[53] He believed that the I.L.P. should co-operate with the U.D.C. to destroy this system. Others, however, felt that it was not enough to advance such a general explanation. It was necessary to examine the specific pattern of events that led to war to see how they could be avoided in the future. MacDonald was usually in this category. Writing in the *Labour Leader,* he contended that Russia had never wanted peace. On the other hand, until Germany hopelessly lost her head owing to her fears of Russian attack, she did want peace. Indeed, 'owing to her pressure and our own, the original quarrel between Austria and Serbia was on a fair way to settlement if Russia had not forced on the European War.'[54]

Most members of the I.L.P., whichever kind of explanation for the war they preferred, gave general approval to the U.D.C. There were, however, some rank and file members who thought that the I.L.P. itself should be careful to reap whatever later benefit might accrue from its stand. Why should it accept the leadership of a group of Liberals, even dissident ones? Keir Hardie, for one, now considered that the old term 'the people' was now 'applicable exclusively to the working class. Many individual members of the other classes will aid in the work, but the interests of the middle class . . . are now so inextricably interwoven with those of the great financial interests that, as a class, it is powerless.' Hardie himself was a weary man. The outbreak of war had apparently broken his heart and a few months later he was dead.[55] Nevertheless, he had successors who insisted that peace would only be secure when the working class took the question into their own hands.

Besides Labour, the U.D.C. was also anxious to gain support from the peace societies. Carl Heath, the secretary of the National Peace Council, accepted membership of the General Committee. So did several other Quakers. However, contrary to what had once been hoped, the other societies did not disband. Its capacity for denunciation unimpaired, the Peace Society struggled to keep the *Herald of Peace* in existence. The National Peace Council still tried to 'co-ordinate' peace activities. Not only did the old societies refuse to die, but the U.D.C. was not the sole newcomer.

Although the great majority of clergy and laity had supported the war, a minority drawn from many different denominations wished to maintain a pacifist witness. One of them, a Presbyterian minister, the Rev. Richard Roberts was typical in believing that the war could conceivably be called just, but to call it a Christian struggle seemed to be going 'beyond fact and reason.' It was therefore time to 'protest against this plain betrayal of the Christian name and of the hope of a sane and peaceful world.'[56] He got together an inter-denominational group which included Edwyn Bevan and the Rev. G. K. A. Bell but he found their attitude too 'pro-war'. Instead, with a Quaker doctor, Henry Hodgkin, he organized a conference of some hundred and fifty people at Cambridge in December 1914. They met specifically to discuss the war from a Christian standpoint. Papers were read by Roberts, Hodgkin and two celebrated preachers, Dr. W. E. Orchard and Miss Maude Royden.[57] With the exception of Lansbury, those present were largely drawn from the professional middle classes. Their common theme was the failure of the churches to accept their responsibility for the peace of the world. Disaster had come because theologians had too easily accepted the idea of two world orders, one natural and one spiritual. The injunctions of the Sermon on the Mount were absolutes, to be followed in and out of season. Christian obligation did not stop short at national boundaries. The churches could not settle international disputes, but they could deal with the spirit of greed and hatred which envenomed them. So many Christians, however, had ceased to believe in self-sacrifice and acquiesced in competition, the very negation of peace and harmony. It was time to create a spirit of 'world adventure'. This approach was very different from that of the U.D.C. The peace with which these pacifists were concerned was much more a matter of the spirit. Although small in number, their singlemindedness and intellectual capacity ensured that they were not completely ignored. Support from such quarters was, however, as much a potential source of embarrassment as of strength to the political objectives of the U.D.C.

This was also true of women. There were many ardent suffragettes like Mrs. Swanwick, editor of the *Common Cause* who felt that man was 'the Playboy of the whole world'. He was playing the 'silly, bloody game of massacring the sons of women.'[58] It was, however, regrettably the case that many prominent members of the National Union of Women's Suffrage Societies were, in Morel's words, 'bitten with the war fever'.[59] In correspondence both with Maude Royden and Helena Swanwick, he made it clear that the U.D.C. would like to see a distinct committee formed of women who would be in broad agreement with its objectives. Mrs. Swanwick pronounced herself 'sick of segregation'. Men and women helped to educate each other. Other women were not so sick. 'I consider we women' a correspondent wrote to Catherine Marshall, the able parliamentary secretary of the National Union, 'must not combine with Morel & Co. yet. . . .' Another felt that the terms of co-operation were 'really very unsatisfactory'. It seemed that the 'leaders of the Union mean that the Suffrage women shall not show as a definite wing of the Peace Movement. . . .'[60] With varying degrees of enthusiasm, the male members of the U.D.C. General Committee professed their support for female suffrage and Mrs. Swanwick joined the Executive. Nevertheless, there was always the possibility that some women would break away on their own. Mrs. Swanwick herself warned Morel that 'We have in the suffrage movement suffered much from the diversity of reasons for which people support us and of means by which people defend us. . . .' She feared that 'the peace movement will have to suffer in just the same way. . . .' There was little that could be done about it. The condition was inevitable if the movement was to be anything other than the activity of a few superior persons.[61]

Her remarks reinforce the fact that although the Peace Movement had 'regrouped' under the impact of the war, its unity was only precarious. The U.D.C. attempted to take over the whole movement but found that old loyalties remained obstinately strong. There was still a great deal of confusion and shifting of ground. Many who had previously been known as pacifists became more fervent in their support of the war than many who had previously rejected that description. They became convinced, or convinced themselves, that this war really was the war to end war. They were more committed to its successful conclusion than those for whom it was just another war. It is tempting here to pursue a parallel with those religious sects which have oscillated between extreme violence and total non-violence in pursuit of their objectives. The pacifists themselves were confronted by a paradox. Peace itself is a negative concept and perfect peace is as sterile as complete security. From his own close personal observation and involvement, J. A. Hobson noted, nonetheless, that 'when a minority group of pacifists is organised against war, it becomes a combative body, conducts 'campaigns', and its leaders are, by natural selection, "fighting men".'[62] The men and women who conducted the 'fight for peace' in Britain after 1914 were to be the victims of harrassment and persecution as the war developed and bitterness increased. They themselves, however, showed scant regard for the integrity of those who considered their outlook to be inadequate.

CHAPTER THREE

Planning for Peace, 1914-1915

By the end of 1914, it was clear that Charles Trevelyan's notion of planning for a peace which would come within six weeks was a little optimistic. The war could still go on for months, even years. Nevertheless, pacifists still believed that they should be ready when it did end. What concerned them was the fear that the government might adopt ambitious war aims without thinking the question through. They wanted a scheme for the preservation of peace to be the first priority at the peace conference. Therefore, while the government began to formulate some war aims, pacifists drew up peace aims. In thinking about the future, it was to some extent possible for 'opponents' and 'supporters' of the war to come together, though the actual war in progress kept tiresomely getting in the way. Some held that it was futile to discuss detailed schemes unless there was a strong possibility that Germany would be defeated. Unless her aggression were repulsed, she would never accept the necessary re-structuring of the world in the interests of peace. On the other hand, there were those who shared a similar concern for the future, but who believed that the war could, and should, be ended by negotiation. They therefore wanted to frame a settlement which could be attractive to Germany. She would then freely join in upholding a new world order.

In trying to keep discussion going, despite the tensions caused by the war, the role of Goldsworthy Lowes Dickinson was crucial. He was a Fellow of King's College, Cambridge, in his early fifties, and a fastidious and successful dabbler in the classics, political philosophy and history. His initial reaction to the war was one of civilized horror. He had always had a feeling that he lived in a world of lunatics, and now he knew it. The sight of so many beautiful young Cambridge men going off to die was more than he could stand. If only what he called 'the peoples' had been in charge, then there could have been no European war 'over such a bagatelle.' The war happened because Russia feared Austria, Germany feared Russia, France and England feared Germany. That is, the governments feared the governments, or the people of one country feared the government of another. The 'cardinal point' was that peoples do not fear one another. The difficulty was, as his friend the architect C. R. Ashbee noted, people did not seem to realize the full significance of what was happening. It was a life and death trial for English Democracy. How was the workman going to come out of it, 'the chap we idealists have put our bob on?'[1]

At first, Lowes Dickinson was completely dejected. 'One's whole life' he wrote 'has been given up to trying to establish and spread reason, and suddenly, the gulf opens and one finds the world is ruled by force and wishes to be so.' Although he was 'against war', he did not see how it could have been avoided in the prevailing state of international relations. That made the peace which was to follow the war even more vital. 'What is not done at the peace' he wrote to Bryce 'will hardly have a chance after it, in a fresh era of competition, fear and revenge.' What he believed ought to be done, and could be done, was to have instead of terms imposed by victors, a general congress, including the neutral powers, and, of course, the United States in particular. So long as people were prepared to come down on the side of working to put an end to war, what they thought about the rights and wrongs of the existing conflict was not important.[2]

Rather reluctantly, Lowes Dickinson did join the U.D.C., but most of his energy went into the private group which he had assembled to discuss the future peace.[3] It included Ponsonby, Hobson, Wallas, Willoughby Dickinson and E. R. Cross, Quaker solicitor to the Rowntrees. On the understanding that everything was to be kept private, Lord Bryce agreed to consider their views and send his own comments. He provided a memorandum, 'When the war comes to an end', advocating national self-determination, limitation of armaments and a league of nations. It is quite possible that Lowes Dickinson was himself responsible for this latter phrase which was to have such wide currency. The group discussed these proposals amongst themselves and with other interested friends through the winter of 1914 and the spring of 1915. Bryce had previously advocated a moratorium on war and now he wished to extend the scope of his idea. He suggested a council to which states should refer their disputes in the first instance. Some members of the group held that it was possible to distinguish between matters which were justiciable and those which were not. Others felt that in principle every dispute ought to be justiciable. The discussions

D

were indeed characterized by disagreement on almost every point of the emerging scheme. Some of differences concerned the form of the council and the role of diplomats and could be reconciled. Others were more fundamental. The majority, including Bryce himself, believed that some kind of international sanction would be necessary; Ponsonby strongly disagreed. He believed that the authority of a council would be all the stronger and more durable because it was not contaminated by force. The members also tried to reach a formula for the limitation of armaments but, when the first version of their proposals was printed in February 1915, they left the matter to be decided by the new international council.

It was on the understanding that the proposals remained private and confidential that they were circulated under the signatures of Bryce and Lowes Dickinson. This reticence was chiefly due to the elder statesman. At this time, he was also ploughing through accounts of alleged German atrocities. He found the German mentality more and more puzzling and was, as a consequence, reluctant to accept the title of pacifist. However, Lowes Dickinson and some other members of the group were less inhibited. They started to lobby potential supporters both at home and abroad, and wrote articles in the radical press.

The members of the Bryce Group were not alone in planning the future. It was only to be expected that Sidney Webb would offer a helpful contribution. The Webbs, however, like most Fabians, firmly supported the war. Mrs. Webb wrote in her diary that the invasion of Belgium had compelled the anti-war propagandists to come out in favour of non-resistance, pure and undefiled. If Belgium was not to be defended, why bother to defend Britain? There was no morality in watching a child being murdered, refusing to interfere until attacked personally and then fighting for your own life.[4] Sentiments like these did not enamour her to pacifists. It is not surprising, therefore, that Webb approached L. S. Woolf with the suggestion that he should draw up a set of proposals for consideration by the Fabian Society. Woolf moved in Bloomsbury circles where pacifism was fashionable, though he was not a complete pacifist himself. He thought Germany and Austria were chiefly responsible for the senseless war, but he thought Britain could have prevented it and in any case should never have become involved. Once the country was at war, however, he thought that Germany had to be resisted and only medical reasons prevented him from going to the front. Lowes Dickinson was a personal friend, though Woolf subsequently wrote that he detected 'a weakness, a looseness of fibre, in Goldie and in his thought and writing, which was subtly related to the gentleness and high-mindedness.'[5]

Woolf published his 'Suggestions for the Prevention of War' in the *New Statesman* in July 1915. He had previously consulted Lowes Dickinson, Wallas, Cross and Hobson. Since he considered the Bryce proposals too general, he went to elaborate lengths, for example, to define the nature of a justiciable dispute. The Fabians also wanted to establish a high court whose decisions between nations would be enforced by sanctions—other than war. While the court would deal with justiciable matters, a council would deal with other disputes. Member states would be required to delay 'warlike' operations or acts of aggression for twelve months, pending a decision. If a member state failed to observe the period of delay, the other states would make common cause against it. Apart from these details, however, what was most distinctive about Woolf's Fabian contribution was its stress on the need to advance to real international government. The council should take on powers which would enable it to deal with many international economic, social and political questions before these reached the stage of crisis. In order to help this work both an international secretariat and a set of functional institutions should be developed.

In this respect, though striking, Woolf's views were by no means unique. Angell, Brailsford and Hobson all wanted to go further than the existing Bryce proposals. They all agreed that it was impossible to return to the international structure of 1914, even if attempts were made to manage it more effectively. Angell warned his readers in January 1915 that pacifists could not insulate themselves from a great war of change. He even dared to suggest that pacifism would have to abandon its old attitude of non-intervention, of refusal to enter upon continental alliances and military obligations to foreign countries. To oppose the renewal of the guarantee to Belgium at the end of the war would be futile. It was, however, the duty of the pacifist to ensure that such a step was 'the foundation of a real union of European states.' [6]

Brailsford, too, considered the old pacifist question—How shall we prevent war?—altogether too narrow. In view of his previous optimism about Europe, he had found the war a great shock. It was 'an issue so barbarous, so remote from any real concern of our daily life on these islands, that I can only marvel at the illusion, and curse the fatality which have made us belligerents in this struggle.' He admitted that Germany undoubtedly pursued economic and imperialistic aims, but the other powers were also influenced 'in some degree' by similar ambitions. Russia, for example, was bent on obtaining the mastery over the Straits, not to mention Constantinople itself. The Germans were attacking and the Allies were maintaining the existing distribution of colonies and dependencies. The stakes in the war lay outside Europe, though the war was waged on its soil. Brailsford believed it mistaken to concentrate on finding a formula for preventing conflict. Change in society was inevitable, and if there was no way of producing fundamental change without violence, 'then war is as inevitable as revolution.' There was a grave danger that pacifists would repeat the mistakes made in the past by diplomats. 'The horror of war' he wrote 'possesses us so strongly that we are apt to conceive our problem too simply as the prevention of war. Our problem is larger; it it to provide for international change without war.' The only certain way of crushing militarism was to internationalize Imperialism.[7]

Hobson advocated a similar policy for pacifists. In his view, the trouble with the pre-war Peace Movement was that it had recognized the evils but it had not suggested radical enough remedies for them. It was useless to attack the arms race without criticizing the international structure of which it was simply a feature. There was even one benefit to be gained from the war. He thought governments might accept that 'by no increase of their armed force will they be reasonably likely to succeed in any aggressive design upon a neighbour.' Obvious motives of self-interest would lead them to reduce armaments when they realized that, under a new system, they were not dependent for defence upon their own forces. The pledge of co-operation would unite all states in a system of 'collective security'. At the same time, the scope of arbitration would be pushed to its limits. All arbitrable disputes, 'irrespective of their importance or the feeling that attaches to them' would have to be submitted to a court. The Sarajevo assassination was an admirable example of the kind of incident which could be considered by a court. Hobson then went on to describe an elaborate system which would aid the process of conciliation. War was so degrading, in his view, not simply because physical force was used unnecessarily and for purely national and interested purposes, but because 'its results or settlement has no assured relation to reason or justice.' He favoured the economic boycott of a state which refused to go to court, but recognized that the chief states in the world would not co-operate with the scheme 'without placing at their disposal, for use in the last resort, an adequate armed force to break the resistance of an armed law-breaking state.' There was nothing utopian about his scheme, he claimed, for all nations would be confronted with the same alternatives. Either they accepted military domination and the reign of war or internationalism and the reign of law. He had little doubt which they would choose. 'What they asked to do' he concluded 'is to insist that the same methods already applied to the settlement of all issues between individuals, groups of individuals, and the smaller societies of cities or provinces shall be extended to the case of the larger social units called States.' Whether or not his plan was implemented depended on the state of mind at the end of the war. It was therefore up to every pacifist to educate the public in the realities.[8]

As a result of such writings, the idea of some kind of new international league had become generally acceptable in progressive Liberal circles by the summer of 1915. Early in May, a decision had been taken to establish a League of Nations Society. A venerable man of the law, Lord Shaw of Dunfermline, was President and the Liberal M.P.'s, Willoughby Dickinson and Aneurin Williams, Chairman and Treasurer respectively. Although they had been critical of government policy in the past, the officers of the Society were supporters of the war. The aim of the Society was to persuade as many states as possible to form a League, binding themselves in the process to use peaceful methods to solve any disputes between them. Justiciable matters would be referred to the court at The Hague, and all other problems would be considered by a council of inquiry and conciliation. In order to put this scheme into effect, the States would unite in any military, economic or diplomatic action that might be necessary. Any civilized state could join and the League was to possess the power, in the last resort, to use force. Unless this power was available, 'the League would become a farce; there would be no security against aggressive States. It does not follow that the force need always be military or naval; it is possible that in certain cases diplomatic or economic pressure might be sufficient. . . .'[9]

Throughout 1915, the plans for a future League or international government underwent continuous scrutiny and revision. Lowes Dickinson remained very busy trying to keep the various groups in touch with each other. Although a prolific writer, his own ideas were less ambitious than those which have been so far mentioned. 'Our worst enemies' he wrote to Ponsonby in April 1915 'are really men like Brailsford and Hobson, who go for federation. They won't get that; but they may easily help to prevent our getting what we ask for.'[10] His own basic remedy was the enforced period of delay, during which a dispute would have to be brought to the conference table. He thought that 'under such conditions, public opinion would not tolerate a war.' He denied that he was abrogating national sovereignty or ruling out war as impossible. His aim was merely to make it 'a good deal less likely than it now is.' Unless there was a fundamental desire to preserve peace, the most intricate of procedural devices would be unavailing.[11]

As for the war in progress, he found the German conduct 'monstrous' but not unique. It was, he stressed, the conduct fostered by the European system. The invasion of Belgium had not caused the war, it happened as an episode in a war already begun. The origin of the war was ambition and fear. It was unjust to present the conflict between Germany and the West as a conflict between domination and freedom. Nevertheless, 'we may say with truth that a victory of the Western Powers, so far as their influence can reach, should make for freedom, while a victory of Germany will make for domination.'[12] Since Europe was deadlocked, he placed great hope on the United States. 'America' he wrote early in 1915 'is ready for very drastic peace settlements. So, of course, am I.'[13] What he wanted to do, therefore, was to get what he considered the best thinking in America on the subject of a new international order in touch with 'European possibilities'. Taking some copies of the Bryce proposals with him, he attended a conference of internationalists from both belligerent and neutral countries at The Hague in April 1915. The conference passed resolutions favourable to the League, and agreed to set up a continuing committee. However, Dickinson reported, the idea was that each country should work out for itself how best to mount its own national propaganda.[14] A start, at least, had been made, although too much contact with Europe might run into official opposition. Contacts with the other side of the Atlantic were more extensive and less open to suspicion. In the United States there was strong interest in the idea of a League, especially among academic and legal circles. There was no man in Britain with more extensive American contacts than Bryce and he frequently exchanged ideas with his friends. In July 1915, the League to Enforce Peace was founded in the United States—as its title indicates, with a stress on the necessity of having coercive sanctions against delinquent states. One of the founders, the political scientist, A. L. Lowell, wrote to Lowes Dickinson a month later that the American organization 'was really founded on the proposals made by your League. . . .' There was, however, a vital difference between the two bodies. 'We feel' he explained 'that the only thing that will prevent war is the certainty that the country going to war will have to meet the world in arms. . . .'[15] There were, in fact, significant other differences, but in the climate of the time it was encouraging to believe that a common Peace Movement with a common objective was developing on both sides of the Atlantic.

Planning for peace after this fashion did not constitute a campaign for peace. None of the groups so far discussed made it their business to press publicly for peace terms or an immediate negotiated settlement. To have introduced this question would have been to break the understanding on which the Bryce Group conducted its business. Bryce and his associates hoped to gain respect from Ministers because they conducted themselves discreetly. They had begun work when there was a Liberal Government and had reason to believe that Grey, at least, was interested in their proposals. They had some grounds for supposing that they could influence the Cabinet. The formation of the new government in May 1915 was therefore rather a blow to Bryce. Although he later thought his fears exaggerated, it seemed at the time to herald the rise of forces less amenable to their work. For the moment, however, Bryce saw no reason to change his attitude.

The mood of the U.D.C. was rather different. Morel preferred pressure to influence. He hammered away at the subject of war origins. Any fresh scrap of evidence which appeared to support his position was immediately published. An editorial in *War and Peace* hinted critically that the whole problem might appropriately be left to future historians, while pacifists concentrated on shaping the future peace.[16] Morel disagreed. Discussion of elaborate schemes for a League of Nations held little interest for him. He believed that only if the government was impressed by the strength of the new radical alliance he wished to promote would the project receive any consideration at all. The formation of the Coalition Government gave him a great opportunity to develop a radical alternative. Such propaganda was more worthwhile than endless academic debate à la Bryce. A series of pamphlets reiterated the main U.D.C. themes. The first, *The Morrow of the War* stated that it was imperative that the war, once begun, should be 'prosecuted to a victory for our country.' It went on to say that the future relationship of the states of Europe should be one of partnership, not of domination. Concern for the common good should override every other consideration. The people could do their part by ridding themselves of the notion that foreign policy was beyond their comprehension.[17] Norman Angell declared that it was impossible to destroy 'Prussianism' solely by force of arms, but admitted that 'it would also be impossible to do it if the Prussians won.'[18]

In the early months of the war, when the U.D.C. stressed that it was not a 'peace at any price' society, the notion of victory was certainly present in its propaganda. After the spring of 1915, however, the desire for victory was softpedalled. Nor was this Morel's initiative alone. Liberals like Denman felt that the change of government released them from their obligation to defend a Liberal Cabinet. Ponsonby and Trevelyan pondered the appropriate strategy in the new circumstances. Writing on 22 May, Ponsonby felt that an attack on the new Coalition would be welcomed by many Liberals. Since the war casualties continued to mount, the government should be pressed for a statement of its policy.

Trevelyan agreed. They had to act because there was no effective party left in the Cabinet anxious for an early peace. 'I am now prepared to base our action' he continued 'on the assumption that, whatever may happen to Austria, Germany can't suffer complete defeat, short of four or five years' war, and that none of the allied people will stand that.' He was hopeful that war-weariness would soon set in and that when it did the nation would say 'here are a few people who realize that the war must be ended on terms.' Morel declared that he would rather be shot than be compelled to fight on after a 'reasonable' German offer had been refused.[19]

The founding fathers of the U.D.C. were not alone in detecting a changed situation. By the summer of 1915, Charles Roden Buxton had changed his mind about the possibilities of negotiation. The previous August, he had helped in the distribution of the MacDonald-Trevelyan-Angell private letter. Then, however, he had been side-tracked. He accepted a mission to the Balkans to try, with the aid of his brother Noel, to prevent Bulgarian adhesion to the Central Powers. It was from the unusual pacifist location of Bucharest that he wrote to his wife in October 1914 saying that he still felt the moment had not come for agitating at home for a settlement of any sort. 'The portentous struggle we are in' he concluded 'is a fact which exists and dominates the situation quite apart from the *origin* of the war. . . . A termination at this stage would, it still seems to me, increase and not diminish the total sum of human misery, if we take a long view. . . .'[20] The long view lasted about six months. Then, he came to feel, as he wrote to Bryce, that the notion of inflicting a crushing defeat on Germany was unwise. It would impose a task of indefinite extent and magnitude, not to mention the fact that it was quite possibly unobtainable. If the war went on without any prospect of a conclusion, disputes might arise between the allies and unrest increase at home. Even if Germany were defeated, she could not be kept a second-rate Power for more than a few years. A sullen and defeated Germany would not contribute to the building of a new European community at the end of the war. Finally, he urged the consideration that Europe might be so exhausted when the war ended that the 'so-called Yellow Peril' might become a reality. He hoped that the government would eschew ambitious schemes of territorial reconstruction and concentrate on restoring the *status quo ante*. There was, he believed, 'a considerable amount of evidence to show that the evacuation of Belgium and Northern France might be secured by negotiations in the near future. . . .' Bryce was unconvinced and declined to sign the memorial.[21]

Charles Buxton was undeterred by the damp reception his memorandum received. Three months later, in September, he circulated another document, 'The Case for Negotiation', arguing that those who were against any attempt to negotiate had to show 'not merely that better terms could probably be gained later, but that terms could be gained which would be *so much* better as to compensate us for the sacrifices which would have to be made in the intervening period.' He accepted that it was natural for statesmen to delay before taking risks but claimed that inaction 'almost always results in delaying negotiations beyond the point when the best terms could have been gained.'[22]

The replies Buxton received illustrate the mood of those who were well-disposed to peace though rejecting the title of pacifist. Bryce thought that there was force in some of Buxton's contentions, but argued that there was little reason to think that the Germans would make peace on any terms a British Government could accept. They would not indemnify Belgium and their peace party was too weak to bring any pressure to bear. Secondly, he wanted to destroy Ottoman power after its efforts to exterminate whole Christian populations. The Turks would therefore have to be defeated. Finally, he believed that a negotiated settlement would leave Germany with her military power and aggressive intentions, thus obliging Britain to keep up a huge army and fleet. The peace would only be a truce. Morley did not see how it was possible to advance to definite ideas of peace and reconstruction 'until military events have shed more light on the relative adjustment of forces.' Courtney of Penwith welcomed the work of investigation that Buxton had undertaken. Nevertheless, he advised against any publication and thought Buxton stated German movements towards peace 'with too little qualification.' Some of the conclusions ascribed to the Liberal politicians of Germany were also rather difficult to accept. The Archbishop of Canterbury expressed a courteous interest but felt that the time was not ripe for public discussion. These were replies from cautious old men, but even Ramsay MacDonald was no more adventurous. 'We have to peg away quietly' he wrote and it was 'too soon to do more than pave the way for it in public. To announce suddenly that there is a party in favour of negotiation now would only have a hardening effect upon public opinion.' On the other hand, he thought there were a great many people ready to receive a little light and 'suggestions that negotiation must not be forgotten even in the midst of the fighting will, I think, bear fruit.'[23]

The only encouragement Buxton received was from R. D. Denman and Lord Loreburn, though it was of a rather lugubrious kind. Denman thoroughly approved of Buxton's efforts but thought the situation hopeless. 'If people really thought we were fighting to secure certain terms' he argued 'they would welcome your memo with open arms.' The reality was that the war had long since become an end in itself. Loreburn approved of the spirit of Buxton's remarks and a good deal of the substance. He thought that the fearful outlook for all the nations if the war continued would have its natural effect soon. The Revolution might finish what folly and incompetence began. A few months earlier Loreburn himself had tried unsuccessfully to persuade John Burns that the time might be ripe 'for saying something that will make people think of the absurdity of fighting on till all the nations are exhausted.' It would not be a 'Stop the War' campaign, but rather an injunction to think.[24]

Buxton was disappointed by the response he received. He and his wife were, however, prepared to devote their private resources to what amounted to a private campaign for peace. Buxton began to speak in public on the subject, where he could find a suitable hall. In November 1915 the Cambridge branch of the U.D.C. was refused permission to hold a meeting which he was due to address in Trinity College. His strong Cambridge connexions were of little avail. He debated with the renowned controversialist and enemy of *Pacificist Illusions,* the historian C. G. Coulton. As a consequence of his actions, he ran into difficulty with Central Hackney Liberal Association who found themselves able to dispense with his services as their parliamentary candidate. His wife was equally active. Early in 1915 she was determined to attack what she considered to be the false division of the world into two arbitrary camps. She published extracts from the foreign press, allied, neutral or enemy. She was fortunate enough to get a government permit for the importing of German papers which she obtained through a bookseller in Scandinavia. Initially, she published her 'Notes from the Foreign Press' in leaflet form but then C. K. Ogden invited her to continue her publication in the columns of the *Cambridge Magazine.* Until 1920 she kept up this private press survey with the help of many willing translators. This service was greatly appreciated by pacifists—and others. General Smuts told Charles Buxton in May 1917 that he had read the column throughout the war and in East Africa it went regularly round his staff too. It was on the basis of his wife's information service that Buxton claimed to have knowledge of a German disposition to negotiate.[25]

The Buxtons' campaign was initially largely personal. In 1915, however, he joined the Executive Committee of the U.D.C. and his views on peace terms were published in its pamphlet series. His brother Noel was more cautious. Even inside the U.D.C., however, the new course advocated by Morel, Trevelyan, Ponsonby and Buxton was not without opposition. Council meetings in October disclosed considerable unease about a motion calling upon the

Allies to take steps to reach a negotiated peace. Ponsonby and Trevelyan raised this topic in the House of Commons in November and their speeches were published. The Bristol Branch stated that it would refuse to circulate copies and it opposed a declaration of peace terms. When Morel was so ill-advised as to write to Josiah Wedgwood for funds he received a strong reply. He was not going to help the U.D.C. to discuss peace terms until the Junkers were beaten to a frazzle. 'I always imagined' Wedgwood continued 'that the Union wanted a settlement on National lines, with the Slovaks, Checks and Serbs free, and Alsace and Lorraine back in France. You have travelled a long way since last year. . . . If that is your Union, it is not for me any longer.'[26]

Fortunately for Morel, however, not all his correspondents replied in such a spirited fashion. He could expect a somewhat more favourable reception both from Nonconformists and the Labour Movement. It was quite common for local U.D.C. branches to meet on Nonconformist premises. Peace supporters found the U.D.C. more vigorous than the Peace Society and it seemed only a matter of time before the latter was completely supplanted. Such prophecy, however, reckoned without the retirement of Dr. Evans Darby and his replacement at the end of 1915 by the Rev. Herbert Dunnico, a Baptist minister from Liverpool who was already an active member of the I.L.P. His aim was to restore the Society to a central position in the Peace Movement.

The relationship of the U.D.C. to the Society of Friends was more delicate. It was unlikely that Quakers would succumb completely to the wiles of Morel. Some Friends, in any case, continued to prefer discussion of abstract principles. The columns of *The Friend* contained lengthy debates on the difference between the civil and military use of force and on the distinction between police and army. However, there was some attention to the immediate circumstances of the war. The Peace Committee urged that the mind of the people should be turned to a settlement in which neither revenge nor national aggrandisement should have a place.[27] Edward Grubb suggested that if the German Social Democrats could see that Britain did not seek an annexationist victory they would be willing and able to control their own government's ambitions. He believed that nationalism was the main enemy of peace and criticized those Friends who had been seduced by its appeal. It was no more possible to remove the peace testimony from the Quaker faith than it was to remove a man's heart and keep him alive.[28] The Yearly Meeting in May 1915 recognized that the peace testimony had not been upheld by all and stressed that there was 'an urgent call to be most faithful.' This debate was, of course, very largely only of interest to Friends themselves—as some

members of the Society were aware.[29] Some Quakers tried to
muster support for the U.D.C.—*The Friend* published an appeal
from prominent members of the Society urging financial assistance
—but it was not clear how far Friends were prepared to commit
themselves politically.[30] There was, for example, disagreement about
the appropriate response to a manifesto issued by the German
Social Democrats on 23 June 1915 calling for a negotiated peace.
The Meeting for Sufferings and the Peace Committee were divided
in their assessment of whether the time was 'ripe' for Friends to
express their agreement.[31]

It was in order to define the relationship between the Quaker
approach and that of the U.D.C. that a conference was sponsored
by Friends in June. Those present included Trevelyan, Ponsonby,
MacDonald, Russell, Allen and Lowes Dickinson. They found that
they had sufficient common ground with each other to produce a
five-fold statement of policy. They agreed that at the end of the
war there should be no annexation of territory contrary to the
interests and wishes of the populations concerned. Every attempt
should be made in such instances to obtain their views by plebiscite
or otherwise. At the peace conference, all nations should agree to
introduce liberty of commerce in their colonies, protectorates and
spheres of influence, or at least equal treatment for all nations. The
work of the peace machinery at The Hague should be expanded.
The nations should agree to reduce their armaments and Britain
should lead the way by announcing her willingness to forego the
right of capture at sea. They finally agreed that foreign policy ought
to be under the effective control of parliaments in all countries.[32]

A programme of this kind could be produced in a day by
individuals who started from very different convictions. It was also
agreed to set up a committee consisting of both Quakers and non-
Quakers to spread these ideas. Although this body does not seem
to have had a very effective life, it is significant that Friends felt
that they ought not to be content with the simple reiteration of
their distinctive religious position. The Yearly Meeting of 1915
was emphatic on this point. While recognizing that the only lasting
remedy for war lay in the supremacy of the spirit, it asked 'May
it not be that our testimony against militarism has lost its effect
because in our social relations we have not lived sufficiently in
the spirit of love, brotherhood, meekness and gentleness and sought
to bring them to bear upon the whole fabric of life?'[33]

Similar language was used by the group of Christian pacifists
who, after their Cambridge meeting, set up the Fellowship of
Reconciliation in January 1915. By the beginning of February one
hundred and seventy people had joined and attempts were made
to form local groups to influence the churches. However, the

members were uncertain how directly political they wanted their Fellowship to be. This small middle-class group was not likely to reach a mass audience and was not even sure that it wanted to. Piously, its committee decided that members should attend I.L.P. meetings in order to familiarize themselves with the atmosphere before speaking at working-class gatherings on the subject of peace. The Chairman of the F.O.R. was the missionary doctor, Henry Hodgkin and he had considerable difficulty in keeping the society together. There were strong personalities in its ranks who were in agreement on little else except that war was always wrong. On the one hand, the F.O.R. attracted those absolute pacifists who had no misgivings about their faith and who wanted to use it as a base for converting the churches to a 'stop the war' campaign. On the other, there were members of the Fellowship who believed that its distinctive note ought to be its 'humble and constructive' outlook. A group of Quaker Socialists added to the difficulties by insisting that Socialism was essential to Christianity, a view which caused embarrassment when they claimed that this was the view of the F.O.R. as a whole. It is therefore not surprising that some members favoured association with a body like the U.D.C. more strongly than others. For its part, the Union approached the Fellowship with caution. Since the Christian pacifists did not believe that any price was too high to pay for peace, they were a doubtful asset at a time when it was being stressed that a realistic and reasonable peace could be obtained by negotiation. It is probably for this reason that the U.D.C. Executive decided in September 1915 not to permit the F.O.R. to affiliate. This move did not prevent individuals from being members of both bodies.[34]

Sympathy and support from Christian bodies was helpful to Morel, but what he really wanted to gain was the allegiance of the Labour Movement. If a 'peace by negotiations' campaign was to be really effective in making the government change its policy, it would have to gain the assistance of trade unions and trade councils. However, at this stage, the U.D.C. leaders were hesitant about identifying their own political fortunes with the I.L.P. In response to invitations they received about this time, Angell, Russell and Morel all refused to join. Russell stated that he agreed 'most warmly with the attitude which the I.L.P. has taken up about the war' and that made him anxious to help, but he was 'not a socialist, though I think I might call myself a syndicalist. . . .' Morel thought he would be 'more useful to the U.D.C. by being identified with no particular body.' F. W. Pethick Lawrence and Mrs. Swanwick also declared themselves in general sympathy but, for the time being, declined to join. Trevelyan thought this was the right course since '. . . it would be fatal to any progress with

Liberals for any one to take a definite step towards political change
of allegiance who is in a prominent position among us.' Nevertheless, although the U.D.C. leadership held back, the 1915 Annual
Report of the City of London branch of the I.L.P. noted that
'a new type of member has been attracted to us, who formerly
held aloof owing to some minor differences. But the attractive
force of the one party which has remained loyal to the principles
of Internationalism and Pacifism, which are also the principles
of the only true civilisation, of ideal Christianity, and of any
Socialism which is more than a catch-word for street-corners, has
overcome all lesser doubts and hesitations.'[35]

The fact that they would not join the I.L.P. did not stop the
U.D.C. leaders trying to extend their influence over it. From the
very beginning, Trevelyan made contacts with I.L.P. stalwarts in
the country. Many of them, like J. H. Hudson in Manchester,
promised that there would be hearty support 'as individuals and
as an organisation.'[36] Personal contacts, however, were not enough.
By the autumn of 1915, the U.D.C. had published fifteen pamphlets
with a total print of half a million. The success of this venture
encouraged the Executive to sponsor a parallel series of leaflets
which put across the U.D.C. message in a simple form for the
workers. The Labour audience was warned that proposals for
'crushing Germany' would involve the 'prolongation of the war
to the utmost limit of German endurance with the maximum of
slaughter on both sides.' If, at the close, Germany was excluded
from the comity of nations, this would result in 'the continued
division of Europe into two irreconcilable camps.' Despite these
critical remarks, the Union had to tread carefully. It was thought
advisable to publish letters from supporters in the army because
it was sometimes suggested, falsely, that the U.D.C. showed 'in
some undefined way, a want of sympathy with the heroism and
suffering of our soldiers and sailors.' Ponsonby was also at pains
to stress that the U.D.C. was not 'Stop the War' writing that 'We
are a body of men and women determined to use every possible
effort to secure adequate reparation for this country.' It almost
seemed as if the only distinguishing mark of the Union was its
belief that if the people were able to exercise their influence it
would be a pacific influence. Morel took the argument a stage
further. The true anarchists, he wrote, were not those who thought
they could reform society by removing its figureheads, but rather
the so-called statesmen and leaders of the nations. A secret and
autocratic diplomacy stood between the peoples and peace. The
false dogma of the Balance of Power had to be rejected. It regarded
nations simply as inert pieces of machinery, not living organisms,
and set up an oligarchy of nations, some of which legislated and

some of which were legislated for. The basic objection to the principle was that it contained no criterion of justice and simply rested international relations on force.[37]

The U.D.C. writers did not restrict themselves to their own pamphlets and leaflets. *War and Peace* offered a regular platform, and, occasionally, *The Nation*. Their basic aim was to show that even if decisive victory were achieved, it would be folly to impose a severe settlement on Germany. Readers were then left to infer that a decisive victory was hardly worth achieving at all. Lowes Dickinson, for example, who privately believed that the outcome of the war would be stalemate 'and that would give the best chance of a lasting peace on the right lines' wrote that the idea of punishment was not really applicable to the settlement after the war. There could be no punishment unless there were definite individual criminals and an impartial court to try them.[38] Similarly, an editorial in *War and Peace* argued that it was pointless to ask whether the Germans merited punishment, the question was rather whether it would make for the happiness of all nations to give it to them. Mrs. Swanwick deplored talk of Germany as a criminal nation. Even if it were true, it was wrong to use force to prove to Germany that force was wrong. Time after time, writers stressed that the victory of the Allies would not, in itself, accomplish anything. Neither military defeat nor crippling indemnity would, according to Charles Buxton, bring home to the German people the fact that they or their government had perpetrated a crime. The only way by which such a result could be effected would be the recognition by the German peoples of the plain fact that their government had failed in its campaign of aggression. He did not explain how this recognition was to come about in the absence of defeat.[39]

The U.D.C. demanded information on the grounds that if public opinion was really going to count then it had to be given 'the opportunity of judging the policies to which it shall give its assent.'[40] On the other hand, it denied that it wanted to know the government's terms for peace in exact detail. Simply by indicating the broad outlines of its policy, the Cabinet 'could make it more difficult for our enemy's Government to continue the war when their own peoples become weary. . . .'[41] In any case, the Union was itself in two minds about public opinion. MacDonald had to admit that 'the people are ready to dance round bonfires to heap them up and to fan them into flames.' Trying to account for this situation, he explained that 'wars are not made by the people but the people furiously carry them on.'[42] The U.D.C. did not really want this 'people' to decide the future, at least not until its propaganda had made a bigger impact. The U.D.C. writers had begun to sow doubts about the purpose of the war but they had made little impact on the working class as a whole. Morel was well aware of this and succeeded in getting an extensive column for himself in the *Labour Leader* in an attempt to improve the situation. Indeed, editorial restraint was necessary to prevent his column absorbing the paper. Week by week he addressed himself to Anglo-German relations in language which was less than cautious. In his view, the country was 'in the grip of a conspiracy against truth' since any attempt to bid the nation weigh carefully and think for itself was to be dismissed as 'pro-German'.[43] Instead of the customary cant, if the British people really felt any pity for Belgium it was time to face honestly 'what the effect upon Belgium would be of a refusal on our part to consider a settlement which would restore her territorial integrity and compensate her.'[44] Contrasting the House of Commons with the Reichstag, he wanted to know why 'no voice has yet been heard in repudiation of the doctrine of destruction, colonial annexation, and economic strangulation.'[45] He thought it worthy of note that the British and German peoples had to go on living on the same planet. As for the supposed 'conflict of ideals', it hardly applied with regard to colonies 'because Germany has never had the opportunity of demonstrating whether she possesses or does not possess the political sagacity to treat great white communities of her own stock overseas as we have learned, by bitter experience, is the right way to treat them.'[46]

Morel was not content to let his words alone make their impact on Labour. In March 1915 he drew up a 'Scheme to secure the support of the organised Labour of the country'.[47] He announced that, after conversations with MacDonald and Anderson, he was going to appoint a full-time organizer whose task it would be to develop contacts with Labour bodies up and down the country. Local U.D.C. branches should help him by developing their own connexions. In May 1915, Councillor Egerton P. Wake was given the job. The aim, as Morel told the General Council in June was 'to gain a solid footing for the Union among the Trade Unions.' It was only the first step in a policy which, he hoped, would 'eventuate in thoroughly infusing the Labour World with the Union's creed.'[48] Thanks to the generosity of the Buxton family, Wake was subsequently joined in this work by J. W. Kneeshaw and J. H. Hudson. Largely due to their efforts, the number of affiliated bodies, chiefly local Labour parties and trades councils, doubled to just over a hundred between June and the end of 1915. It was claimed that over three hundred thousand people belonged to affiliated organizations. Nevertheless, aware that this exaggerated the extent of U.D.C. influence, Morel warned the politicians of the

U.D.C. that they ought to begin 'to form clear notions of the port they are steering for'. Only if they actually became members of the I.L.P. might they be able to direct the movement in the way they wanted. Morel could be well pleased with the year's work.[49] There was still a long way to go, but the Union was already a body to be reckoned with. It was strong enough to launch, in November, its own monthly, *The U.D.C.* with, inevitably, Morel himself as editor. He now felt strong enough to persuade the Executive to ignore letters from the Bristol branch and elsewhere deploring the attempt 'to press on the Government and the nation any directly pacifist policy—at any rate until the situation, both political and military, is improved.'[50]

Despite the satisfaction with which the U.D.C. Executive viewed the developing links with the organized working-class, there was, beneath the surface, considerable tension between the U.D.C. and the I.L.P. For some, the principles of the Union were not revolutionary enough. Had not Arthur Henderson, on resigning from the U.D.C. when he joined the government, declared that he continued to support its principles?[51] Those principles did not apparently prevent him sharing in the government's policies. Of course, his decision to join the new Coalition Government in May refuelled the controversy on the war within Labour's own ranks. Philip Snowden played an increasingly prominent part in this debate. He launched a bitter attack on Henderson for accepting office. As an independent force, Labour might have rendered powerful help in shaping the peace terms; now its voice would be lost. Labour had also forfeited 'its claim to represent any distinct phase of democratic thought and action in Great Britain.'[52] Other leading I.L.P. figures like Bruce Glasier and Alfred Salter did not want to associate with the U.D.C. Liberals—even Snowden was somewhat compromised in their eyes. Glasier, a fierce critic of bourgeois radicalism, and Salter, a thoroughgoing Christian Socialist revolutionary, thought the U.D.C. only tinkered with the problem.[53] There was little point in endlessly turning over the actual circumstances of the war. The fact was that for years the International Socialist movement had forecast the likelihood of war. That was enough. Now it had happened. The whole system of 'militarism' was at fault. The enemy of the pacifists was no longer simply 'war', but the whole political and economic complex which was mobilizing the nation at arms. This new Militarist Imperialism had two roots; capitalist fear of losing the foremost place in the scramble for the world's wealth and the desire of the ruling classes to regain political command over the democracy and keep the wage-earners in industrial subjection.[54]

The Annual Conference of the I.L.P. at Norwich in April 1915

E

brought this confusion on the question of pacifism into the open. The Chairman, F. W. Jowett, located the cause of the war in the antagonisms which tore capitalist society apart and in the policy of colonial dependencies and aggressive Imperialism. Nevertheless, Jowett did not accept as a correct representation of the I.L.P. position the view that the British Government ought to have declared for neutrality. He agreed that it was honour bound by its secret understanding with France to declare for intervention. In acknowledging this however, there was even more reason to speak out in order to ensure that 'never again would the witch's cauldron of secret diplomacy brew the war broth of Hell for mankind.' When discussion followed, there was considerable controversy. The series of pamphlets which the I.L.P. sponsored, 'Labour and War', was criticized from diametrically opposed standpoints. Pamphlets were attacked both for omitting to stress the crimes of the Central Powers as well as those of the Allied Governments, and for including the phrase 'obviously the war must be finished now'. MacDonald was deputed to elucidate the latter statement. 'It was no use at the present moment talking about a mere "Stop-the-War" movement' he said. 'They had first of all got to lay down under what conditions the war had to be stopped.' J. R. Clynes found the party's position distinctly puzzling. The leaders rightly said that Belgium had to be freed and compensated. How could they say that and then calmly leave the task to others? Since Clynes had 'gone over to the militarists' his question was ignored. On the motion of C. H. Norman, the conference was quite happy to accept by an overwhelming majority that there were only two issues in the war. One was that between Germany and Russia in the Balkans. The other was the Anglo-German naval rivalry in which the British government had conducted a policy which had driven the country to a warlike solution.

This unanimity disappeared when the conference considered a motion by Dr. Salter on 'Socialism and War'. He urged that in future Socialists should refuse to support every war entered into by capitalistic governments, whatever the ostensible object of the war and even if it was nominally of a defensive character. A speaker then moved the deletion of the words 'capitalistic government'. Miss Ellen Wilkinson then wanted to know how the resolution affected miners fighting capitalists in Colorado. Not at all, answered C. H. Norman. It specifically referred to conflicts between nations. Another speaker suggested that it was not possible to preserve the sanctity of human life without defensive war if necessary. The Woolwich branch wanted to delete 'whatever the ostensible object of the war' and substitute 'except for the purpose of repelling an actual invasion of territory'. J. H. Hudson declared

that the Woolwich amendment would justify the British Government's stand in the Boer War. Salter announced that he accepted
the first amendment, but there was a protest against appearing to
identify the I.L.P. with non-resistance. After a vote, it was clear
that the conference was equally divided. Where exactly the party
stood was therefore mysterious. It opposed war as an instrument
of national policy, but at that point agreement stopped.[55]

Younger members of the party were not satisfied with this vague
state of affairs. The most critical voice was that of Clifford Allen
who, at twenty-five, was widely held to be the voice of the coming
generation. After Cambridge, where his opinions moved steadily left-
wards, Allen became secretary of the new Labour daily, the *Daily
Citizen* in 1912. In this capacity, he mingled with the great men
of the Labour Movement. He was a member of the Fabian Society,
and in 1914 led the small minority who felt that it was wrong for
Britain to fight at all, whether or not Belgium was the real cause
of the intervention. 'German policy' he had then declared 'was
a defensive one' and the violation of Belgian neutrality was 'a
necessary part of that policy.' He argued that International
Socialism would recover from the blow it had received. Shortly
afterwards, he published a pamphlet, *Is Germany Right and Britain
Wrong?* When his newspaper supported the war, Allen was free
to find the appropriate forum for his talents. 'I am not content
with our present activities' he told his fellow members of the
I.L.P. The U.D.C. should continue its valuable work, but 'let the
I.L.P. take up as its particular burden a campaign for the
immediate statement of the Government's peace terms and thus
force its opinion once more upon public attention.'[56]

Allen's call met with a mixed response. Ellen Wilkinson agreed
that the U.D.C. was too cautious a body. She found its four points
commonplace. In some parts of the country its members were
unwilling to attack the Liberal Government of 1914 for its part in
bringing about the war.[57] MacDonald, on the other hand, was
disturbed by Allen's extremism. In his judgment, every letter from
Germany showed the devotion of the German people to the Kaiser
and it was 'no use perverting or suppressing the facts.'[58] His advice
could not repair the breach between those who thought that the
I.L.P. should wait patiently for the rest of the Labour Party to
see the light and those who wanted to see the I.L.P. wash its hands
of the parliamentary body and strike out in a new direction. The
infectious enthusiasm of Allen was regarded with suspicion by
those with more experience than he possessed of the intricacies of
party politics. On such bodies as the War Emergency Workers'
Committee, it was quite possible for Labour men to work together
regardless of divisions on the war.[59] Refusing her signature to a

manifesto urging negotiations, Beatrice Webb replied that it was better for those with little knowledge of foreign affairs to remain silent. 'What I am concerned with is the Labour question after the war.'[60] There were many rank and file members who agreed with her and who found the enthusiasm for peace which characterized members of the party who had never done a day's manual work in their lives somewhat oppressive.

One thing is clear from this confused pattern of activity in 1915; the Peace Movement had revived. The U.D.C. and the I.L.P. were both, potentially, considerable centres of dissent. To what extent they became 'anti-war' would probably depend on the war itself. Already, by the end of 1915, they and the other peace bodies had succeeded in launching the idea of 'peace by negotiation', though it was a propaganda phrase rather than one with any precise content. They had also begun to undermine the reputation of the men who had taken the country into battle, and started to discredit the official explanations for the war. There was an increasing emphasis on the physical and economic cost of the war and the fact that it could still be years before victory could be achieved. Skilfully used over many months, these assertions could reduce government confidence and, conceivably, lead to a change of policy. There were, however, few signs that the campaign had yet been successful. The Cabinet had been far too busy in the first fifteen months of the war with the immediate problems of survival to spend much time drawing up plans for peace. Sir Edward Grey was personally interested in some sort of League of Nations at the end of the war and Lowes Dickinson did inform him of the international movement and its objectives, but there is little sign that his policy in this matter was directly affected by outside influences. Nor did the Cabinet, either before or after the formation of the Coalition Government, respond to the call for a clarification in detail of its war aims. After the Constantinople agreement and the Treaty of London, ministers well knew that the war was no longer simply for the restoration of Belgium, yet they kept silent. They had little private enthusiasm for these steps, which had been taken in the interests of the allied war effort as a whole. The future of Belgium, however, did remain vital. Doubtless, as some pacifists urged was the case, Germany would be prepared to settle on the basis of the existing *status quo,* but the Cabinet would not give the plan a moment's thought. Indeed, even a peace on the basis of the *status quo ante* would be inadequate. The war could be long and exhausting, but there was no disposition in 1915 to abandon the struggle.

Nevertheless, although the politicians knew that public opinion was not, on the whole, hostile to the war, they were aware that in parts of the country there was no special enthusiasm for it. Events could develop in such a way that centres of disaffection might appear. It was for this reason that the activities of the U.D.C. and the I.L.P. were closely scrutinized.[61] Morel was a favourite target in the pro-war popular press. Accusations about his sympathies and the source of his funds were freely made. Old scores from the days of his Congo agitation were paid off. When U.D.C. speakers ventured on public platforms, their meetings were occasionally broken up amid violent scenes. Critics asserted that the various peace societies and groups had the common aim 'to bring about a conclusion of the war on terms which shall not be unfavourable to the Germans.' Ponsonby and Trevelyan sought the advice of Sir John Simon, the Home Secretary, but despite their previous political association with him, received little satisfaction about future protection. When their meetings were disrupted, they received letters of sympathy from those, like Gilbert Murray, who disagreed with them.[62] Nevertheless, pacifists felt that they were being cold-shouldered and ostracized. Their ties with former colleagues became strained and, inevitably, they saw little future for themselves in Liberalism. They thus found themselves in a paradoxical position—though one which apparently did not trouble them—that public opinion was the voice of peace and that public opinion needed to be converted to their convictions. In November 1915, the official, but 'anti-war' Labour candidate at Merthyr Tydfil for the seat made vacant by Keir Hardie's death lost to a 'patriot'. It was clear, both to pacifists and the government, that there was still some way to go before the Peace Movement swept the country.

CHAPTER FOUR

The 'Fight against Militarism'

Preparing for peace was only one aspect of the Peace Movement's activity. From the beginning of the war there was great anxiety that within a short time 'militarism'—the subordination of all values to the needs of war—would be introduced. One by one, it was foretold, the freedoms of Englishmen would crumble before the onslaught of the militarists. The nation would become so regulated and regimented that it would resemble that very Prussian militarism which it was supposed to be dedicated to defeating. There were dark hints that once the shackles had been put on, they would not be removed when peace returned. The chief fear was the introduction of compulsory military service. The pre-war advocates of conscription would surely revive their demands. Initially, however, this proved not to be the case. The rate of voluntary recruitment was such that it was all the government could do to make sure that the new force was properly equipped. The Prime Minister, assured that conscription would be unpopular in the country, saw no reason to introduce it. An army of eager volunteers was better than one of reluctant conscripts. So long as recruiting remained steady, there was little ground from which to challenge Asquith's assertion that conscription was unnecessary. The moment the figures fell, as they did in July 1915, he was vulnerable, especially since his Cabinet now contained some members who actively supported its introduction. The demand was raised in a number of parliamentary debates. In the same month, Milner became Chairman of the General Council of the National Service League and condemned a policy of 'drift' on the subject. Northcliffe gave these views wide coverage in *The Times* and the *Daily Mail*. In face of pressure from these, and other sources, Asquith retreated slightly. Since it was unclear just how many men

were available for military service, he made provision for a
National Register to be taken in the middle of August. It was discovered that over two million men of military age were not in the
services. The production of this figure did not, however, lead to
agreement on the appropriate next step.

The situation in the Cabinet was delicate. Some of the Prime
Minister's leading Liberal colleagues, like Grey, Simon, Runciman
and McKenna were firmly opposed to conscription. There was a
serious danger that the Cabinet would break up unless Asquith
explored every alternative. In October, acting through Kitchener,
he appointed Lord Derby as Director-General of Recruiting with
instructions to conduct a vigorous new canvas. Derby, himself a
conscriptionist, undertook the task on the understanding that if
his drive failed, some form of compulsory service would be
introduced.[1] It was an arrangement which suited the Prime Minister.
If sufficient recruits were forthcoming, the demand for conscription
would lessen. If they were not, he could tell his reluctant Liberal
colleagues that he had no other course. Precisely how the drive
was to be deemed a success or a failure was left unclear. When
Derby reported to the Cabinet on 15 December, he was able to
report considerable progress, but nevertheless the drift towards
conscription could not be halted. Asquith had already given a
promise that married men who had attested under the Derby
scheme would not be called on until the pool of single men had
been fully exhausted—if necessary by conscription.

A Cabinet Committee was set up to provide the details of a
new Military Service Bill. Speed was now the essence of the matter.
Asquith wanted to present the measure as a further development
from the Derby Scheme, not as something revolutionary in
character. The Draft Bill was therefore applied to the same class
of men as had previously been canvassed by Lord Derby. Because
there was no civilian department of state to hand, the War Office
was given the responsibility for supervising the call-up. There was
no provision in the draft for the exemption of men who objected
to military service on the grounds of conscience.[2]

When the Cabinet considered the Bill on 28 December, its out-
line was approved, but McKenna and Runciman dissented and
reserved their position. Grey also made it clear that if they found
it necessary to resign, he would do so too. Simon, the Home
Secretary, was known to be strongly hostile. Perhaps with the
exception of Simon, they did not object to the principle of compulsory military service so much as the sapping of the financial
and industrial security of the country which, they believed, it would
entail. However, in return for some rather insubstantial under-
takings to have a look at the overall cost of the war, Grey,

McKenna and Runciman stayed on. Simon resigned alone. Nevertheless, if he used his formidable debating talents, he might manage to raise a substantial parliamentary opposition to the Bill, composed of unhappy Liberals, Labour and Irish members. A substantial protest in the Commons might encourage the opposition to conscription in the country and, conceivably, make the new law unworkable. The Prime Minister wanted to present the measure as a demonstration of national will and determination. Probably, therefore, the short-term need to reduce the threat posed by Simon, rather than a fine concern for 'tolerance' led Asquith to insert in the revised Draft Bill that exemption could be claimed 'on the grounds of a conscientious objection to bearing arms.' This new proposal set a host of problems, both of definition and administration, which had to be settled speedily before parliament met to consider the Bill. Asquith refused to listen to military pleas that exemption be restricted to those with historically authenticated religious objections. He also changed the wording, at the last moment, from an objection to 'bearing arms' to an objection to 'undertaking combatant service.' The proposed system of appeal tribunals was strengthened and was placed under the general direction of the Local Government Board. However, in the haste, a crucial ambiguity in the wording left it uncertain whether these tribunals were empowered to grant exemptions from all military service or only from combatant service. At the time, it was not expedient to focus too much attention on this 'conscience clause' because this would compromise Asquith's contention that what he was asking his party to accept was not really a conscription bill at all. When Asquith rose to speak on 5 January 1916 he was fully aware that in making this last minute concession he ran the grave risk of upsetting the Tories. It could only be justified if he succeeded in carrying the day.

The opposition to the proposal that Asquith was about to present seemed formidable. As usual, however, it was composed of widely differing opinions which made it less effective in practice. If Asquith had attempted to introduce his measure without a 'conscience' clause, the critics might have been more formidable. However, the provision of exemption—before its complexities were properly appreciated—disarmed one set of opponents. Even so, many Nonconformist Liberals, who had not until this date associated themselves with pacifists, were disturbed. The central ground occupied both by these Liberals and by pacifists was that conscription was the beginning of militarism. As the Peace Society declared, 'were it only a method of military procedure, it would not interest us, but it involves the whole advance of a military system which is threatening to swamp and engulf the national life.'[3]

Whatever Lloyd George might think, *War and Peace* argued in November 1915, 'the introduction of compulsory service does raise very grave and very controversial questions of principle.' Its adoption would be 'the greatest blow which has been struck at the principles of liberty and civil government for generations.'[4] Morel, writing in *The U.D.C.* argued that voluntaryism had proved a magnificent success. There was no call for hasty legislation. The attempt to stampede the country into conscription was part and parcel of a general policy 'and should be recognised as such.'[5] In the *Socialist Review*, Ramsay MacDonald lamented that governments found it so hard to be convinced of the truth of Fox's words, 'Liberty is order; liberty is strength.' He contended that if the war went on and discontent among the people were to spread, 'The Defence of the Realm Acts and the trials and prosecutions already taken under them will, in spite of their iniquity, be but a foretaste of what is yet to come.'[6] Bruce Glasier was even more forthright. 'Compulsory military service' he wrote 'stands in a category of tyranny by itself and calls for our utmost moral and political resistance. No ordinance of oppression that a Government, even if backed by the majority of its citizens, could devise, strikes so fundamentally at the root of personal liberty, or so mortally at the human spirit, as the enforced bearing of arms for organised human slaughter.'[7] The *Nation,* too, lamented that there was a type of Liberal 'whose idea of patriotic duty during war consists in throwing to the wolves one after another of his Liberal principles . . . Free Speech, Free Press, Habeas Corpus, Voluntary Service, Free Trade—let them all go in this war for liberty!'[8]

The tone of these remarks was impeccably defiant, but the 'great revolt' so confidently forecast, showed little sign of developing. One reason for this may have been the ambivalent attitude of the peace societies. The Fellowship of Reconciliation, for example, both opposed conscription and at the same time felt that its members should be prepared to suffer the consequences of their refusal to serve. Similarly, it at once welcomed the provision of an exemption clause and warned that members of the Fellowship would probably not seek its protection. Its committee decided that the F.O.R. would only join in protests about the act which were of a definitely religious character.[9] It would not allow its funds to be used for political purposes. The Society of Friends, on the other hand, was very anxious to insist on the right of conscientious objection. In September 1915, the Meeting for Sufferings addressed a memorial to both Houses of Parliament. It eschewed consideration of the military and political arguments and did not base its opposition on any abstract doctrine of the right of the individual to be free from the control of the state. Friends believed that it was the duty of every citizen to serve his country in peaceful ways in order that Britain should perform its true service for humanity. What Friends did deny was 'the right of any Government to compel its subjects to do things that their conscience disapproves.'[10] The attempts of the government in January 1916 to meet the Quaker position were appreciated, but Asquith was warned that 'a large number of conscientious objectors are not prepared to accept compulsory service, whether combatant or otherwise, under the military authorities.' To attempt to compel persons with such views to accept service required by the military authorities would be 'a violation of freedom of conscience.'[11] Nevertheless, under the proposed legislation, Quakers could reasonably expect that the popular identification of the Society of Friends with pacifism would stand them in good stead when their claims for exemption were considered.

The position of the U.D.C., however, was more complicated. In the first month of the war, F. W. Hirst, the editor of *The Economist* and a strong opponent of British entry, wrote to Morel observing that there was 'one vital omission' from his programme. It was vital that the Union should do all it could 'to prevent a military despotism being established in this country bringing with it conscription, protection and a substitution of martial law for trial by judge and jury.'[12] However, opposition to conscription was not included in the official statement of the U.D.C.'s aims.

When fears revived in the summer of 1915, opposition to compulsory military service seemed to some members of the Executive to be an ideal way of linking the U.D.C. with the Labour Movement. Other supporters of the U.D.C. took a different view. In June, Lowes Dickinson wrote to Russell advising against such a course. People who had joined on the basis of the four points would have a legitimate grievance if other points were included to which they might be strongly opposed. The Union had a heavy enough burden of misunderstanding and misrepresentation to carry without adding to it. He himself had 'always thought that the propaganda of the U.D.C. dealt with after the war, not with the way of carrying on the war' and he might feel compelled to resign. He thought there was no case for conscription but was not prepared to say that the necessity for such a step might not arise in a life and death struggle. Notwithstanding such objections, in the same month, while Morel was absent, the Executive passed a resolution pledging the U.D.C. to 'oppose to the utmost any attempt to impose compulsory service either for military or industrial purposes . . .'[13]

Morel was not pleased when he heard of this action, calling it a 'grave step'. If 'to the utmost' was anything more than rhetoric, it would mean that the U.D.C. was committed to resisting a measure which might well become the law of the land. Rather surprisingly, he chose this occasion to declare that he was not a Quaker. It might seem jesuitical, he wrote, but he drew a distinction between compulsion for home defence and compulsion for service abroad. He held that the utmost a man could be compelled to do was to enlist for home defence, adding 'I should find it impossible to resist that call.' He was most anxious lest the U.D.C. find itself stranded, for if Labour did not revolt, it would be 'beating the air'. If the government did make out an overwhelming case for compulsion—something he felt unlikely—then the U.D.C. could only resist it 'by taking up the attitude that we don't mind whether England is beaten or not.'[14] While, no doubt, these were his personal views, Morel may also have been aware that the Executive was rather out of step with the branches on this matter. At the General Council in October 1915, a strong resolution saying that no case had been made out for compulsory military service, and that its introduction would be 'disastrous' to the principles of liberty, was defeated by the votes of eighteen branches to ten. The Executive's original resolution would probably have been defeated by an even larger margin.[15] Morel may also have calculated that conscription would bring home to many men the reality of the war. He may well have hoped that an increasing number of families would ask themselves whether it was worth continuing the fighting for such uncertain objectives. Doubts of this kind would make them more receptive to U.D.C. propaganda.

In the event, therefore, the Union condemned conscription but did not concert opposition against it. It did, however, release one of its paid organizers, Bernard Langdon-Davies, to become secretary of a new body, the National Council against Conscription —which later continued its activities under the name of the National Council for Civil Liberties. Its objects were to work for the repeal of the Military Service Act, to prevent conscription from becoming a permanent part of British life, and generally to safeguard all civil liberties which appeared to be under attack. On its executive were familiar names like Clifford Allen, Charles Ammon, Margaret Bondfield, Dr. John Clifford, Alex Gossip, Dr. Henry Hodgkin, George Lansbury, F. W. Pethick-Lawrence, Robert Williams and H. W. Massingham. Significantly, this list contained both 'pro-war' and 'anti-war' advocates in a common campaign against the iniquities of compulsion. The N.C.A.C., however, never became a large body. Most of the people who graced its platform were more active in other bodies. As so often in the Peace Movement, 'co-ordinating' activity meant in reality establishing another small organization.

Morel's caution concerning the Labour revolt against conscription was well justified. For months, commentators had been stressing the profound objections which existed among the workers. J. H. Thomas, for example, warned Asquith in August 1915 that its introduction would give 'those in our ranks—who from the first opposed the war, such an opportunity which they certainly would not be slow to take advantage of. . . .'[16] It was often suggested that South Wales and Clydeside would come out in open opposition to the war. In retrospect, however, it seems likely that such discontent as existed was caused by the industrial aspects of the measure. The so-called pacifism of Clydeside was in any case a complex phenomenon. David Kirkwood, a prominent member of the Clyde Workers' Committee, was basically anxious to defend the position of the skilled workmen. As he told Lloyd George, 'We will not allow the patriotic sentiment abroad at this moment to be a cloak under which to introduce low-paid labour and reduce us to the level of the textile workers of Lancashire.' Kirkwood maintained that he was not 'Stop the War' in his outlook. On the other hand, since he also stated that he could not support the continuation of the war until Germany was defeated, he must be classified as an advocate of peace by negotiation.[17] It is not therefore surprising to find him being criticized both by patriotic workers and by those who wished to sabotage the war effort. In this confused situation, it was difficult for Lloyd George to grasp the real objectives behind the demands which were put to him during his noisy Christmastime visit to Glasgow in 1915. The Workers' Committee did seem to be asking the government to take over all industries and introduce a considerable element of worker participation in management. The grounds for advocating this step, however, included greater efficiency in meeting the needs of the nation at war. In their turn, Marxists like Maclean, Gallacher and MacManus were sceptical about the intentions of the Committee and alleged that the anti-war sentiments of the working class were being left on one side. The Marxists themselves were not pacifists in the sense that they abhorred violence in the pursuit of all political objectives, but they opposed the war in progress because its outcome could be 'no concern of the workers one way or the other.' Urged on by Bruce Glasier, they tried to organise a strike, both in Glasgow and elsewhere, in protest against conscription, but they failed to raise sufficient support and the agitation fizzled out by the end of January. In this confused and highly rhetorical situation, it is almost impossible to judge how strong 'anti-war' sentiment was. All that can be said is that while the government was sufficiently alarmed to suppress some of the local political broadsheets and, a little later, to arrest some of the local leaders, the promised 'Revolt on the Clyde' did not take place.

There was, however, one source of opposition which remained undimmed: the No Conscription Fellowship proudly proclaimed its defiance of government policy. This body had been formed as the result of a letter sent out in November 1914 by Fenner Brockway, then working on the *Labour Leader*. Brockway, son of Congregationalist missionaries, was in his mid-twenties. In his letter he foretold the coming of conscription and asked all men who would become eligible for military service to join him in a fellowship of those who would refuse to enlist.[18] It was, above all, a movement of young men, most of them members of the I.L.P., who wanted to run their own campaign without the restraint of their elders. Clifford Allen found in the call the outlet for his talents for which he had been searching since the outbreak of the war. He quickly became chairman of the new body. Other enthusiastic young men who joined at an early stage included C. H. Norman, the Quaker Socialist Barratt Brown, and J. H. Hudson and Morgan Jones, elementary school teachers and active I.L.P. speakers in Manchester and South Wales respectively. Edward Grubb, the respected Quaker writer, became treasurer. Bertrand Russell, a rather older young man, found the N.C.F. more exhilarating than the U.D.C. with which he was also associated. He was, at least at the beginning, very enthusiastic. Miss Catherine Marshall, who had been prominent as a suffragette, offered her considerable organizational abilities. Her regard for the chairman went rather deeper than simple comradely concern.

The response to Brockway's letter was therefore sufficient to warrant the establishment of an office in London early in 1915. From then on, letters of advice and instruction were circulated to supporters all over the country in an attempt to counteract the pressure for conscription. The N.C.F. did not specifically advise its members against registering under the measure of August 1915, but warned that, in its judgment, registration meant that conscription was near. However, despite this activity, it was only after the first National Convention in November 1915 that the Fellowship really came to life. Allen used the occasion to describe the basis of its concern. It did not consist of people whose objection to conscription was 'merely military or strategic'. He sympathised with those who objected to conscription because it would be the gravest possible blow to the free institutions of the country and to the activities of the trade union movement, but that was not the reason for the existence of the N.C.F. either. What really united all the members, he claimed, and brought them together was their belief 'in the sanctity of human life . . . that whatever else a State may or may not effect, there is one interference with individual judgment that no State in the world has any sanction to enforce;

that is to tamper with the unfettered right of every man to decide for himself the issue of life and death.' He warned members that the way ahead might be full of suffering, but the cause would flourish to the degree that they were prepared to suffer for it. They would all have to be prepared to undergo whatever penalties the state might inflict—even death itself—rather than go back on their convictions. In the words of its statement of faith, the N.C.F. was 'an organisation of men likely to be called upon to undertake military service in the event of conscription, who will refuse from conscientious motives to bear arms, because they consider human life to be sacred, and cannot, therefore, assume the responsibility of inflicting death.' It denied the right of governments to compel anyone to bear arms. A national committee—with Allen, Grubb, Brockway, Ayles, Brown, Hudson, Norman, Jones, Russell and Salter the most prominent members—pledged itself to frustrate the government's plans.[19]

However, when the Prime Minister rose to address the Commons on 5 January 1916, he did not seem unduly perturbed by the protests of the various peace bodies. No doubt he was more conscious of the number of honourable members in the chamber who were dressed in khaki. His speech was deliberately flat, all of a piece with the notion that no fundamental change was being proposed. When he came to the fourth ground for exemption, the conscientious objection to undertaking combatant service, his announcement was greeted with long and contemptuous laughter from one section of the House. Asquith resumed by claiming that the provision was in accordance with British traditions. The men who would receive such exemption were, he supposed, ready to perform other duties. He led M.P.'s to believe that they would receive exemption only from military combatant duties, though this was not, it seems, the interpretation placed on their decision by some other members of the Cabinet. Whatever ambiguity the Prime Minister left behind, however, he had succeeded in his task. Simon, speaking later in the debate, argued that 'the condition that compulsion should only be adopted by general consent has been abandoned in favour of the condition that compulsion shall be adopted without any regard to the numbers to be compelled or the strength of the opposition . . .' but he was ineffective. Llewellyn Williams, however, spoke for many Liberals when he said that he would have preferred such a Bill 'from a Tory Government which believes in compulsory service, than at the hands of gentlemen who profess their unbounded devotion to the voluntary principle while cutting its throat.'[20] Refusing a plea from Arthur Balfour not to disturb national unity by forcing a division, Simon and his followers went into the lobbies. There was little consolation for them in the result. The voting figures showed 403 for and 105 against, with about 100 Liberal abstentions. Approximately half of the votes against had been cast by Irish Home Rulers. Since the measure did not in fact apply to Ireland, they subsequently abstained, and in the debate on the second reading the opposition could only muster 39 votes.

During the Bill's passage through parliament a number of changes were made. The emotions which had been aroused lost their intensity and it was agreed on all sides that Walter Long, the President of the Local Government Board, handled his measure with great tact. Attempts to limit the ground of exemption more strictly were defeated. On the other hand, a Liberal proposal that it would be sufficient for a man to declare his conscientious objection on oath was also rejected. Long continued to believe that local tribunals would be able to discriminate effectively and honestly between the applicants who came before them. He could have had little idea of the extraordinary variety of grounds on which exemption would in fact be claimed. More serious than this, however, was the failure to give clear guidance to the tribunals on their powers. The ambiguity both in the original drafting and in the Cabinet's own mind remained. Different ministers appeared to express different opinions on the question of whether or not it was possible to give the conscientious objectors complete and absolute exemption. The government did, however, accept an amendment moved by the Quaker M.P.'s, Arnold Rowntree and Edmund Harvey, which would allow conscientious objectors an exemption from all military service provided the applicants concerned undertook work of national importance. There was no attempt to define what 'work of national importance' was, with the result that local tribunals were to be reluctant to suggest this alternative. In hoping that its measures would avoid an open clash, would avoid men either being sent to prison or being ignored in their resistance, the government was being unduly optimistic.

The passage into law of the Military Service Act on 10 February 1916 marked a decisive stage in the evolution of wartime pacifism. Until this point, if one led a quiet life, being an 'opponent of the war' was largely a matter of private conviction without public significance. Now it became a matter of general concern to the state. For eligible men, a choice between fighting on the one hand and accepting or refusing the alternatives offered on the other, could not now be avoided. It is not surprising that the new situation produced much indecision and confusion of counsel among pacifists. The Peace Society, for example, could only say, rather feebly, 'We are free to confess that it was not easy for us to determine whether Conscientious Objectors ought or ought not to state their objections to compulsory service before the Tribunals.'[21] Nor was the Fellowship of Reconciliation any more forthright. Some pointed out that there was no work which did not indirectly or directly help the conduct of the war. If pacifists starved to death rather than fight they made food available for those who were prepared to do so. It was widely believed that the alternative which pacifists were being offered was quite inadequate, though a minority welcomed it. That minority was divided, however, between those who objected to their consciences being tested and those who thought that a test was justified. The ubiquitous Dr. Salter, this time speaking as a member of the F.O.R., remarked ironically that the war might come to an end before they came to a clear decision of policy.[22] There was, however, more vigour in the debates among Friends. The work of Edmund Harvey in securing the provision of work of 'national importance' for those who refused to fight was appreciated, but the Meeting for Sufferings felt that the scheme had great dangers because it 'might have the effect of obscuring our testimony or committing us to the seeming support of the conditions created by the Military Service Act.' It stood by its previous decision that exemption from combatant duties 'does not meet the objections of the great majority of our members and of those who think with us.'[23]

If the established peace bodies were all somewhat embarrassed by the conscription issue, the N.C.F. professed to welcome the challenge. Its leaders were unimpressed by the concessions the government had made. In March, Allen and Brockway informed the Prime Minister that the proposed Non-Combatant Corps was not an acceptable alternative. Such a force would be, in every sense, 'part of the military machine'. Asquith should appreciate that the N.C.F.'s objections applied to 'any form of military service, combatant or non-combatant, and also, for all but a few of us, any form of civil alternative, under a scheme whereby the Government seeks to facilitate national organization for the prosecution of war.'[24] This letter was written just at the time when the first cases were being considered before local Tribunals up and down the country. The leaders of the N.C.F. were determined to frustrate the operation of the Act for their aim was to 'cause the removal of Conscription from the life of the country of free traditions.'[25] Therefore, while members were of course free to follow their consciences, they were nevertheless urged early in February to apply for absolute and complete exemption 'for thus we can advance our real objection and make our testimony effective in the country.'[26] Writing in the newly established N.C.F. journal, the *Tribunal*, on 8 March, Allen claimed that if the local tribunals refused even to recognize conscience, and the Appeal Tribunals maintained their decisions, the government would ultimately have to face the problem of imposing penalties. It was therefore essential that the conscientious objector should be seen to be prepared to suffer rather than be false to his faith.[27] Five days later, his own claim for absolute exemption was turned down by the Battersea Tribunal. Speaking as a non-religious Socialist, he made it clear that he could not accept any distinction between combatant and non-combatant service. It was war that was wrong. As a result of this experience, Allen claimed that the Tribunals were a farce. It would be better for the government to face up to the problem. It should treat those conscientious objectors whose cases had not been considered as the Act intended; they should be left to continue usefully employed as they had been hitherto.[28] In taking this stand for absolute exemption as opposed to alternative service it was the intention of the N.C.F.'s leaders to make nonsense of the Government's scheme. They were helped by the fact that it took some time for adequate administrative provision for alternative service to be made.

On 8 April 1916, the second National Convention of the N.C.F. was held in London. There was a representative selection of speakers from the different peace groups. In his address from the chair, Allen rallied the conscientious objectors by linking their objection to conscription and their objection to war in general. Their alternative to conscription was not the maintenance of the voluntary system. It was, rather, that the country should immediately enter upon peace negotiations. Not everybody agreed with this contention although it was not discussed further. The major source of controversy was, instead, the status of alternative service. Allen reiterated his basic objection to the whole idea of a Non-combatant Corps. The fact that such a provision had been made showed how completely the Government misunderstood their position. In fact, however, not all pacifists were as opposed to the scheme as he claimed. Some simply had a personal objection to being placed in a position where they would be expected to kill another human being. Exemption from this possibility was all they asked and non-combatant service would meet their case. Others both objected to fighting and to non-combatant service under military control, but would be prepared to accept work of national importance. Others refused even this. To accept such alternative service would only mean releasing other men for fighting and thereby prolong the war. They demanded the right to do whatever they chose as though no war was happening at all. Beatrice Webb, a hostile observer, felt the N.C.F. was not really interested in the right to refuse military service, but in the inauguration of 'a strike against war by the armies—actual or potential—of all warring peoples.' She recognized at the meeting a combination of 'professional rebels' and undoubtedly superior young people whose reiterance of 'we are the people whose eyes are open' was rather irritating. Although Allen explicitly denied it, her conclusion was that 'They *want* to be martyrs, so as to bring about a revulsion of feeling against any prosecution of the war. They are as hostile to voluntary conscription as they are to conscription . . . not so much conscientious objectors as a militant minority of elects, intent on thwarting the will of the majority of ordinary citizens expressed in a national policy.'[29]

While the desire for martyrdom was undoubtedly present among some N.C.F. members, the immediate objective of the leadership was the clarification of the law. Churchmen, academics and politicians were all approached to use their influence to this end. In a letter to *The Times,* the Bishop of Lincoln claimed that the Act explicitly stated that 'the conscientious objector to war is to be exempt from service.' The conduct of the Tribunals was therefore a scandal. Allegations about the iniquitous behaviour of the Tribunals were frequent, though, as a recent study of their practice and composition establishes, these allegations were somewhat exaggerated.[30] The Tribunals did make mistakes in some instances, but the exact state of the law made for confusion on all sides. In an attempt to clarify the situation, Allen and Miss Marshall had a session with Lloyd George on 11 April to explain their grievances, but it produced little immediate improvement. All the while, the N.C.F. leaders bombarded sympathetic contacts with information about the fate of individual conscientious objectors and their own general standpoint. 'We who believe that it is wrong to fight' Russell wrote to Gilbert Murray 'are bound not only to abstain from fighting ourselves, but to abstain from abetting others in fighting. What would you and the police think of a man who had a conscientious objection to being a burglar, but was willing to undertake "non-combatant service" by standing in the street and giving warning of the approach of the constable?' As for work of national importance, accepting alternative work to one's ordinary employment liberated others for the trenches and assisted in the national mobilization for war. To ask someone who objected to war to take part in its organization was to ask him to be utterly inconsistent with his principles. All such schemes 'seem to many of us to embody a compromise which we could not accept without fundamental treachery to all that we believe.'[31] Nevertheless, the day after Russell wrote this letter, and despite the pleas of the N.C.F., the High Court ruled that the Tribunals had no power to grant absolute exemption. If Russell's exposition of the N.C.F.

standpoint was correct, it seemed that an open confrontation between the objectors and the government was inevitable.

It was not a confrontation which the Prime Minister wanted. Although he did not agree with Russell, Murray was sufficiently impressed by the seriousness of the situation to approach Asquith. The two men lunched together on 30 April. A decision taken the previous day by the Cabinet, to extend compulsion to all men of military age, provided an opportunity to clarify the law. Asquith himself was prepared to abandon the provision that non-combatant work should be under military control. His colleagues, it subsequently appeared, were not prepared to go so far. However, when the new law was announced the following month, it contained an explicit assurance that Tribunals were in fact empowered to give absolute exemption. It was not, of course, stated that they should normally give such absolute exemption. Long himself supposed that this power would be used but sparingly, otherwise there was a danger that the whole scheme would be overturned. There were many like him who found it quite unpalatable that objectors should be totally exempted from all service to the state in this emergency. Their mood was not helped when Allen, who had been allowed to find work of national importance when his case was heard on appeal, wrote to the Tribunal of 11 May claiming that his work as Chairman of the N.C.F. qualified. Blatant non-co-operation of this kind must have hardened the Cabinet against any further concessions to conscientious objectors. Even Charles Gore, Bishop of Oxford, who wrote to the Prime Minister that he was anxious to prevent a 'root of bitterness' emerging in the community, did not dissent from the view that absolutist objectors should be punished. However, the important point was that they should not be punished as soldiers; they should be transferred to civil authority for this purpose.[32] For the time being, though, attitudes on both sides hardened and Tribunals were sparing in the use of their power to grant absolute exemption.

In different ways, both the Cabinet and the N.C.F. committee were embarrassed by these developments. The Cabinet now had to face the fact that there were conscientious objectors who had been refused exemption but who continued to hold to their principles after their enlistment. There were allegations that such men were subject to serious ill-treatment. Even more important, was the question of whether objectors were to be shot for refusing to obey orders. Asquith never intended that this should happen. Writing on his behalf to Miss Marshall, David Davies M.P. assured her: 'I have ascertained that directions have been given to Sir Douglas Haig that no conscientious objectors in France are to be shot for refusal to obey orders.'[33] The problem now became to devise a scheme which would take the position of these men into account without undermining the verdicts of the Tribunals. In consultation with the Home Secretary, Herbert Samuel, it was decided that men who had been court-martialled for refusal to obey orders should have their cases reconsidered by the Central Tribunal and if their pleas were accepted, they should remain technically in the Army, but in practice be set apart for civilian employment. The Brace Committee was set up to work out the details of such a scheme. Those intransigents who had refused to accept military jurisdiction had reason to hope that they had won the day.

The N.C.F. also had its difficulties. The bold 'all or nothing' approach sounded magnificent, but it did not represent the views of all conscientious objectors, or even of all members of the N.C.F. committee. The ringing declarations of the 1500 delegates to the April Convention certainly did not represent the views of the purported 15,000 supporters of the N.C.F. In private, the committee was quite aware of this fact at the time. Russell wrote to Miss Marshall that it was clear to him that a scheme of 'national importance' could be had if the N.C.F. would take it. On the other hand, 'total exemption cannot be got till a good many have suffered severely.' In these circumstances, he had come to the conclusion that 'a large number of the N.C.F. will, individually, become willing to accept work of national importance after a period of solitary confinement on bread and water.' If I thought most would hold to what they voted in the Convention' he concluded 'I should think the vote right; but I dread their yielding.'[34] There was more realism in these comments than in the strong language he used about Edmund Harvey 'and a few other elderly Quakers' in a letter to Murray a week later. He complained that they had 'arrogated to themselves the right to say what conscientious objectors ought to do, and have concealed from the authorities the fact that they disagreed with those for whom they professed to speak.'[35] In fact, even without solitary confinement on bread and water, it was clear that more men were prepared to accept either non-combatant service or work of national importance than the absolutists liked. Some members of the N.C.F. committee wanted it to do more to help such men. Most, however, agreed with Miss Marshall who, at this stage, wrote that she could not possibly accept any conditional exemption herself and thought it 'essential for the official policy of the Fellowship to be absolutely uncompromising too.' On the other hand, she admitted that freedom of the individual conscience was 'the very bedrock' of the N.C.F. The problem for the committee was to reconcile the intense individualism which it professed with the need for a common policy.[36]

The strain of this demand began to tell on the leadership. Allen was never physically robust and the pace of his life was wearing him out. Police raids on the *Tribunal, Labour Leader* and *Forward* offices were a reminder, if one were needed, that the activities of the conscientious objectors were not highly regarded in government circles. 'It will soon be illegal to publish the Sermon on the Mount' was Allen's wry comment. He lived in daily fear of arrest. An elaborate plan existed whereby the utmost publicity would be gained from this event when it occurred. Every day came news of fresh arrests. Some, like Morgan Jones, writing from the police cells at Bargoed on 29 May, were cheerful. 'We have the happy reflection' he reminded Allen 'that the future is with us. Our Fellowship is dealing smashing blows to militarism in this country, and it is my confident belief that it will never recover.' Others were less confident.[37]

There were many non-pacifist sympathizers with the conscientious objectors, but it was difficult to give effective help because of the N.C.F.'s own attitude. Lord Hugh Cecil, for example, ardently supported the right of exemption, but made it clear that he did not 'desire to associate myself with any persons prominently connected with opposition to the Military Service Act or to conscription.'[38] Cases of ill-treatment continued to come to light. In one instance, that of C. H. Norman at Wandsworth prison, Murray did bring the matter to ministerial attention. 'It seems to me' he wrote to Miss Marshall on 11 June 'that the treatment of the C.O.'s is at present getting worse.' He attributed this to the desire on the part of 'the military people' to terrorize them before they were handed over to the civil prisons.[39] In this particular instance, the protest was effective. The Commandant was sacked and fresh warnings about the treatment of prisoners were issued. Paradoxically, more was achieved in such cases by supporters of the war, like Murray, than by some of the pacifist societies. Replying to a request from Miss Marshall that the F.O.R. sponsor an appeal to the churches on the question of the outrage to conscience, G. M. Ll. Davies replied that the matter had been frequently discussed by its committee. However, the F.O.R. 'felt that the outrage of conscience does not appear to be such a favourable ground for appeal to Christian ministers as the whole outrage of war. . . .'[40] Nevertheless, late in June 1916 a combined delegation of Quakers, F.O.R. and N.C.F.—the nucleus of what was later to be a Joint Action Committee of the three bodies—saw a sympathetic group of M.P.'s. The politicians were clearly of the opinion that if all conscientious objectors could be brought under civil custody—and that was the way things seemed to be moving— then the outstanding problems could be resolved. Though she agreed, Miss Marshall warned the sympathizers against agreeing to any conditions which would allow the War Office to have power over the men at a later stage.[41]

The feeling that some such solution was in sight had repercussions within the N.C.F. There had always been a faction which had never wanted to bother with the question of exemption at all. Now it began to assert itself. A statement from the committee at the beginning of August attempted to meet both sides, agreeing that the N.C.F. should make 'the exposure of militarism and the spread of pacifists views its principal object' but that it should also 'endeavour to obtain for its members those forms of exemption which are acceptable to them.' In order to rebut his critics, Edmund Harvey wrote in the *Tribunal* that objectors to military service showed the spirit of citizenship most effectively 'by accepting without complaint the humbler tasks which the community now offers to many who would help it in an hour of great need.' To some N.C.F. members, such a statement was rank collaboration and totally unacceptable.[42]

The controversy was stilled for a while by the arrest of the Chairman of the N.C.F. in early August 1916. Allen looked forward to his departure. It would, he hoped, 'be the proudest experience of my life. I am glad we Socialists have been involved in this business; it has given the Socialist Movement its great chance. . . .' When arrested, Allen reiterated his determination never to accept 'the degraded slavery of civil tasks imposed by a Military Service Act.'[43] He was sent off to Wormwood Scrubs. He went away, Miss Marshall warned Brigadier-General Childs, the Army Director of Personal Services with whom she dealt in matters affecting conscientious objectors, 'believing that the chance of coming out alive is very small, and the chance of his coming out otherwise than permanently crippled in health, nil.' It was for this reason that even the most firm critics of exemption showed anxiety for Allen while at the same time not wishing to ask for special treatment. Edmund Harvey sympathized with Miss Marshall in the dilemma in which she found herself, but he took 'a somewhat gloomy view of the prospects of a change for the better in the position of the "Absolutists" while Mr. Lloyd George remains Secretary of State.' Allen, in turn, did not weaken in his resolve.[44]

In his enforced absence, Bertrand Russell became acting Chairman of the N.C.F. Although also active in the U.D.C., it was to the cause of the conscientious objectors that he gave most of his time. His views on the war were idiosyncratic. While being prepared to work with Quakers, non-resisters and Socialists, he delighted in telling Quakers that he thought many wars in history had been justified and in telling Socialists that he dreaded the tyranny of the state. It is not surprising that he was regarded with a certain suspicion by the committed. 'If I belonged to a neutral country' he wrote 'my sympathies would be against Germany. And as an Englishman, I believe that there is far more hope of reform in the foreign policy of my own country than in that of Germany.' As for the war itself, it was not being fought for any rational end but because 'at first, the nations wished to fight, and now they are angry and determined to win victory.' Future peace depended on the success of Socialism for 'its internationalism makes it the surest force in modern politics, and the only large body which has preserved some degree of judgment and humanity in the present chaos.'[45]

Although he sometimes gave the impression that he was an absolute pacifist, he also made it clear in other writings that he was not. He distinguished four types of war—wars of colonialism, wars of principle, wars of self-defence and wars of prestige. Although regretting that the methods and objectives of colonialism seldom coincided, he approved of wars in his first category. As for wars of principle, he thought that it was seldom that any principle of genuine value could be propagated by force. Wars of self-defence were absurd. The only thing that surprised him was that nations still bothered to use this excuse. Finally there were the wars of prestige. In the present case, 'until the war had actually broken out, it was almost the only thing involved, although as soon as the war began other and much more important matters came to be at stake.'[46]

He did, however, give some consideration to non-resistance. 'If England had no army and no navy' he maintained that 'the Germans would be hard put to it to find a pretext for invasion. All the Liberal elements in Germany would oppose such enterprises. . . .' Passive resistance would be desirable providing a nation were convinced of its goodness, 'yet it is rather to the ultimate creation of a strong central authority that I should look for the ending of war.' Although hopeful of Socialism in one breath, he was critical in another. It was too ready to suppose that better economic conditions would make men happy. Men also needed more freedom, more self-direction and opportunity to experience the joy of life. He asserted that 'The ultimate fact from which war results is not economic or political, and does not rest upon any mechanical difficulty of inventing means for the settlement of international disputes.' The ultimate cause of war was that a large proportion of mankind had an impulse to conflict rather than to harmony.[47]

Russell subsequently denied that he was a non-resister, yet at the time close associates like Mrs. Swanwick believed that he was.

'Your non-resistance faith is the one about which I feel the least certainty,' she wrote. 'I think it is the ultimate faith, but it seems to me that we shall have to apply it nationally before we can apply it internationally. I see little hope of its working between nations till it has worked between individuals or groups.'[48] In the fastidiousness of his pacifism, Russell typified the superior refinement of that Cambridge-Bloomsbury circle to which he belonged. The notion that G. E. Moore's philosophical outlook was responsible for their attitude to the war, suggested by Keynes' biographer, seems contradicted by statements from Leonard Woolf, David Garnett, James Strachey and Duncan Grant. Keynes, however, captures the outlook of his friends when he described them as being among the last of the Utopians. They believed 'in a continuing moral progress by virtue of which the human race already consists of reliable, rational, decent people, influenced by truth and objective standards.'[49] Keynes himself was strongly criticized at the time by his friends. On the one hand, he seemed to use language which suggested that he was, if not a conscientious objector himself, at least strongly sympathetic to their cause. On the other, he continued in the service of the government. As Lytton Strachey put it, their set were all special cases and it was no use pretending otherwise.[50] E. M. Forster developed conscientious objections while serving in the Red Cross at Alexandria but he never felt any obligation to return to England to face a Tribunal. Clive Bell initially wanted to join the Army Service Corps because ill health prevented him joining a fighting regiment. Somewhat later he wrote the pamphlet *Peace at Once*. Lytton Strachey went round making weary remarks about how little difference it would make if the Germans did arrive. He was, in any case, secure in the knowledge that he had established the standard reply to a standard question asked by Tribunals. He had done his bit. Russell formed the link between these clever people and the serious activity of the N.C.F. He was often whisked away for week-ends to Garsington Manor by the dashing Lady Ottoline Morrell. There, far from the madding crowd, amongst other matters, they could discuss the future policy of the Peace Movement.[51]

Where Russell was different from these associates, at least initially, was that he possessed both vestigial backbone and a modicum of physical health. Noting that Russell was working day and night with the N.C.F., Strachey wrote cynically that he was 'at last perfectly happy—gloating over all the horrors and moral lessons of the situation.' Russell, in turn, was disgusted by Strachey's unwillingness to make any contribution to the cause of pacifism in which he apparently believed.[52] Already, Russell had become a public figure. He stood trial on 5 June 1916 for his part in publishing a leaflet 'Repeal the Act'. In his defence, he claimed that 'we pacifists owe a great debt of gratitude to the Government for this prosecution . . . whether I personally am acquitted or condemned is a matter of no great importance, but it is not only I that am in the dock; it is the whole tradition of British liberty. . . .' He was fined £100. Snowden spoke for many pacifists when he described the speech as a 'magnificent performance'. It was necessary for pacifists to be ever vigilant and counteract the growing audacity of the military and the police.[53]

Undeterred, Russell continued to say publicly whatever he wanted to. At the end of June he started on an extensive speaking tour in South Wales. At Cardiff on 6 July he revealed to his audience that he could not make up his mind in regard to Belgium whether 'given the obligations we have entered into, we were doing a worse act in keeping those obligations or in breaking them.' He stated that he did not believe for one moment that 'men in high places who spoke about the destruction of German militarism when this war began, ever intended or desired such a thing.' He did not claim to know, but it was not unlikely that 'one of the things we are fighting for now is to prevent the liberty of Poland.' He concluded, 'quite deliberately', that he did not believe that the British Government or any other Government in Europe desired a permanent peace. It was performances of this character which led to an embargo being placed on lectures 'on the general principles of politics' which he proposed to give in Scotland and the North of England. When the matter of the embargo was raised in the Commons, however, it got short shrift from Lloyd George. He did not care in the least what title the lectures were given, 'they undoubtedly interfere with the prosecution of the war in this country, and lead to weakness, inefficiency, and, if tolerated, would hamper us in the prosecution of the war. It would be an intolerable weakness on our part if we allowed it.'[54]

The most celebrated deprivation to which Russell was subjected was the loss of his college lectureship at Trinity. He was not, in fact, at this time a Fellow of the College. The action, following the fine in the courts, was taken by the College Council on which the more elderly dons predominated. Lowes Dickinson wrote to Russell that the expulsion seemed to snap his own last link with Cambridge. He rejoiced to hear that the *Manchester Guardian* had given the Fellows a good trouncing. E. D. Morel also expressed indignation at the 'abominable way' Russell had been treated. 'That the Government should fear you I can well understand' he wrote, '— their case is so groggy that to let out a man to lecture on philosophical problems lest he should tell the truth on other matters may well have terrified them: but the action of Trinity College is beyond words. But what effect is there likely to be in America!'[55]

Russell's status as prophet and oracle did not help him when he came to tackle the internal problems of the N.C.F. The crisis in its affairs, temporarily stilled by Allen's arrest, now resumed. There was common ground in the condemnation of militarism. 'Our opponents' wrote Fenner Brockway 'may say that it is better to live under home-made militarism than German. We reply that to us, militarism is the enemy, not a particular brand of it.' Russell took a similar line. He described the N.C.F. as a pacifist body engaged in a fierce fight. It was true that it was by passive resistance, 'but still we do and we must fight; we are against various things that are strong in the world just now—militarism, ruthlessness and the denial of liberty.'[56] To descend from the general to the particular, however, led to difficulty. Miss Marshall continued to investigate individual cases of alleged ill-treatment of conscientious objectors. She either saw General Childs herself or worked through sympathetic intermediaries. Shown a letter from Childs to Rev. Dr. F. B. Meyer concerning two particular cases, she replied to Meyer that it confirmed 'the opinion I had already formed of him. I am confident that he takes infinite trouble to ensure that his provisions for C.O.'s shall be strictly carried out. When the provisions are good, the result is good.' She appreciated that he was under pressure from those who felt that too much leniency was being shown to objectors, but that made the work of the N.C.F. to balance this pressure all the more important.[57] At the mid-October national committee meeting, however, there was an onslaught on her activity. Barratt Brown complained that the N.C.F. had lost sight of its original vision and had become bogged down in matters of method and detail. W. J. Chamberlain was even more critical. The Fellowship had degenerated into a society for the entertainment of Cabinet Ministers and War Office officials. He had never dreamed that a time would come when officers of the N.C.F. would be in direct communication with the War Office and be able to get the soldiers to do as they requested. W. H. Ayles agreed. He had foreseen the danger of helping the Government to administer the Military Service Act and now it had happened. Dr. Salter, as usual, disagreed with everybody. It was wrong even to have tried to press for exemptions in the first place. The conscientious objector would now never be listened to as he would have been if he had gone to prison without protest.[58] Russell tried to calm the atmosphere and claimed that the N.C.F. had not changed its policy in any way. He himself wished that the whole Fellowship were absolutist, but facts had to be recognized. The same kind of issue recurred in December when there was a move afoot to stop the N.C.F. from having anything to do with members of the

Non-Combatant Corps unless they declared their intention to leave the Corps. Miss Marshall 'felt exactly as if someone had run a bayonet through my heart' and contemplated resigning the Secretaryship.[59]

The critics were right to the extent that the original policy of the N.C.F. had failed. The Military Service Act was still on the statute book. The cause of peace, equally, had not been further advanced. Partly as a result of the support received from non-pacifists, the issue had increasingly been presented as simply one concerning the 'rights of conscience'. Indeed, rather to its dismay, the N.C.F. found that a large number of conscientious objectors were often quite a-political in their outlook. Indeed, from a numerical standpoint, they were more significant than those who are normally considered to be 'the pacifists of the First World War'. For these objectors, the kind of N.C.F. argument was largely outside their conceptual framework. The only war in which they were interested was the Battle of Armageddon; ordinary world wars were trivial matters of little concern. Other sects, like the Christadelphians, refused to accept military discipline but were prepared to work in munitions factories. Freedom of conscience might be 'the bedrock' of the Fellowship but, if so, it produced some strange bedfellows. Strange, that is, for those who regarded their consciences as infallible. In this situation, it became more and more difficult to say what the N.C.F. stood for.

Edward Grubb repeatedly testified to his fellow Friends that the movement was of essentially moral and religious character. He wanted to persuade the more sceptical that it was not a revolutionary body.[60] Fenner Brockway was normally engaged on precisely the opposite explanatory task. There was, in his view, a 'ruggedness and directness' about the N.C.F. leadership which contrasted with the U.D.C. whose leaders were 'bourgeois to their fingertips. They were suave, gracious, cultured. They might have been lifted out of any gathering of the gentlemen of England.' His message was simple. No one state was responsible for the war. The blame rested in fairly equal parts on the ambitious Pan-Slavism of Russia, the bumptious and brutal militarism of Germany, and the secret diplomacy of France and Britain. He saw the remedy in the complete abolition of capitalism. The N.C.F. would become the vanguard of a new kind of Socialist pacifism which, this time, would persuade the Labour Movement that 'an absolute repudiation of war would be the surest defence a nation could have.'[61] In advocating a programme whereby the Fellowship would continue to press both for Absolute Exemption and for an honourable Alternative Service, he insisted at the same time that both of these objectives should be put on one side. The N.C.F.

should instead concentrate on pacifist propaganda. Whether or not Brockway's new course succeeded, it was clear that it would have to be tried. The fate of conscientious objectors would not, of course, be ignored, but by the end of 1916 there was strong pressure both from within and without the Fellowship to recall that the achievement of peace was really its main concern.

CHAPTER FIVE

The Beginning of the Peace Campaign

It is not surprising that pacifists considered 1916 their year of opportunity. The casualties of war were already great and no end seemed in sight. In the opening months of the year, British politicians were privately somewhat gloomy about their chances of victory. Writing in January for the illumination of his colleagues, the Foreign Secretary forecast exhaustion on both sides within a year. If things remained as they were, he wrote, 'I think that there will be a sort of general collapse and inconclusive peace before next winter.' He drew the conclusion that the only chance of victory was 'to hammer the Germans hard in the first eight months of this year'. If that attack failed, then it would be best to settle for an inconclusive peace.[1] His assessment was, of course, based on facts and opinions not available to pacifists, nevertheless, they also saw stalemate as inevitable. Their conclusion, however, was different. There was not even any point in a further eight months of hard hammering. At the very least it was time to make a clear declaration of terms.

'Finding out' Charles Roden Buxton continued to claim 'does not necessarily mean arriving at a settlement, as to that, it leaves us perfectly free.' In any case, according to Pethick-Lawrence, 'The sooner we divide off the jingo militarist elements of our enemies from the reasonable section of their peoples who want to return to the normal avocations of life, the sooner we shall end this war. . . .' It was in this mood that a rash of pacifist proposals emerged. In February 1916 Brailsford put forward what he called a 'peace by satisfaction'. In order to endure, the peace settlement would have to deal with the fundamental causes of strife and give impartial justice to both friend and foe alike. He therefore insisted that Belgium be restored, Serbia reconstituted and French territory evacuated. In turn he urged that her colonies be given back to Germany, or some equivalent compensation made elsewhere. He did not favour the break-up of the Habsburg Monarchy. The Poles, Czechs, Serbs and Croats would have to be content with self-government within the Empire. If the inhabitants of Alsace-Lorraine agreed, the provinces would be returned to France. The Allies, however, would also have to make certain concessions. Germany was to be allowed to form a close economic union with Austria-Hungary. Turkey would also come within the German economic sphere, though with guarantees for the trade of other Powers. In addition, all countries would agree not to perpetuate differential tariffs in their tropical colonies. Surprisingly, in view of his pre-war agitation, Brailsford was prepared to allow Russia, besides the Armenian province of Turkey, an ice-free port on the Persian Gulf and a formal protectorate over Persia itself. Germany would have to assent to some scheme of permanent international conciliation and the reduction of armaments. Britain would have to consider changing her views on the 'Freedom of the Seas'.[2]

Proposals of this kind can be found, with some variations, in many pacifist journals about this time. What is striking in Brailsford's plan is its strong conservatism. Despite his radical convictions, he was advocating minimal changes in the pre-war territorial *status quo* in the hope that all the countries concerned might be persuaded to agree that the war had been a mistake. The purpose of such plans was to counteract what Charles Buxton described as 'the greatest danger of the moment', that the idea of 'unconditional surrender' should overpower the opinion of reasonable men and women. He continued to address meetings up and down the country. After one of his speeches the *Morning Post* complained of the fact that the police had been present to ensure order. 'It seems hard' the paper declared 'that the public services should at this time be taxed and bothered in this way. If these meetings must needs be permitted, why should the police be required to protect them?' In March, Buxton wrote to Sir Edward Grey to state that although he had become associated in the public mind with some people who merely protested against the war, he was 'far from being willing to accept any kind of peace, and regard it as essential to concentrate on the terms of settlement, rather than on the protest against war.' He added that he had spoken at over eighty meetings, half of them in public, and claimed to have been disturbed at only five of them. It was his 'strong impression' that there was 'a large body of opinion which is anxious for sober and reasonable discussion of the settlement and which is not set upon the idea of a "dictated" peace.'[3]

Buxton's campaign was still largely personal, nevertheless, his activities largely forced the U.D.C. in the spring of 1916 to try to draw up an agreed 'peace settlement' for speakers under its auspices. After considerable discussion, a sub-committee agreed on a programme. Germany was to undertake to restore the sovereignty and independence of Belgium as a condition of negotiation. She should also make reparation to Belgium, evacuate Northern France and restore Serbia. If Germany still desired a Colonial Empire equal in extent to her pre-war possessions, it should be given back to her. There was to be no transfer of Alsace-Lorraine without the consent of the population.[4]

Morel himself believed that it was Britain's responsibility to take the initiative in reaching a settlement. He assumed that Germany would withdraw from her conquests in Western Europe. He refused to commit himself on what the inhabitants of Alsace-Lorraine and 'Poland' really wanted. Europe was not in fact the chief focus of his concern. The colonial future was vital because he believed that 'the closing of the Colonial markets to Germany was one of the main fundamental causes of the war.' Britain should take the first step leading the world back to sanity. It would be a mistake to let feelings of moral superiority stand in the way. Germany could be described as militarist 'just as and no more than any other of the European Powers with conscript armies. We are in a fair way to becoming militarist ourselves.'[5] In these, and succeeding months, Morel was under considerable strain and his judgment more than usually erratic. He was under constant press attack, from the *Morning Post,* the *Daily Express,* and other dailies. Cecil Chesterton in his *New Witness* singled him out for special attention. An Open Letter appeared in the issue of 27 January accusing 'Morel' of being an agent of the German Government. 'I accuse him' Chesterton continued 'of having been its agent for many years before the war. That is not an "insinuation". It is a charge. If it is false I can be sent to prison. If it is true, "Morel" ought to be sent to prison. . . .' The charge was not taken up, though Morel's friends angrily rejected it. Despite his hectic activity, Morel about this time confessed to Russell that he felt inadequate. He described 'the repulsion, which amounts to positive physical and mental pain, I have of sailing under false colours and being pitchforked into the position of appearing to be an authority on such problems as the U.D.C. is up against.' He felt like giving everything up. Edward Grubb was among those who persuaded him to carry on—'the work to be done is tremendous, & we can't spare you.' No one else had the same knowledge and the same power of putting things forcibly. Morel carried on—'I can't help myself'.[6]

Part of the reason for the depression some pacifists felt can be found in the military situation. The German attack on Verdun

had started towards the end of February. As bloody week followed
bloody week, the outcome assumed deep symbolic significance. If
the Germans broke through, it was supposed that they would go
on to win the war. At no matter what cost, they had to be held.
By the end of June, after much slaughter, they had been. While
the battle raged, politicians were not likely to be attracted by the
academic exercises of pacifists. Besides, pacifists themselves were
divided in their reactions. While he found the casualty figures
appalling, Norman Angell wrote that a German failure was likely
to strengthen the influence of the moderate party in Germany. It
would stimulate war-weariness and dampen enthusiasm. It would
to some extent undermine confidence in the military clique which
controlled the Government.[7] Others felt that, on the contrary, a
German failure would only strengthen the determination of the
military party and increase their support. The only thing that
would end the war would be a realization by both sides that the
war in its entirety would become a kind of extended Verdun with
a terrible toll on both sides. Such pacifists almost found themselves
in the peculiar position of wanting to see the maximum slaughter
possible at this stage. Viewed in this light, Verdun could provide
an opportunity for a fresh start to the peace campaign; in unity
the various societies would find success.

Such an expression was, of course, little more than conventional
rhetoric. The notion that the Peace Movement would be likely to
be able to compel the British Government to negotiate was little
more than encouraging fiction. It was customary to speak of its
various 'wings': the Political (U.D.C., N.C.C.L., I.L.P., N.C.F.),
the Religious (Peace Society, Quakers, F.O.R.) and the Women's
(Women's International League for Peace and Freedom—W.I.L.).
The wings, however, had no common commander. The three
groups most concerned with conscientious objection, Friends,
N.C.F. and F.O.R., did have a joint action committee for certain
purposes. Here, it was claimed, rather optimistically, was a happy
precedent. The societies could all do so much better if they worked
together. A high level meeting was held on 28 April to consider
a common petitition urging a negotiated peace. Among those
present were delegates from Friends, F.O.R., I.L.P. (Dubery),
N.C.F. (Miss Marshall), W.I.L. (Mrs. Swanwick), Peace Society
(Dunnico) and the U.D.C. (Roden Buxton). After much discussion,
with promises of financial support from Buxton on his own behalf,
the U.D.C., the W.I.L. and the N.C.F., it was decided to form
a Peace Negotiations Committee. The intention was to sponsor a
petition to the Prime Minister which would make it clear how many
people favoured a negotiated peace. Dunnico of the Peace Society
became secretary and the new committee operated from the offices

of the society.[8] 'Such harmony of all our peace forces has been attempted before' was one comment, 'but the obstacles have been great. At last in the presence of unprecedented militarism, we have looked one another in the face and discerned that our common humanity and common idealism transcend our differences.' The snag in the project, as the *Labour Leader* pointed out, was that if pacifists failed to gain a large number of signatures, their cause would be more discredited than if they had never conducted the experiment.[9]

The Peace Negotiations Committee made slow headway partly because in practice the different societies were absorbed in their own particular problems. Behind the call for a negotiated peace existed wide divergencies both of method and objective. There was serious division within the Society of Friends. In March, for example, the London and Middlesex Quarterly Meeting informed Charles Roden Buxton that he would no longer be able to hold his open meetings on their premises at Devonshire House. He was told that 'misleading statements' which had appeared in the press had 'evidently created a great deal of uneasiness amongst those who have not been able to be at the meetings.' In this situation, Friends had rather yielded to the wish for 'respectability'.[10]

On the opposite wing, a group of radical Quakers banded together to publish in February 1916 a new monthly, *The Ploughshare*, subtitled *A Quaker Journal of Social Reconstruction*. On its advisory council were well-known Friends such as Barratt Brown, J. H. Barlow, J. E. Hodgkin and Lucy Morland. They stressed the need for wide debate on social questions, not simply those relating to 'war and peace'. The tone of the journal was visionary, even apocalyptic. Members of the Society were reminded that they belonged almost entirely to the 'Haves'. They would have to decide which side to take in the approaching culminating struggles in the age-long war of the classes. They should recognize that the existing social order was in fact one of war and its logical outcome was international conflict. Fenner Brockway took the opportunity to remind Friends that the ultimate aim of the Labour Movement was the same as theirs. J. W. Graham, on the other hand, criticized the view that nothing would cure the world of war except the abolition of capitalism.[11] At a conference in April a specially appointed 'War and the Social Order' committee examined the question. Speaker after speaker claimed that the 'unsound economic system' was the cause of the war. The theme that 'The peoples, unless inflamed by their preachers, teachers, politicians and press in the interests of and with the ideas of the privileged classes, know scarcely anything of national hatred' was frequently enunciated. The committee reported that 'though we

G

could not show that the present social order has its inevitable outcome in war, yet the converse seems true, at least of modern wars,
that they have their origin in the social system in which we all too
readily acquiesce.'[12] The *Ploughshare* group was not satisfied with
this conclusion, insisting that it was not enough for the Society to
testify against war when it arrived without concerning itself
sufficiently with the root causes. If there really was to be an attempt
to establish a permanent peace this would not be achieved by
making balanced statements. 'The warning against dabbling in
political action, against joining with peoples whose convictions
were moral rather than religious' they felt 'came with little force.
The Society has found its hedges broken down.' They were to find,
however, other members of the Society who were anxious to patrol
the boundary.[13]

This tension between the 'political' and the 'religious' also
affected the F.O.R. The Fellowship's membership was steadily
increasing—it was to reach 5,500 by the end of the year—but its
basic role was still a matter for debate. It sponsored a volume,
The Ministry of Reconciliation, which discussed various aspects of
Christian pacifism. The writers did not base their pacifism on
particular texts in the New Testament, rather they claimed that it
suffused the whole. To use deadly weapons for self-defence was to
obscure witness to the Divine Reality. Dr. Cadoux, a Congregationalist theologian, argued that since the Church had fallen on
evil days, only a bold stand in faithful adherence to the great
commandments of the Master would remedy matters. Richard
Roberts felt that the principle of nationality could be a source of
co-operation rather than of conflict. Carl Heath, the secretary of
the National Peace Council, wanted to go deeper. Was the peace
which pacifists sought a negation of life or would it prove an
inspiration? Was the abolition of war an end in itself or was it an
aspect of the establishment of the City of God? Questions like
these were discussed endlessly by the members of the F.O.R. at
their meetings and conferences. Like the Quaker Socialists, they
evidently did not want the issues of 'war' and 'peace' to be
narrowly defined. As Dr. Orchard wrote, 'the pacifist who is concerned about war as if it were the only evil is not only rightly
open to condemnation for neglecting the other elements in the
teaching of Christ of equal demand on our obedience, but brings
upon himself the suspicion of possessing a patchy conscience.'[14]
Nevertheless, although agitation for peace had strong support in
the F.O.R., other members were adamant that its spiritual ends
would thereby be compromised.[15]

The same issue also affected the Labour Movement. Christian
pacifists were primarily interested in peace and sought co-operation

with Labour because they believed that social transformation would help to create the conditions of peace. The *Labour Leader* agreed that the cessation of the war was 'more important than any other issue' but other members of the I.L.P. did not want to see the party concentrating exclusively on this one problem.[16] They wanted social transformation for its own sake and were less concerned about pacifism. Herbert Morrison, for example, described himself as 'anti-war', but feared that members of the I.L.P. were 'too inclined to make opinion on the war the supreme test.' They should not forget that 'there may need to be fighting between the workers and some of the middle-class people who agree with us on the war, but not on our Socialist and Labour position.'[17] The political order in Europe still seemed relatively stable, so this division of opinion remained for the moment theoretical. If the situation changed, it could become very important.

Despite Miss Marshall's prominent association with the Peace Negotiations Committee, the N.C.F. was preoccupied with its immediate concerns. As has been seen, it was only by the end of 1916 that agitation for peace gained high priority. Indeed, in the summer, Russell was actively trying to persuade other leading figures in the Peace Movement to forsake their own peace societies and devote themselves to the cause of the conscientious objectors. Mrs. Swanwick refused to allow herself to be drawn away from the W.I.L., though she admitted that many of its supporters had taken up new work. 'I think women have got to organise women' she wrote 'and to make them think as women. Men generally won't trouble to organise women at all, but if they do, it is always to think as men and work, in a one-sided way, for men.' She did not consider Russell an exception to this rule. She fully admitted that the N.C.F. was fighting the battle against militarism 'in one of the most effective ways possible', but that did not mean that 'all the anti-militarist women should just throw themselves in with the N.C.F.' The W.I.L. would do what it could for the conscientious objectors, but 'to get peace negotiations is I believe our most urgent work.' In fact, she tried her own persuasion, urging Miss Marshall to play a smaller role in the N.C.F. and come back to the W.I.L. for most of her time. Miss Royden also pressed her to return, writing that she respected the N.C.F. in much the same way as she respected the militant suffragettes. Their mistakes were 'only possible to very fine people' but they were still mistakes. Miss Marshall resisted their pleas and, in fact, resigned from the W.I.L. in September.[18]

Naturally, since Dunnico was secretary of both bodies, the Peace Society was committed to the Peace Negotiations Committee. Dunnico himself saw the new body as a way of regaining prestige for his rather moribund Peace Society. It was its centenary year and he wanted to find a cause which would demonstrate its continuing vitality.

It was, perhaps, partly because he did not wish to see a revived Peace Society that Morel was rather wary of the P.N.C. The fact that the U.D.C. was associated with it at all was largely due to Charles Roden Buxton. Morel wavered between full support for the Committee and a belief that the U.D.C. would do better to strengthen its links with the Labour Movement directly. In this regard, the status of the Liberal M.P.'s and candidates on the U.D.C. Executive was still a difficulty. From November 1915, Ponsonby and Trevelyan began to speak in the House of Commons more frequently than they had done in the first fifteen months of the war. Trying to enlist the support of John Burns, Trevelyan wrote that they felt that the time had now come when some kind of discussion ought to begin in parliament in order to encourage people generally to think where they were going. His constant theme was that German militarism would not survive if the Allies proposed reasonable peace terms. Ponsonby was convinced that there would not be difficulty about any of the European or colonial problems. It was the cry of 'Victory before Peace' which stood in the way and for the moment destroyed all hopes of negotiations. Their speeches, however, had little impact on the House, being mostly received in stony silence. They were little more than demonstrations 'to keep the flag aloft' as J. W. Graham put it.[19]

Would joining the I.L.P. increase their influence? In early April a meeting took place between leading I.L.P. and U.D.C. figures. MacDonald, Ponsonby reported, had been very helpful but he suspected F. W. Jowett of being after U.D.C. money.[20] Nevertheless, the following month Ponsonby still refused an invitation to join the party. He replied that his views might not differ materially from the I.L.P. but he did not desire a fresh political label. He did not want to alienate his Liberal colleagues by precipitate action but rather to 'endeavour to urge them along the same path which I myself am treading. . . .'[21] The problem was a delicate one because the U.D.C. had to make up its mind about what to do at by-elections. In April, the Executive agreed to support I.L.P. candidates if, in turn, the I.L.P. would be prepared to assist independent candidates who had a U.D.C. platform. Once this had been satisfactorily settled, Trevelyan favoured putting up I.L.P. and Peace candidates as often as possible. His eagerness, however, was not universally shared. A sub-committee in May felt that the U.D.C. should not try to promote candidatures, though it could give general support to any candidates who were in sympathy with its policy. In July, it was agreed to meet with the N.C.F. and the

N.C.A.C. to discuss the whole question of by-election strategy.[22] An agreed policy might only be possible if broader political differences between the societies were resolved. In August, for example, Morel was pressed to say why he did not declare himself a Socialist since he was so anxious to gain I.L.P. support for the U.D.C. 'How can you imagine that I am anything else but a Socialist' he replied 'if Socialism means, as I take it to mean, the betterment and increased happiness of humanity?' As far as the tenets of the Socialist creed were concerned, he went a long way, 'but the existing framework of society cannot be revolutionized by a stroke of the pen.' Shouting slogans like 'Down with Capitalism' was not enough. He wanted to make people understand that concentration upon the internal condition of their respective countries was insufficient.[23] Dogmatic Socialism he continued to find irritating.

In any case, in the summer of 1916, Morel was not in a calm frame of mind. The arrest of his erstwhile associate, Sir Roger Casement, in connexion with the Easter Rising in Dublin in April 1916, naturally led to further suspicion falling upon him. He admitted privately that the whole affair was 'a beastly complication', but held that he could not be responsible 'for the action of a man ten years after I first came in touch with him. Of course you must set against that that he and I were known by a lot of people to be friends. . . .'[24] In turn, Morel became more and more certain that the war was being continued for reasons which had little connexion with the reasons officially advanced. It would have been out of keeping for him to believe that responsibility for the failure of governments to start negotiations lay anywhere other than in London. If it was true, he wrote in March, that Britain had allowed Italy Dalmatia as a reward for joining the war, such a promise knocked the bottom out of the case for denouncing German conduct towards Belgium. He also expressed his fear that Russia had similarly been promised Constantinople. It was no accident that articles appeared in the *U.D.C.* on Lithuania and the Ukraine. 'Suppressed nationalities' were not confined to the Habsburg Monarchy. These suspicions made Morel even more uninhibited in his criticisms.

One further piece of evidence which seemed to confirm the malignity of Allied intentions was the plan for 'economic war at the end of the war.' The notion that Germany was poised to make an onslaught on third markets at the end of the war was treated seriously by the British Cabinet. It was under pressure both from some of its Conservative members and from the French Government to devise a system to protect the future position of Allied trade. The Australian Prime Minister, William Hughes, was particularly anxious to exclude German trade and capital from the British Empire. The subject was discussed at an inter-allied Economic Conference at Paris in June. However, apart from general resolutions about the need for the Allies to keep themselves economically independent of the Central Powers nothing very specific emerged.[25]

The U.D.C. saw these developments very differently. It was a subject which J. A. Hobson made particularly his own. At the beginning of 1916 he had proposed to the Executive that it should add a fifth point dealing with the question of the 'open door'. It should be the objective of British policy to secure greater freedom of trade between nations. However, when the matter was discussed at the end of January there was disagreement and a decision was postponed. In May, however, an emergency General Council was held. Hobson then introduced a motion in favour of free trade and the open door, demanding that the European conflict should not be continued by economic war after the military operations had ceased. This time the Executive was more sympathetic. It deplored a situation in which British workers would be asked to approve a relentless economic feud against the workers of Germany. Such a course would lead to 'the continued divisions of Europe, the perpetration of war, the maintenance and aggravation of militarism in all its forms and the increasing poverty and subjection of the working classes.'[26] When he heard of the intention of the Allies to safeguard their trade, Hobson exploded against the ignorant and foolish politicians who, in his view, completely misunderstood the nature of the problem. The idea of 'Germany' seeking 'domination' over the products and markets of the whole world was an 'intolerable joke'. Lowes Dickinson was another to join in the attack on the Paris conference. He pointed out that Germany would have to be present at a peace conference and it was therefore essential that the proposals she be asked to entertain would lead to permanent peace. The policy of Paris would only lead to disaster by making such agreement impossible. In the event, the Russian Government refused to ratify the Paris resolutions and their force was diminished. By then, however, the episode had gained a symbolic importance for pacifists. 'We are not "fighting for our lives" ' wrote Morel in June. 'We are not fighting to destroy militarism. We are not fighting to crush Germany. What, then, are we fighting for now?'[27] Morel thought he knew the answer.

Looking back over British foreign policy since 1906 he became more and more convinced that it was 'one vast lie'. The great majority of the British people—he did not include public men in this estimate—believed that Germany alone prepared for war and that her conduct of it was the great obstacle to a reasonable peace.

While the Government could feel confident that the people continued to hold such views, they had the support they required 'to ruin our country and to sacrifice British lives to Russia's ambitions, to revenge, to French madness. . . .'[28] He proudly revealed that he was setting out to shake that confidence by publishing *Truth and the War*, a collection of articles on aspects of pre-war diplomacy, together with suggestions for future improvements. He admitted that German diplomacy had been short-sighted, immoral and treacherous, but in this it was only like any other diplomacy. The history of Morocco, for example, 'revealed a record of treachery and deceit towards the British and French peoples, towards Morocco and the rest of the world, by the French and British Foreign Offices, with few parallels even in the annals of diplomacy.' He concluded the book with a quasi-poetic epilogue 'To the Belligerent Governments' who 'lied and plotted and spied, span webs of intrigue, dug pits, laid traps, contrived ambushes . . . and one and all you betrayed your peoples.'[29] The book was widely distributed in pacifist circles, though some found its tone too strong for their taste. Morel complained to Bertrand Russell that the *Cambridge Magazine* treated him as though he had the plague. Some Socialists, on the other hand, felt that Morel was attacking the wrong target. Walton Newbold considered it extremely unlikely that war over Africa was ever imminent between France, Britain and Spain. The cause of the war was not to be found in the policy of one nation or another but in Capitalism. He doubted whether Germany had been seriously aggrieved by Morocco but rather had used the opportunity to cause friction between France, Britain and Spain. Morel did not agree that 'Capitalism' was so important. Besides economic impulses there were also 'personal ambitions and prejudices whose powers of embroiling peoples in war are terrific, because of the diplomatic procedure tolerated by the peoples.' If Morel was unsound from a Socialist standpoint, his latest diatribe against Governments was a little too vehement for his close associates. Trevelyan had no doubt about the facts Morel cited, but wondered whether they necessarily led to the 'magnificent explosion of wrath' contained in the epilogue. For him, the tragedy was not that the rulers were specially bad men, but that there was 'no statesman anywhere in Europe who has the greatness of soul and intellect to rise above the passions of his own nation.'[30]

Trevelyan's reference to any statesman in Europe was deliberate. Despite the stirrings of disillusion which they occasionally professed to see, many pacifists, despondent about their ability to influence the British Government, transferred their affections and even their activities across the Atlantic. Norman Angell, indeed, spent most of his time after the summer of 1915 in the United States, with only occasional visits to Britain. He went initially as Director of Studies at a Summer School on International Relations at Cornell University, He then became, in effect, a member of the staff of the *New Republic* for a lengthy period. He saw himself as supplying the Americans with ideas while attempting—not very successfully—to raise money which could be used in Britain by the U.D.C. Quite independently of the *New Republic,* Angell claimed to have his own contacts with President Wilson, mainly through Colonel House. He certainly succeeded in floating his views into the White House, though how many settled there is another matter. His chief importance was as a middle-man who introduced British articles by Brailsford and Wallas to American periodicals and at the same time sent back his own assessments of developments in America to Britain. As early as February 1915, Angell had written that if Britain and America were in substantial agreement about the future shape of the world 'we have every interest that America shall play as large a role as possible at the settlement.' Angell, however, remained an individualist. When in the United States, what seemed to him important was to clarify the sort of world order which Britain and America could both support. If substantial agreement could be reached, he wanted the Americans to abandon their neutrality and throw all their weight behind a future just settlement. Reporting in February 1916 on the prospects of American intervention, he urged Britain to offer the United States a share in exercising sea power 'for objects that we both have in common.' In other articles in the following months he urged the Americans to reconsider the doctrine of neutrality. In urging such a role upon the United States Angell can hardly be termed a strict pacifist and some of his erstwhile associates in Britain regarded his activities with suspicion.[31]

The more frequent hope among British pacifists was that President Wilson would hover above the battle, prepared to mediate between the belligerents and create the conditions in which a negotiated settlement was possible.[32] At the same time, he would propound a basis for peace which would ensure that war would be no more. Such objectives were indeed in the President's mind, but the problem was how to achieve them. House had already made one unsuccessful European tour in 1915. In February 1916 he again came to London for talks with the Foreign Secretary. This famous exchange hardly improved Anglo-American understanding. Presidential suspicions of British policy deepened. When in London, House renewed his acquaintance with critics of the government like Lord Loreburn and F. W. Hirst of the *Economist* who assured him that a movement for a negotiated peace was developing. Over the next few months, House received similar assurances from Roden Buxton, J. H. Whitehouse and other radical politicians. In July, Noel Buxton visited the United States for further consultations. Rather more cautious than his younger brother, he was nevertheless now convinced that the time was ripe for negotiation. He drew up a memorandum on his talks in Washington in which he claimed that, with American assistance, it would be possible to bring about a settlement.[33] The British Ambassador, Sir Cecil Spring-Rice, was greatly perturbed and wrote to the Foreign Office hoping that Buxton could be dissuaded from launching any organization to push Wilson's ideas in England. Could Buxton not see that for Britain to agree to the President's proposals at once would be to bring about what it was the objective of German propaganda to achieve; the driving of wedges between the Allies?[34]

Sir Eric Drummond replied that it was doubtfully wise to prevent the formation of such an organization. While there was general agreement that the terms of peace would have to be settled between the belligerents, it was possible that there might be a second peace congress at which President Wilson's ideas might be discussed. In his draft he added that Noel Buxton was 'looked upon here as rather fanatical and I doubt whether he would secure much influential support for his proposals.' The Foreign Secretary ordered this reference to be deleted before the reply was sent.[35] Sir Edward Grey was in a very difficult position. On the one hand, he wished to maintain good relations with the United States at a time when some of his colleagues were inclined to take a stronger line. However, he found the apparent American refusal to discriminate between the belligerents as to the causes of the war most annoying. He still believed that it would be possible to achieve a decisive victory, though at the same time he wanted to be in a position to summon American mediation if the situation deteriorated. It was possible therefore, that, carefully handled, the concept of the League of Nations might prove the vital link between the British and American Governments, the British Government and British pacifists, and between pacifists on both sides of the Atlantic.

At this juncture, the League of Nations tended to mean whatever anyone wanted it to mean. It was, therefore, a very useful idea; that is, until attempts were made to go beyond the stage of acclamation and discuss particulars. The work of clarification, however, was essential and in this process Lowes Dickinson remained the key figure, writing for a wide variety of journals and speaking to many different groups. In his contribution to the volume *Towards a Lasting Settlement* he surveyed the factors that made for peace. Not, he thought, religion, science, or learning. In his experience all these served war as much as they served peace. There was 'one only that works for peace, that human reason which is also charity. With that white sword alone we can prevail. Will the people seize and wield it as it drops from the hands of those who should have been their leaders?' He worked out his ideas more systematically in *The European Anarchy*. In a subsequent autobiographical fragment he admitted that he had made no special study of international relations, but 'knew enough to know that Europe had long been a powder magazine, and I saw that nothing would cure that, no victory, no defeat, except a complete and radical change of policy, not in this or that state, but in all states.' It was necessary to give up the tiresome habit of dwelling on the peculiar wickedness of the enemy. Instead, in future, all states should agree to submit to 'law' and to 'right' in the settlement of their disputes; then they should agree to refrain from using force except against the lawbreaker. In order to do this effectively, they should construct rules which would enable them to determine who the lawbreaker was.[36] Dickinson's clear willingness to contemplate using force in this manner probably arose from his contacts with the American League to Enforce Peace. He had visited the United States in the spring with his friend, C. R. Ashbee the architect, lecturing on the League idea at Universities in the East and Middle West. On his return, he reported to Lord Bryce that the American organization was in good hands. His impression was that the idea was regarded as acceptable and practicable wherever it was put forward. President Wilson, of course, had still to commit himself, though Dickinson was optimistic that he would do so.[37] Ashbee reported in similar terms to the Foreign Secretary, adding that the American leaders would 'welcome some move on our side—even if it were only some little word of encouragement privately conveyed from yourself.' Grey replied that he had given general approval of the League idea in a message for an American newspaper and, for the moment, he did not think it wise to do more.[38]

These exchanges were encouraging, but it was unlikely that British politicians would want to commit themselves much further. To associate too closely with Dickinson was not advisable. Indeed, at this juncture he was trying to persuade C. P. Scott to move the *Manchester Guardian* into the 'peace by negotiations' camp. Everything, he claimed, favoured such a shift of opinion—the military deadlock, the destruction of civil liberties and the growing Peace Movement. Above all, declarations by Grey and Wilson in favour of an international agreement to keep the peace were perhaps 'one of the most important events in history, the significance of which this nation seems completely to miss.'[39] Scott still had his reservations and Dickinson had sadly to acknowledge that everybody, and especially everybody with a reputation to lose, still felt that 'the time is not ripe.' It was not possible to get a single name of real weight given to the League of Nations Society.

President Wilson's public declaration in August in favour of a League seemed to give its British supporters the chance they had been waiting for. Even Bryce was moved to write to Colonel House that the speech was 'by far the greatest step made towards the goal.' Hitherto, because of the public preoccupation with the events of the war he and his friends had 'thought it best not to press the whole League of Peace question to the front at the present. . . .'[40] The implication was that Wilson's declaration might make him change his mind. When Grey also made a public statement in October which favoured the League idea, Dickinson thought that the time was at last ripe for a more vigorous propaganda campaign. There was, however, still very great reluctance on the part of League supporters to declare themselves in public. They wanted to go to great lengths to make it clear that they were not associated with the 'peace by negotiations' campaign. Aneurin Williams, the treasurer of the L.N.S., stressed that 'any terms which Germany would accept could not possibly be acceptable to the Allies at present. Lamentable as it is . . . the struggle should go on until Germany is prepared to make very much larger concessions than any she would make now.' Bryce too stressed that he was 'one of those who while wishing no evil to the German people and opposed to permanent hatreds, think that for their sake and the world's sake it is necessary that the military caste in Germany should be distinctly defeated and that the people should know it.'[41] The *Arbitrator* which published an article by the American, Theodore Marburg, on the League in its October issue also featured a series of replies to the question of whether the Allies should offer peace terms to Germany. To its satisfaction, G. J. Wardle M.P., Chairman of the Parliamentary Labour Party answered 'emphatically in the negative.' Organized Labour was strongly averse to such a proposal. The journal stressed that the League idea and a negotiated peace had no necessary connexion.

The League idea was simultaneously in difficulties from the opposite standpoint. To many pacifists it seemed to represent a compromise and would hinder their efforts to abolish war completely. In June, the Society of Friends Peace Committee decided to hold a conference on the question of the League and peace. Edward Grubb advised Friends to go carefully. 'It would be a disaster' he wrote 'if, because of our sense of the extreme danger of these proposals for the use of force, we opposed altogether the formation of a League of Peace. We cannot afford to divide the

Peace party. . . .'[42] Lowes Dickinson, who was invited to speak on the question, agreed that the idea of a provision to employ force would alienate some possible supporters, but asked Friends to remember that such a provision would also gain many who would not otherwise be secured. He doubted whether a League without this power of coercion would receive the support of Sir Edward Grey and President Wilson.[43] The Quaker conference took place in the middle of October and it did not prove possible to reconcile all points of view. A statement issued at its conclusion declared that '. . . as individuals we shall certainly take various views of our duty to the League' but as a whole, the Society could not support it. 'We believe that any scheme which we as a religious society can support should not bind the constituent powers before-hand to take up arms but should leave each issue to be decided, as it arises, in the best way that the public opinion of the time permits. . . .'[44] Some Friends felt strongly that the potential use of coercion would destroy, not enhance, the value of the projected new organization. The discussion between the two sides in this argument had been vigorously conducted, though some felt, as a result of the debate, that the world needed both the temperamen-tally idealistic and the temperamentally political pacifist.

This issue, of course, did not simply trouble Quakers. Lowes Dickinson and Bertrand Russell had both been present at the conference and had taken opposite sides. Although Dickinson admitted that the general sentiment of the meeting was against his proposal to include force he was unrepentent. 'The essence of the "force" part of it' he explained to Miss Marshall 'is that you compel people, under threat of force, to attempt a peaceable settle-ment before recourse to war as you compel a citizen in a state to go to the courts and not to take the law in his own hands.' He was convinced that if anything at all was done to cure international anarchy after the war, it would be on such lines. 'Unless' he added 'you can conceive a popular revolt demanding disarmament. I cannot. Short of disarmament I think this is the only plan. . . .'[45] Miss Marshall then turned to Russell for his view of the question. She had to confess that the very title 'League of Enforce Peace' made her dubious. Russell replied that he did not agree with the proposed provision to use force, the very point which had gained the support of the Foreign Secretary. However, he had to confess that he was 'not even against this part in *principle* or in the long run.' Under existing circumstances he believed it would give a dangerous opportunity for 'disguised militarism'. It was not possible, he thought, to abolish force in international affairs 'except by passing through the stage where such force as is used is subordinated to law.' Therefore, he believed, 'something like the

League to Enforce Peace will have to be formed, as soon as a majority of civilised Governments desire to preserve the peace more than to promote their own power.' Miss Marshall was not impressed. 'For once' she wrote 'I think your reasoning is thoroughly unsound. There's impudence for you!' Russell replied that he was not surprised. He had just had a 'fearful rumpus' about force at an N.C.F. meeting. 'I have begun to find it difficult to go on pretending' he added ominously.[46]

Sooner or later, wrote Graham Wallas to Herbert Samuel in early October, all wars reached a point 'where in all the belligerent countries there are two parties, one desiring a comparatively inconclusive peace, based on the conception of the general good of mankind, and the other desiring a conclusive peace based on the annihilation of their opponents.' As things stood he believed that ninety-nine out of a hundred Englishmen desired success for British arms and believed that German victory would be a world disaster. He added, however, that as the winter wore on, he expected to find that nearly all of them who were Liberals by principle would be driven into opposing the combination which would effectively control the Government.[47]

If he could have known other reactions to Lloyd George's 'Knock-Out Blow' interview on 28 September he would have felt even more confident in his view that some change in the balance of political forces was likely. Of course, comment in the pacifist press was scathing. 'To save civilisation' the editorial in the *U.D.C.* observed 'Mr. Lloyd George is prepared to sacrifice civilisation. That is not an investment: it is a speculation.'[48] More significant were the reservations of some other members of the Cabinet. Grey complained that the American President would now put pressure on Britain. Personally gloomy about war prospects, the Foreign Secretary added that he had always held the view that until victory was certain the door should be kept open for Wilson's mediation. Lloyd George's speech had closed it for ever.[49] No one could pretend that the war was going well. While the destruction wrought by German submarines worried Grey most, McKenna and Runciman worried about the financial strain which continued war would bring. Runciman wrote to Charles Roden Buxton in significantly different tones from earlier letters on the war. It would be difficult, he now confessed, to find anyone outside 'the cheapest circles' who was not perturbed by the Lloyd George interview. At the same time, he still thought there was a long road to travel before English public opinion was ready for such peace terms as were reasonable.[50]

During these weeks the Cabinet was engaged on a rather desultory review of the war. Despite the doubts raised by Grey and

Runciman, the general impression remained that it was necessary to inflict such a defeat on Germany as would deter her from future aggression. Although for some months, the Foreign Office had been busy producing suggestions for a territorial settlement in Europe, they were not specifically considered by the Cabinet. It was, as Hankey put it, 'impossible to contemplate with equanimity the prospect of a discussion of peace terms at any date, however remote, until the balance of advantage has inclined far more decisively than at present to the side of the allies.'[51] Nevertheless, a few days later, on 5 November, Lord Lansdowne submitted a memorandum in which he discounted the possibility of losing the war but which questioned the chances of winning it 'in such a manner, and within such limits of time, as will enable us to beat our enemy into the ground and impose upon him the kind of terms which we so freely discuss?'[52] In reply, the Chief of the Imperial General Staff set out to combat the 'unfounded pessimism' which seemed to be growing. He poured scorn on 'cranks, cowards and philosophers' (not apparently honouring Lansdowne by including him in any of these categories) who somehow thought that there was more to gain by losing the war than by winning it. Germany should be defeated and the nation could only win if it set about the task with utter singlemindedness.[53] However, when he later claimed that the whole Cabinet at this juncture in the war came to the unanimous conclusion that peace negotiations before military victory would be disastrous, Lloyd George was only formally correct. There were many who in private wondered whether this desirable victory was, after all, obtainable.

This Cabinet debate was, of course, confidential, yet the Peace Movement seemed to sense that events were moving to some sort of crisis. Pacifists believed that public opinion was changing. Leading representatives of middle-class commercial Liberalism were becoming uneasy. Since the summer, men like R. D. Holt, A. G. C. Harvey, E. T. John and S. Arnold had begun to think seriously about a negotiated peace. Ponsonby welcomed these converts, though he found them 'very shy' of Labour.[54] Their vigorous public spokesman was F. W. Hirst, whose views on the war made his tenure of the editorial chair of the *Economist* increasingly precarious. He had completed a formidable tome on *The Political Economy of War* which forecast a gloomy financial future if the war was not ended. On leaving the *Economist* he launched a new weekly, *Common Sense,* in October. His backers included Sir Hugh Bell, the ironmaster (C. P. Trevelyan's father-in-law), Molteno and Holt.[55] All those associated with the paper resisted the extension of State control, defended Free Trade and feared that the Northcliffe Press would so dominate the Government that it would virtually run the war. An editorial in the first issue declared that it would be folly not to fight on until the right terms could be won. Equally, however, to fight on after the right terms could be secured for the sake of what was called 'in bruising circles' a 'Knock-out' was no policy at all. Molteno now agreed with Charles Roden Buxton that 'This talk of fighting to a finish is sheer madness' and he hoped that there would soon be a return to reason. So did Holt, though he confessed that many of his friends who deplored Lloyd George's statement had 'the feeling that Germany only wants peace now to get a breathing time for a fresh start' and he himself could not find evidence that the German Government wanted to relieve Europe of the incubus of militarism.[56]

This movement of opinion was very welcome to those who had hitherto been designated pacifists. As Philip Morrell put it, 'The only people who can now give effective help are those who were in favour of the war (or at least not openly against it) when it started, and have since come to see that peace is possible.' A combination of Capitalists and Socialists in the cause of peace might be rather bizarre, but it might also be effective.[57]

Quite apart from the situation inside Britain, there was one further ground for optimism among pacifists in November. President Wilson had just been re-elected. The Buxton brothers, J. H. Whitehouse and others had not relented in their campaign in favour of American mediation. Now that the President was confirmed in office, they led Colonel House to believe that there was a strong drift of public opinion towards a reasonable settlement with Germany. They also stressed that there was pressure from military and conservative circles for a fight to the finish. If the President intervened, he could tip the balance in favour of negotiations. Wilson told House that it was indeed very nearly the time, if not the time itself, when the peace move should be made. On 24 November the British Ambassador in Washington warned the Foreign Secretary that the President wished to see peace with himself as mediator. There would be a lot of talk about the future of the world being guaranteed by a League to Enforce Peace. The Ambassador thought this was no more than a pious wish since it would prove impossible to ensure the required amount of force. The Foreign Office therefore awaited the American initiative with as much anxiety as pacifists awaited it with enthusiasm.[58]

Very suddenly, early in December the British context was completely changed. Lloyd George became Prime Minister. His previous statements had hardly been encouraging from a pacifist standpoint, yet there were a number of concurrent developments, at home and abroad, which led them to hope that at last there was a chance of a negotiated peace.

CHAPTER SIX

A Time of Hope, December 1916-July 1917

Pacifists regarded the new Prime Minister equivocally. They detested his recent bellicose speeches and his evident determination to win the war at whatever cost. They feared that he would commit the country to an even more terrible struggle. Yet he was in their estimation so unprincipled that he might abruptly about turn and become the man to negotiate peace. 'I fancy he is clever enough' wrote Morgan Jones from detention 'to try to arrange peace even though he may be bellowing ever so loudly about organisation for war. Does he *want* peace do you think. I fancy he does.'[1]

On 12 December, the German Chancellor, Bethmann Hollwegg, informed the United States Embassy in Berlin that Germany, while confident that her own position was impregnable, had no wish to crush or eliminate her adversaries. The Central Powers were ready to enter into peace talks. A day later this news was in the British press. *The Times,* like most other newspapers, was unimpressed by this simultaneous display of power and rectitude. The War Cabinet met and decided to await a precise statement of the German terms. According to Lord Robert Cecil, a key figure in these matters, 'negotiations begun without any definite basis would be a mere mockery.' There is, indeed, little evidence to suggest that the new government seriously contemplated peace. It was only too clear that the military advantage in Europe rested with Germany and that the peace terms would be bound to reflect this ascendancy. However, there was the danger that some of the Allies might be attracted by the German move, in which case Britain might be forced to negotiate. Immediate steps were therefore taken to minimize such a possibility. There was also some anxiety lest a curt dismissal of the German note would offend the United States. The Cabinet was well aware of Wilson's interest in the question of peace and it was difficult to tell how he would react. If the United States cut off supplies of money and munitions then Britain's position could become very grave.

Pacifists believed that the German note gave them their great opportunity. If the President could be persuaded to intervene then there was a good chance that the war could be brought to an end. They were prepared to trust Bethmann Hollwegg and considered that it would be possible to reach a settlement on 'reasonable' terms. Letters from Trevelyan, Whitehouse and others flowed across the Atlantic urging the President to take action. He was told that British public opinion would prefer a negotiated peace to war under a virtual military dictatorship. The Peace Negotiations Committee chose this moment to present a petition to the Prime Minister. It was signed by over two hundred thousand individuals and it was claimed that three times that number of people belonged to organizations which had also given their support. The petition was sent across to Washington by W. H. Buckler, a special assistant at the American Embassy whose task it was to keep in touch with the 'negotiation group'. Ponsonby appealed to Lloyd George not to reject the German approach in a peremptory fashion. He also talked of the strength of 'moderate opinion'. It is difficult to tell how much importance was attached in the White House to this 'other Britain'. The President could not seriously have supposed that Lloyd George was 'unrepresentative'. For his part, the Prime Minister made it clear that Britain would not negotiate without hearing Germany's terms. The proposals would have to involve more than a return to the *status quo* of 1914. His speech was thus a clear commitment to victory, the only danger from a British point of view being that Germany might, after all, state terms which would appear plausible.

Despite Lloyd George's initial reaction, on 18 December President Wilson sent a note to the belligerents. He drew attention to the fact that both sides claimed to have the same objectives in the war. They even talked about some kind of new international organization to emerge at its conclusion. He declared that he was not proposing peace, or even offering mediation. He merely wished both sides to state the precise terms which would satisfy them. Although Berlin now suspected a plot between London and Washington, the note was generally interpreted in British Government circles as favourable to Germany. Its chances of success did not seem very great, nevertheless pacifists were delighted. 'Wilson seems to have done them to a turn this time', wrote Morgan Jones. 'They seem to be fearfully annoyed—and yet they may be secretly glad.' Miss Marshall felt that now was the time for action, though she did not know what would be the best course to follow. She was glad to hear that Bertrand Russell had written a vigorous appeal to the President, but she felt that something else was needed. The chances of success depended on 'a right handling of the moods and sensibilities of the chief persons concerned, and the promulgation of ideas *through the right media.*' The temptation was 'to come out with a united demand from pacifists for a definite statement of terms at once' but perhaps it was better 'to exercise a little patience and let the demand come from *new* sources. . . .'[2] Other peace journals saw no need for such restraint. *The Herald* wanted Lloyd George to put all his cards on the table and forget talk about victory and righteousness; Germany might not really be prepared to negotiate, but he should be willing to try. *Common Sense* stated that emperors and statesmen could not seriously expect their peoples to commit suicide or to mortgage the whole revenues of their countries. 'The whole fate of the world' Lowes Dickinson wrote to Ponsonby 'seems to me to depend on America.' Trevelyan did not see how the belligerents could now, with any semblance of reason, avoid stating their terms. If they did, pacifists would be placed in a most powerful position for agitation.[3]

Although Buckler reported to Washington that the British Government knew that peace sentiment in the country was too strong to be taken lightly, there seems little sign that this consideration was uppermost when the Cabinet debated its reply to President Wilson's Note of 18 December. The British position had been made easier by the reply already sent by the German Government. This discounted any possibility of American mediation and suggested direct negotiations between the belligerents. It was, in effect, a snub for the President. However, the Allied reply to the German note, handed over on 30 December, ruled out the possibility of direct talks. The German proposals were dismissed as mere sham designed to create dissension among the peoples of the Allied countries. In this they had not been successful.

It was not until ten days later that the reply was sent to President Wilson. It had been very carefully considered. The Note listed German crimes and stressed the worthlessness of German promises. It rejected 'in the friendliest yet the clearest way' the notion that the aims of the two belligerent groups were similar. For their part, the Allies had 'no difficulty' in answering the President's request for a precise definition of their war aims. Belgium, Serbia and Montenegro were to be restored and compensated; France, Russia and Rumania were to be evacuated with just reparation; Europe was to be reorganized, principally on the basis of respect for nationalities, specifically the liberation of the Italians, Slavs, Rumanians and Czechoslovaks from foreign domination, and the release of the populations subject to the bloody tyranny of the

Turks. The Emperor of Russia would create a free Poland. Such a reply was a vigorous challenge to Wilson. The British were keen to have their terms as widely known as possible in neutral countries. In Berlin, it was correctly assumed that Bethmann Hollwegg's initiative, whatever its real motivation, had failed. His policy was in ruins and he was in no position to resist its alternative —the declaration of unrestricted submarine warfare. In Vienna, it was feared that the references to the Slav peoples meant that Allied policy was moving towards the destruction of the Monarchy.[4]

The reply of 10 January had been framed with an eye to its international impact. No less important, however, was its significance at home. For many months, pacifists had been clammering for a statement of terms. Well, now they had them. They were not very pleased with the result and began to wonder whether they would not have been better to have remained in ignorance. 'My instinctive dread' wrote Brailsford on 15 January 'of the consequences of forcing a declaration of terms is, I think, justified.' It had become clear that the Entente Powers were committed to a total victory which would involve the dismemberment of Austria and the expulsion of the Turks from Europe. The tiresome aspect of the statement was that 'the phrasing was just clever enough to prevent a moderate revolt.' The only thing for pacifists to do was deplore the policy of pure conquest and to cry '*A bas* Lloyd George'. To talk of a League of Nations on top of such a policy was 'pure hypocrisy'.[5] Brailsford's irritation is an indication of the extent to which the Prime Minister's announcement had successfully embarrassed the pacifists. Lloyd George well knew that, before the war, many of them had keenly supported the 'suppressed nationalities'. They could hardly denounce Lloyd George's supposed concern for their future as wicked. The most they could say, like Charles Roden Buxton, was that to lead small states and oppressed nations to believe in some vaguely conceived 'ultimate triumph' which would give them all they had ever hoped or dreamed, would be 'grossly unfair' to them. The destruction of both the Habsburg and Ottoman Empires appealed to impeccable Liberals like Bryce and prevented them from straying to the side of the Government's critics. While admitting that he was perhaps unduly bitter, Brailsford could not conceive that the Prime Minister would 'move on to any vision of a good peace, even if he learns by six months' trial that he can't "knock-out" Germany.' Noel Buxton regretted that a great opportunity had been lost. He was convinced that the desire in Germany to see militarism overthrown and discredited was intense. Bertrand Russell foresaw peace in the autumn after Lloyd George had drunk the blood of half a million young Englishmen in a further ineffective offensive. Not that Lloyd George was worse than the rest of mankind, on the contrary, he belonged to the best ten per cent. 'It is the human race that is vile' he wrote to Miss Marshall. 'It is a disgrace to belong to it.'[6]

Disgrace or not, most pacifists could find no alternative, and the outlook seemed once again rather bleak. In the end, Lloyd George might be forced to accept a compromise peace, but that time still seemed some way off. Despite the rebuffs he had received, President Wilson had not completely given up hope that he might yet emerge as the peacemaker. Throughout the next couple of weeks he worked away at the speech, delivered on 22 January, which became famous as 'Peace without Victory'. In this address he declared that victory would mean a peace forced on the loser; only a peace between equals could last. At the end of the month, however, came the decision by Germany to embark on unrestricted submarine warfare. Relations between Germany and the United States deteriorated. Far from being able to bring the belligerents together to settle a peace, it looked increasingly to pacifists as if the United States would intervene on the side of the Allies. Such a trend confronted them with a difficulty. The declared war aims of the Allies seemed both sinister and absurd; the undeclared aims were probably more sinister and more absurd. They gave help and comfort to the militarists among the enemy. Pacifists were therefore reluctant to suppose that President Wilson endorsed such objectives. Before America had entered the war, Morel wrote that it was inconceivable that the Americans would support such a policy as was indicated in the worst features of the Allied reply. After April, when the United States did join the conflict, the only consolation was that the White House would surely use its influence to curb the ambitions and emotions of those states with which the United States was now associated. American intervention might therefore mean that, while the war would go on, the objects for which it was being fought would be purified. Wilson's refusal to enter into a formal alliance with Britain and France was seen as an encouraging sign. Pacifists hoped for the situation which the British Government feared, that America would be able to dictate terms. A few agreed with Lord Bryce that an American expeditionary force might shorten the world's suffering by many months. The majority shared Snowden's anxiety that war fever would develop in the United States. He saw little reason to suppose that the American people would long remain actuated by the noble sentiments in the President's war speech. Bertrand Russell, too, stressed that militarism would grow across the Atlantic and he believed that 'the help of America is quite as likely to lengthen the war as to shorten it. Without America, universal exhaustion might have driven all the nations to a compromise peace—obviously the best in the interests of international concord.' With America, it might be possible to go on for a further three years in the hope of gaining a final military victory.[7]

In any case, whether American entry would shorten or lengthen the war, President Wilson had lost some of his attraction. For the moment, British pacifists were more excited by the news of the March Revolution in Russia. Initially, many British newspapers tended to interpret the events as a decisive blow against the pro-German influences at the Russian Court. The *Morning Post* proclaimed 'Germanism overthrown' and even the *Manchester Guardian* declared on 16 March 'It is certain that as a result, Russia will go forward to the end with her allies, and will fight with greater efficiency and with a better heart.' For pro-war Liberals in particular, the embarrassment of having an autocratic ally was removed. Naturally, pacifists did not agree with such interpretations. They preferred to stress that within a week Russia had been transformed into the most free country in Europe. It was time for Britain to learn lessons in civil liberty from Petrograd.[8] When the new Provisional Government issued statements calling for a peace settlement without forcible annexations and based solely upon self-determination, Morel rejoiced. It proved the folly of trying to exploit the Russian Revolution in the interests of the 'knock-out blow'. The British Government would soon discover that the Russian people, like all people, wanted peace. The U.D.C. modestly declared that now both the American and the Russian Governments accepted its principles. It claimed to be able to discern that the real war in every country was on the home front. The enemy consisted of 'The Extremists', whatever their nationality. It was time for the men of goodwill in every belligerent country who accepted U.D.C. principles to come together, for when the peoples fully realized the truth about the war which was being waged in their name, they would stop it.[9]

The events in Russia, followed by the American intervention in the war, meant that once more the political situation seemed more hopeful for pacifists. For its part, the British Government knew that the prospects of immediate military success were slight. Russian power was failing and it was increasingly feared that it would collapse completely. It would still be many months before the effect of American assistance would be felt. Lord Cecil minuted in April that it seemed increasingly probable that 'we may have to accept an unsatisfactory peace.'[10] Such pessimism was not, of course, common knowledge. After taking various soundings, the Prime Minister was convinced that Germany would consider peace only if she were allowed to keep the conquests she had made during the war. He was not prepared to abandon his recently declared objectives without a struggle. Nevertheless, it was increasingly feared that a combination of internal subversion and loss of will on the part of her Allies would force Britain to retreat from her stated aims. The Government could not control feelings in other countries, but it could attempt to restrict the activities of British pacifists still further.

At this critical juncture in the war, pacifists had some slight reason to believe that public opinion was moving a little in their direction. In February, a by-election was held at Rossendale in Lancashire. The result, with nearly a quarter of the electorate supporting the peace candidate, pleased, among others, the old Radical Sir William Byles. He was convinced that there was a very large body of opinion in the country favouring a negotiated peace and believing that Germany was ready to entertain reasonable proposals.[11] This relative success encouraged the peace groups to contest other seats as they fell vacant. The joint by-election committee became more active. However, despite reports of favourable receptions for U.D.C. speakers in the North of England, the result at Stockton-on-Tees in March was a disappointment. Edward Backhouse, a respected local Quaker, secured only 596 votes in a total poll of 8,237.[12] A couple of months earlier, J. E. Hodgkin of Darlington had informed F. W. Hirst of his 'firm conviction that a very decided change is coming over the county, and specially over the more thoughtful section of the population, in regard to the war.' People, he claimed, were beginning to realize that they had been deliberately misled by the Government and by the Press both as to the causes and the facts of the war.[13] In April, at Aberdeen South, F. W. Pethick Lawrence stood as a 'peace by negotiation' candidate and was supported by prominent pacifists. At stormy election meetings he proclaimed that it was possible to gain a reasonable peace. He believed that such a settlement could be guaranteed by international courts. It would be terrible to continue the war simply to break up the Habsburg Monarchy. He obtained 333 votes in a total poll of 5,123.[14] In May, Charles Roden Buxton wrote in a private memorandum based on his experiences that 'We are no longer the preachers of a desperately unpopular doctrine. A year ago we were treated with contempt, as a negligible minority. Today, we have become strong enough to be feared and . . . tomorrow, we shall be resisted but we shall be a formidable fighting force, not capable of being suppressed. . . .' He exaggerated, but less so than he had done in the past.[15]

However optimistic Buxton and others were, the results of the by-elections showed that they still had a long way to go. An alternative strategy for pacifists was to contemplate following the Russian example by organizing a revolution. The British industrial situation seemed promising for such an attempt. In 1916 the number of days lost through labour disputes was the lowest for nine years but during 1917 the number of stoppages steadily increased. The most serious strikes occurred in the engineering industries in March, April and May 1917 involving nearly two hundred thousand men and causing the loss of a million and a half working days. From the Government's standpoint, there was a real danger that the frustrations and hardships might wear down the patriotic sense of the workers. The growth of the Shop Stewards' movement and the demand for 'workers' control' were further causes for alarm.[16] Discontent was increasing in such areas as Clydeside and South Wales. Feeling certain that the difficulties were being caused by German agents and pacifist agitators, Frances Stevenson was strongly critical of their activities. Commenting on a letter from C. P. Trevelyan to a friend in Petrograd which had been intercepted she described it as 'a most malicious document' which gloated over the fact that the poor would soon be hungry and ripe for revolution.[17] Her master, the Prime Minister, reacted to the general situation by appointing special commissions to investigate the mood in different parts of the country. Lord Milner urged greater government support for a loyal association, the British Workers League. 'What I do believe in' he wrote to the Prime Minister at the end of May 'is systematic work by Labour men, who are on our side, to counteract the very systematic and active propaganda of the Pacifists. . . .' He told a journalist that he wanted to go both for bullying, profiteering and unscrupulous employers and for the agitators.[18]

An extraordinary Labour Convention held at Leeds early in June, a few days after the announcement of the special commissions, seemed to confirm that the situation was indeed serious. Over twelve hundred delegates from Trades Councils, Trades Unions, the I.L.P., the B.S.P. and various other bodies met to celebrate the Russian Revolution. The British Government was called on 'immediately to announce its agreement with the declared foreign policy and war aims of the democratic government of Russia.' Another resolution demanded the release of political prisoners in Britain and the restoration of political and industrial freedom. The Convention also decided to establish Councils of Workmen's and Soldiers' Delegates in every town. The atmosphere was exhilarating and emotional, although punctuated by some unpopular questions from Ernest Bevin. The Pethick Lawrences were typical. They 'enjoyed the Convention enormously. It was splendid to see such unanimity and enthusiasm.'[19] Milner wanted the press to be instructed not to 'boom' the Leeds Convention. His reason was clear. 'I fear the time is very near at hand, when we shall have to take some strong steps in this country, unless we wish to "follow Russia" into impotence and dissolution.'[20] Whilst it reveals Milner's state of mind, this comment seems in retrospect too alarmist and may well have seemed so to some of his colleagues. The Leeds euphoria did not last long. The committee to promote the British Soviets proved ineffective. By the middle of July the Government had received detailed information about the causes of discontent and took action to remove some of the immediate grievances. The prospect of a revolutionary summer began to fade. Nevertheless, it was apparent that the domestic situation was more uncertain than it had been at any stage since the beginning of the war. In future the Government could not rely on an easy consensus.

Perhaps fortunately for the Cabinet, pacifists were not agreed about the use to be made of their political opportunities. The Peace Movement was still divided into various sections who professed the common aim of peace but seemed unable to co-operate between themselves. They all continued to insist that they stood for a distinct aspect of the truth. Each apparently had a particular concern which no other body could deal with effectively. The National Peace Council had sponsored a rather surreptitious Peace Congress in London in January at which the speakers included Dr. Hodgkin, Miss Marshall, Mrs. Swanwick, Bruce Glasier and Robert Williams but it could not be said to be co-ordinating pacifist activity. The International Arbitration and Peace Association even withdrew from membership of the Council. The Association felt that in the clamour for negotiations the claims of justice were being overlooked. The *Monthly Circular* of the N.P.C. regretted the parting but commented sharply that it was 'worse than useless to attempt co-operation with colleagues who, quite sincerely, made a dogma of what is only held to be true by a small minority of the world peace movement. . . .'[21] In June, in the post-Leeds enthusiasm, Charles Trevelyan wrote to Bertrand Russell urging, once again, that 'something ought to be done to prevent the overlapping of pacifist societies. The political work for peace ought really to be done by the I.L.P. and the U.D.C. The actual helping and advising of C.O.'s needs no doubt a separate organisation: but the maximum of good for the whole movement has probably been obtained now by the C.O.'s.'[22] Despite the fact that many of the leading individuals were all, in theory, supporters of each other's societies, nothing very much came of this initiative. Not only did the groups maintain their distinct identities, they were all themselves internally divided on important questions of policy. The prospect of peace, dim though it might be, brought into sharper focus the fact that pacifists did not really know what peace was.

The relationship between the cause of peace and Socialism was especially vexatious. A speaker at the I.L.P. Annual Conference in April pointed out that some of their peace friends, such as Mr. Morel, were not working for the overthrow of capitalism. The primary goal of the party, however, was the introduction of Socialism. The end of capitalism would certainly mean the end of war, but that was, as it were, an incidental benefit. Of course, Socialists loathed the war but there would be little consolation if it ended with capitalism still firmly entrenched. It was possible, on the other hand, that the continuance of the war might promote conditions favourable to socialist revolution. Other speakers did not wish to rule out the possibility that in the future a Socialist state might need to defend itself against counter-revolutionary forces. The issue was an extremely delicate one. At this particular conference, Dr. Salter gained the day for a motion that pledged Socialist parties in all countries against any war entered into by their respective governments, whatever the ostensible origin of the dispute. MacDonald spoke against the motion. He agreed that the distinction between offensive and defensive war was meaningless, but equally he did not want the party to make a general pronouncement of this kind which 'when they thought about it, really meant nothing.'[23] Socialists had to remove the cause of war. After keeping out of the limelight for some months, MacDonald now sensed his opportunity. In a book on *National Defence* he made light of the conscription issue. Once war had come it was almost inevitable. He stressed again and again that it was necessary to deal with the roots of conflict before disaster occurred. Fine-sounding words and postures would not make much difference thereafter. It was necessary to approach the problem more rigorously than had been done in the past by sentimental pacifists. 'We can have Hague Courts by the score' he mocked 'and Arbitration Treaties by the thousand, but without this diplomacy of democracy there can be no guarantee of peace.'[24] The new diplomacy which Labour would inaugurate would not need armed force or citizen armies. It would be sufficient for the people to become knowledgeable and take over power.

Such an argument did not explain how the people were to win power. MacDonald had always opposed seizing control by force. His appearance at the Leeds Convention seemed to some to be an indication that he was becoming rather 'revolutionary'. His lack of clarity at this stage is, however, understandable. No one wanted plain-speaking on the question of peace and revolution. George Lansbury's *Herald* described the Russian revolution as 'a proletarian revolution and therefore a *pacifist* revolution.' It was explained that in this context 'pacifist' meant 'non-aggressive' rather than 'non-resistant' but otherwise the reader was left to decide for himself what the statement meant.[25] For the *Socialist Review*, the enthusiastic cheering of the speakers at Leeds in proportion to their repute as 'traitors', and the 'pacifist and revolutionary' tone of their remarks, was encouraging.[26] It was, however, quite happy to link together the adjectives 'pacifist' and 'revolutionary' without comment. Yet, it was clear that if revolution was to occur in Britain in 1917 it could only come about by violence. The *Ploughshare*, organ of the Quaker Socialists, was enthusiastic about the revolution in Russia, rejoicing that the policies of military conquest and domination had been repudiated. It was, however, unhappy about the Leeds Convention, writing that pacifists surely, and Quakers among them certainly, would not countenance the use or stimulation of mutiny or wholesale desertion from the army. 'We have no right' it concluded 'to call ourselves pacifists, to challenge war at all times and in all places, and then to set to organising committees, the success of which is to depend on the potential use of the Army. . . .'[27] Revolutionaries would no doubt claim that they only used force to end force but nevertheless this was not the same as pacifism. The profession of pacifism did not, of course, mean indifference to social reconstruction. On the contrary, some of the most ardent advocates of social change were also the most ardent pacifists. The tension that resulted can be seen most clearly among the members of the No Conscription Fellowship.

In January 1917 the possibility of industrial conscription led to demands for a reconsideration of the N.C.F.'s basis. The Quaker Socialist, Barratt Brown, proposed that the members should describe themselves as men and women who would 'refuse from conscientious motives to allow their occupations to be changed for war purposes, because they consider human life to be sacred, and cannot, therefore, take any part in war.' They would deny the right of Government to change their occupation for such purposes. . . .'[28] The subject was debated by the national committee on 20 January. Supporters of the motion argued that since the avowed purpose of industrial direction was to increase efficiency for war purposes, pacifists should oppose the scheme. On the other hand, it was argued that Brown's wording made it impossible for those who had accepted Alternative Service or work under the Home Office scheme to remain in the N.C.F. The proposal was defeated. It was also felt by some among the majority that 'the State ought not to be opposed, even in time of war, except in so far as its energies are devoted to carrying on the war, and that any citizen ought, even at this time, to be prepared to assist it in those of its activities which are concerned with objects that would be

equally important in time of peace.' Rather confusingly, the committee then resolved to oppose industrial conscription but simply
on 'the pacifist objection to the conscription of men and women
for war purposes.'[29]

Although highly topical, the industrial question was really only
an expression of the continuing division in the N.C.F. on the issue
of alternative service. Russell admitted privately that the national
committee had been more or less paralysed by this problem for
many months. At the same January meeting, a motion was moved
that the Fellowship should give full publicity to the witness of its
members but should not make any efforts, direct or indirect, 'to
alleviate their conditions, or obtain for them exemptions of any
kind, devoting its energies solely to arousing the public conscience
on war and conscription for war.' This motion was also lost, with
the result, according to Russell, that the committee was now 'free
to do much more than before on behalf of alternativists and men
in Home Office camps, and we are desirous of making full use of
our liberty.'[30] Writing in the *Tribunal* he proclaimed 'We pacifists
are, at the moment, the guardians of the principle that every man
should be free to follow the guidance of his or her own
conscience.'[31] A new period of unity seemed about to dawn. The
problems of the Home Office scheme, in particular those at the
work centre at Princetown—Dartmoor Prison—upset this prospect.

The predominant feeling in parliament was that the men on
the Home Office scheme should have been grateful for their release
from prison and be prepared to accept whatever work and conditions the Brace Committee prescribed. In practice, however, the
scheme proved very difficult to operate. Men who had been released
from prison under its provisions did not like the work they found
they were expected to do. Conditions were not good. Concerted
idleness began to make its appearance. The authorities tried to
devise new rules, but the lack of suitable employment, which
might make the scheme a success, was critical. There were only
two work centres, at Wakefield and Warwick, to take all the men
released from prison. It was to meet this situation that Dartmoor
was turned into a work centre in March 1917. It held twelve
hundred men by the autumn. This large group contained men with
a bewildering variety of moral, political and religious opinions.[32]
They strained the patience not only of the work centre administration but also of the N.C.F. national committee. In order to make
its own position clear, on 3 March the executive sent out a
document setting out its views on 'The Position in the Home
Office Camps.' It admitted that some men in the Camps were bent
on defeating the scheme by evading work as much as possible.
Such a spoiling policy appeared to be open to objections 'of the

same kind as we should feel against a policy of joining the Army with a view to undermining discipline. We feel that, in signing the undertaking, men subject themselves to an honourable obligation either to carry out its provisions to the best of their ability, or to announce to the authorities that they no longer intend to carry out its provisions and are prepared to accept the consequences. . . .' Quite apart from the moral aspect, the committee felt that the effect upon public opinion of a policy of evading work would be so bad as to cause 'serious damage to the whole movement. . . .'[33]

This concern for gentlemanly conduct was touching, but it had little connexion with the babel that was Princetown. It was difficult to maintain contact btween London and the men at the work centre and misunderstandings easily arose. One N.C.F. member sent the committee a detailed description of the various schools of thought at Princetown. Stressing that the atmosphere was most unpleasant, he believed that the 'wretched Scheme seems to have as terrible a power of corrupting men as the Army itself. Having accepted the scheme for himself, he considered that he had a duty to help other conscientious objectors make the best of it. He would, however, be misrepresented as 'helping to run the Scheme for the Home Office.' A former member of the N.C.F. national committee, C. H. Norman, was organizing a group which was deliberately setting out to wreck the project.[34] Russell replied that he did not support wrecking. It was very bad for those who engaged in it and did the cause of the conscientious objector no good. At a time when attacks in the press were mounting in frequency and intensity, the refusal of some men to co-operate made effective defence very difficult.[35] C. H. Norman was not impressed. His judgment was that 'the position of the conscientious objector, owing to the revolutionary action of the Russian soldier and the situation in America is graver in England than ever it was. The capitalists recognise now that we are a challenge not only to the military machine but to the capitalist order of society.' Talk of 'keeping a contract' or 'rendering service' angered him. The idea of freely working in a community, paying taxes and generally leading the life of a citizen 'does not seem to me to be opposing militarism.' The national committee had failed to grasp that 'the men in the camps were more living witnesses of the defeat of militarism than those in prison; because in prison you are behind the wall. In the H.O. camps you are outside—*not* wearing the insignia of militarism.'[36]

The national committee discovered that Norman's view was gaining ground. The atmosphere in Dartmoor was getting worse. Disgruntled men were turning against the scheme altogether. It was now in a precarious position. On 26 April, Miss Marshall was informed by General Childs that he had in his possession certain incriminating documents which could damage the cause of the conscientious objector. He read an extract from a letter in which the author spoke of his intention of undermining the Home Office scheme by systematic slacking. It was, in the General's view, not an honourable statement. The men concerned were disclosed as really absolutists who were trying to wreck a scheme provided for alternativists. Miss Marshall then took it upon herself to tell Childs that the national committee did not support such men who were, in any case, very largely outside the ranks of the N.C.F. She repeated this view in a letter to a Home Office official the following day. She added that the N.C.F. did not consider the Dartmoor scheme perfect, but felt that it could evolve into something quite acceptable. It would be 'very disappointing and regrettable if the action of a small number of the men who do not represent any of the organised bodies of the Conscientious Objectors is allowed to frustrate such a desirable development.'[37]

When news of Miss Marshall's actions reached Dartmoor, they provoked C. H. Norman to fury. The national committee, he considered, had shown quite extraordinary bias in the matter. Its willingness to give information to the military was quite disastrous. In his judgment, work under the Home Office scheme was 'penal work just as prison work is, only it is done under somewhat freer conditions: there is no moral duty so far as I am aware to obey military, prison, or Home Office regulations.' Turning the tables, he alleged that the press onslaught against slacking under the Home Office scheme had only started because the contents of the Executive's own letter of 3 March had reached the ears of Northcliffe. With Miss Marshall herself, Norman was even more frank. 'Surely' he wrote 'the N.C.F. has not got to the stage when its officials are to supply the common enemy with munitions. That is the unwitting result of your action.' Warned by Russell that the camps were 'ablaze', Miss Marshall tried to clear herself. She claimed that her motive was simply to prevent the N.C.F. from being unjustly criticized.[38] Norman was not appeased. Meanwhile, at Dartmoor itself, discipline was tightened and he accused the national committee of collaboration. Both Russell and Miss Marshall were beginning to find the situation a great strain on their nerves. The national committee tried to calm tempers, recognizing that 'Under the influence of persecution, men tend, not unnaturally, to become hostile to their persecutors, thereby losing the spirit of human brotherhood', but since pacifists believed in the power of the spirit 'when we adopt the spirit of the Militarist, we are bound to fail, since force is not on our side.' This was the ideal, but the

Quaker, J. W. Graham, was right to remark at the end of May
'. . . I am afraid our C.O. resembles the Apostle Paul, in that there
are fightings within, and fears without. . . .'[39]

Tension within the Fellowship was not confined to the problems
of the Home Office scheme. From prison, Clifford Allen wrote
an Open Letter to his colleagues declaring that he and many other
absolutists were coming to feel more and more firmly that their
opposition to alternative service, or any form of service arising
from the conscription situation demanded that they should, in
principle, cease to work in prison. Allen had just been sentenced
at another court-martial to two years' hard labour. He was now
at the cross-roads of his career. His experience in prison had
helped to convince him that mere propaganda to expose the horrors
and futilities of war was useless. It could only be along the path
of social reconstruction that there would be any headway made
against war. Pacifists and Socialists had to work together.
Incarcerated as he and other pacifists were, however, the leadership
in this reconstruction looked like going elsewhere. Catherine
Marshall sent Robert Smillie a message from Allen expressing his
profound regret that circumstances beyond his control prevented
him attending the Leeds Convention. The significant point, however, lies in her second paragraph, 'C. A. was deeply hurt—and I
am too—that the N.C.F. has not been invited to take part in the
Convention. Surely the C.O.'s are putting up as great a fight for
freedom and democracy as any body of men in the country.'[40]
Allen's determination not to co-operate with the prison authorities
was, therefore, in part a bid to regain lost prestige. It was time
to launch a new campaign for absolute exemption for the thousand
or so men who would not accept any form of alternative service.
He made it clear that he would not be prepared to accept any
special treatment for himself.

On 31 May, therefore, Allen addressed a lengthy appeal to the
Prime Minister. He declared that the Government's policy was
nothing less than deliberate persecution of genuine opinion. He had
therefore decided to refuse all orders during the remaining term of
his imprisonment, no matter if this meant solitary confinement and
extreme privation. He would not condone conscription in any
shape or form, nor the various alternatives that had been offered.
The hearts of the men in prison might be broken, but their spirit
would never wilt.[41] Miss Marshall was delighted to hear that this
appeal was supposed to have caused serious embarrassment to
Lloyd George. However, it was also a serious embarrassment for
the N.C.F. leadership. C. G. Ammon, who did a great deal of
political liaison work for the Fellowship, considered Allen's statement 'ill-advised and impossible to turn to good account. It might

succeed in securing his discharge but will not achieve anything
further. . . .'[42] Influential members of the national committee were
so opposed to Allen's proposed course that they wanted to ban
any reference to it in the *Tribunal*. 'Dramatic action' wrote Dr.
Salter 'like a work or hunger strike will achieve nothing for our
cause. The most that could be hoped for would be the compas-
sionate release of a few individual men who had been brought near
to physical and mental death.' Barratt Brown disagreed with Salter
and resigned from the national committee. He could not be party
'to a policy and method which in my view are calculated to relax
our uncompromising opposition to conscription and to facilitating
the working of the Military Service Acts.'[43]

What was at stake in this dispute was the extent to which
pacifism involved passivism. The division was very largely between
'religious' and 'non-religious' objectors. The mood of the F.O.R.
in these months was especially quietist. Its general committee could
not decide how far it should associate with the U.D.C., the I.L.P.
or the N.C.C.L. The General Council decided in March that 'just
now it would be a mistake to construct the message of the Fellowship into any specific line of action. . . . The duty of the F.O.R.
was to show that the Christian ethic is heroic and demands the
giving of the highest both for individuals and nations.' Miss Marian
Ellis appealed to members to declare that political methods ought
to be based on the laws of the Kingdom of God.[44] Her sister, Miss
Edith Ellis, wrote to Miss Marshall on behalf of the Friends Service
Committee to say that the Society of Friends would not press for
the release of conscientious objectors. It was not an easy attitude
for those with relatives behind bars to take, but Friends felt there
was grave danger in letting the public think that conscientious
objectors could not face hardship willingly as soldiers did.[45] For
her part, Miss Marshall despaired of being able to communicate
her viewpoint to her Quaker colleagues. The essential characteristic
of the N.C.F., she considered, was that it gave direct practical
expression to an idealistic faith, but also showed that pacifism
was not inconsistent with vigour and valour. She feared that circumstances were causing men in prison to lose this desirable
balance in one direction or another.[46] Allen, indeed, now wanted
to achieve the practical success of getting out and 'defeating the
system'. Labour, he thought, would become increasingly contemptuous of the silent minority. Pacifists would be cut off from the
growing spirit of revolt in the country, and it was 'so important

that we should use our intelligence to restrain violence in the new revolutionary movement. . . .' He was prepared to accept sacrifice but he did not want martyrdom.[47]

The issue of Socialist Revolution was not the only matter which tested the nature of pacifism. The problems posed by the idea of a League of Nations witnessed another kind of encounter between the politics of absolutes and the politics of pragmatism. The notion of a League was more widely discussed in early 1917, but the very fact that Governments were considering its feasibility meant that some pacifists were suspicious. They feared that the League would be 'militarized'. Politicians in power, on the other hand, were inclined to be sceptical about the extravagant claims made by some of the League's supporters. Enthusiasts had therefore to protect themselves from criticism from both flanks. In their anxiety to do so, they veered uneasily one way and then the other.

Lowes Dickinson began 1917 by regretting that, with the departure of Asquith and Grey, the change of government had involved the loss of 'the only two men who have explicitly stated that they believe in a reform of international relations after the war on the line of a "partnership of nations".' Lloyd George was indifferent and the rest of the new Cabinet either sceptical or avowedly hostile. If this was the case, there was a need for an effective public movement in favour of a League to Enforce Peace. The difficulty was that no movement would 'go' unless there were eminent men to give it backing. He recognized the obstacles—the fear of press hostility and allegations of being 'pro-German'—but, in his view, those like Bryce who felt that the moment was still not ripe for public discussion were allowing opponents of the idea to have full sway. Dickinson admitted that he was himself 'irrevocably tainted' and that the committee of the L.N.S. was not strong, yet it was the only such body in existence. He saw no alternative but to 'endeavour a more active propaganda in ways that are possible. . . .'[48] Bryce remained careful 'lest the question should in any way be confounded with that of stopping the present war. . . .'[49]

In this situation, the intellectual framework continued to be laid by Dickinson, Brailsford and Hobson, all three of whom were 'tainted'. In mid-February Brailsford published a full-scale work specifically on the League. It was described a little later by Lowes Dickinson as 'much the ablest book' on the subject.[50] It went through several impressions and was widely acclaimed. The author was not so much concerned with complicated organizational details as with the general problem of creating any kind of League at all. His main theme was the necessity of moving from force to conference in relations between states. He believed that it would be sensible to base the future peace on a policy of trust rather than distrust. To take a risk with a defeated state was unquestionably a gamble with human nature; but it might be splendidly vindicated. There were, however, no short-cuts to peace. Unlike some pacifists, he considered that an international conference in the summer of 1914 would not have averted war, simply because the world in 1914 was not ready for a solution of the problems involved other than by force. Although it was true that pacifist thought was quite flourishing in pre-war Britain, it was a different story in Serbia or in Germany. This was not because of the peculiar psychology of other peoples. In this matter, everything depended on the varying urgency of the need which nations felt for fundamental change. If, therefore, a League attempted to keep international society rigid, it would surely fail. Only if it provided for peaceful change would it survive and play a useful role. He believed that its chances of success would be helped if, at the end of the war, there was as little change as possible in the general framework of Europe. There was little point in supposing that special alliances and connexions between states would wither away overnight. The hope would be that the League would gradually elicit its own loyalty from states. An international League could tolerate associations and parties within itself provided there was loyalty in all to the general good and obedience to the general will. If a German Government pledged itself to enter a League based on arbitration and conciliation, that would offer a better chance of destroying Prussian militarism than a peace of punishment. However persuasive his arguments, Brailsford was in private not very hopeful. Lloyd George would not like the League simply because President Wilson had taken such a fancy to it and the credit in history would not be his. He was convinced that, despite the pious talk, the Prime Minister was keeping ready a subtle invulnerable under-water torpedo which would kill the project at an appropriate time.[51]

J. A. Hobson wanted to see the League system in the wider context of social transformation. Pacifists should cease to regard war as an isolated aberration. It was militarism, not war, that needed to be abolished, for militarism was the state of affairs which made war acceptable. Hobson had no doubt that it would be a difficult task for he refused to link the existence of militarism with capitalism in a simple-minded way. In examining instances of aggression, he wrote, 'We still find that other non-economic considerations often seem to outweigh the distinctively economic ones.' In these circumstances, democratic control was the only certain remedy. If oligarchic control was allowed to remain in any single sphere then all other forms of popular self-government would be almost worthless. The full spirit of democracy had to be roused and organized for a general attack. He admitted that 'the people, as a whole, have not the intelligence, the knowledge and the persistent will needed to make democracy effective.' This ignorance, however, was not invincible and would vanish when the management of public opinion by the ruling and possessing classes had been overcome. The League of Nations would be the way of asserting this democratic control in the international sphere.[52]

Lowes Dickinson also stressed that pacifism was at one with the whole movement of social transformation which was vaguely referred to as the coming of democracy. He was sure that, as an ideal, war would fade into the past and peace take its place. The problem was to relate these assertions to the complexities of foreign policy. It was vital that international relations should be made more comprehensible by the ordinary man or woman going about everyday life. He did not think this would be difficult since the masses instinctively felt that internationalism was inevitable. He contended that it was the absence of adequate machinery to deal with disputes rather than their insoluble nature which led to war. The League of Nations would be a way of solving these difficulties. It would not be a super-State and would not possess its own international force, nevertheless he continued to agree with Hobson that the sanction of force was, in the last resort, essential. Pacifists should not be distressed, since such a sanction would mean that force would invariably be used in the service of law. There was, therefore, a choice to be made. At the close of the war either the nations would perform a great act of faith in themselves and in one another or they would succumb to an era of new wars. Privately, he was not very optimistic about the right choice being made. 'I get so cynical about all public persons' he wote in May, 'Governments appear to me to exist for the sole purpose of destroying mankind, which, however, shows every willingness to be destroyed. The only people to admire and respect are the Russian workmen's committees....'[53]

Dickinson's cynicism was slightly mitigated by the fact that, at long last, public persons agreed to speak publicly on the question of the League. The first open meeting was held on 14 May in a packed Central Hall, Westminster, with Lord Bryce in the chair. The principal speakers were the Archbishop of Canterbury, Lord Buckmaster, Lord Hugh Cecil and General Smuts. The concluding resolution, moved by Smuts, stressed the need for some machinery for the maintenance of international rights and general peace. The meeting attributed such a scheme to President Wilson and commended it to the British people.[54] Lowes Dickinson, much encouraged, wrote to Bryce that people, like Smuts himself, who seemed to think that there was going to be a long period of bitter fighting after the war, should remember that less than twenty years previously the General was fighting the British Empire. Bryce too was pleased with the meeting. In his opinion, the American entry into the war had made a great difference to the support they had received. Previously, 'the movement would have been discredited as "pacifist".' He agreed that the next step would be to persuade the Government to take up the idea in a practical manner.[55]

Public meetings in favour of a League continued throughout the summer. Yet there was no real agreement among its protagonists about the detailed machinery which would be needed if the idea were ever to become reality. For example, the views of those who attended the annual meeting of the L.N.S. in July—they included Willoughby Dickinson, Lowes Dickinson, Lord Parmoor, Aneurin Williams, Noel Buxton, F. N. Keen, R. Unwin, L. Woolf, C. D. Burns, A. E. Zimmern and J. A. Hobson—varied from support for an embryonic international government to endorsement of a limited machinery for imposing a 'cooling-off' period. As a body, the L.N.S. went out of its way to show that it was not opposed to the use of force as a last resort. A reference in the objects of the Society to the need for members of the League to unite in any action necessary to preserve peace was made more specific. It was now stated that the members should jointly use their economic and military forces against any one of their number that goes to war or commits acts of hostility against another.[56] As well as public meetings, a host of pamphlets appeared during these months outlining proposals. Those of the Bryce Group were at long last published.[57] Some of these writers argued for a minimum of machinery, others for a consultative or semi-legislative conference whose final decisions could be embedded in law or treaty. While this debate went on, Bryce forwarded a memorandum, dated 8 August, to the Government together with a covering letter to the Prime Minister. It urged that the declaration of support by the Government for the creation of some machinery to preserve a permanent peace would have an excellent effect in America, Russia, and even among the better sections of the German people. The Cabinet should move from general approval to specific proposals.[58]

The Government had in fact been giving some consideration to the idea of a League. A committee under Milner's chairmanship had reported its findings to the Imperial War Cabinet on 26 April and 1 May. It did not endorse the programme of the American League to Enforce Peace or envisage institutional changes which would lay the foundations of international government. The subject of its interest was the idea of a moratorium: a League which would include all the major Powers, with some other states, and which would operate principally in times of crisis. The Imperial War Cabinet agreed that some kind of sanction would be necessary to enforce the moratorium, but the precise form it would take was postponed for later discussion. It was not thought advisable to go beyond this and enforce the conclusions of the international conference. If states still insisted on going to war, only the strength of public opinion would be able to restrain them. It is clear, however, that Lloyd George was not satisfied with these proposals. There was nothing in them about disarmament or enforcing the decisions of a League. The Prime Minister seemed to be contemplating an institutional League with some executive power.[59]

Officially, therefore, it was difficult to tell where exactly the British Government stood in relation to the project. It may well be that Smuts, in collusion with Lord Robert Cecil, used the public meeting of 14 May as a device to gain some clarification of the Cabinet's thinking.[60] Cecil wanted to appoint a League Commission to act jointly with the United States to produce firm agreed proposals. He believed that the British Government should act to gain American agreement to a scheme which it would have had the advantage of drafting. His strongest argument for some action of this kind was that such a step would have a good effect on domestic public opinion. In the wake of the Leeds Convention the War Cabinet on 5 June decided that 'the time had come to undertake an active campaign to counteract the pacifist movement which at the moment had the field to itself.'[61] However, his colleagues seem to have thought that such an exercise would only have aroused suspicions among the Allies and brought differences into the open. Balfour, the Foreign Secretary, was not hostile to the League idea but he did not want it to swamp consideration of other important questions involving Britain and the United States. The Cabinet was also perturbed by the possibility that a commission might produce such an attractive scheme that in the excitement the primary need to defeat Germany would be overlooked. It might be necessary to reach a patched-up peace in the end, with the League as one ingredient in the settlement, but it would be a mistake to encourage such an idea. By the middle of the summer, it became clear that neither the British nor the American Governments wanted to have a commission.

Public interest in the idea of a League was a factor in the British Government's handling of the question. Nevertheless, the Cabinet, as this episode shows, was not forced into action by outside pressure. Quite apart from the merits of the proposals, the L.N.S., with Bryce as its most prestigious supporter, was not the kind of body to have much influence on Lloyd George at this juncture. It was politically useful for the Government to keep open a channel of communication, but the composition of the Cabinet was such as to make it somewhat sceptical about the whole enterprise. Despite the fact that Bryce had written of the May meeting that the great thing in organizing it would be 'to avoid utopian cranks who talk about a "World State" and the immediate and final abolition of all war', the prominent role of Lowes Dickinson lent colour to charges that the League idea was connected with a negotiated peace.[62] The irritating problem for Bryce and his associates was that, on the whole, other pacifists had little sympathy with some of the 'militarist' ideas they were urging upon the Government.

There was strong opposition from Quakers and Christian pacifists generally to any kind of sanction of force behind the proposed League. To compromise on this issue was to destroy the ideal for which they were struggling. For example, despite a visit from Lord Buckmaster to talk about the League, the Peace Society, on the whole, was unimpressed. Old Dr. Darby told the Annual Meeting in May that he had never been enthusiastic about the idea. 'You cannot enforce peace' he argued 'and for a League of Nations to come into existence with military force at its back, however you may conceal the fact, is simply a repetition of what has already convulsed the world. . . .'[63] Most Quakers were also suspicious, though the subject was divisive. Guy Enock, a delegate to the National Peace Council from the Peace Committee, resigned his post because he reported that he could neither oppose nor condemn the practical stages in the setting up of better international relations simply on the ground that they did not coincide with his own views from a Christian pacifist standpoint.[64] On the other hand, Pethick Lawrence, though not a Quaker, wrote a strong attack on the very idea of the League. Readers of the *Ploughshare* were informed that he also found the very idea of enforcing peace a contradiction in terms. He found the analogy between the individual policed within the nation-state and the nation-state policed by a League quite inadequate. There was no central sovereignty to enforce the decisions of such a League. Advocates of 'police' action against an offending nation were only deluding themselves if they thought that such action differed in any significant respect from straightforward 'war'.[65] In a review of Brailsford's book, J. W. Graham sought a way out of this impasse by urging Friends to 'work earnestly for such a League of Nations as is immediately conceivable, but also let us not keep silence anywhere about what we hold to be the ultimate ideal.'[66] Other writers argued that the problem of 'force' and the League had been unduly magnified.

Within a national state, the force which the Government in fact had at its command was often known to be inadequate, yet its existence strengthened the authority of the state. The great need was to create an international body which could count on a similar degree of support with only a minimum display of force. If, in order to accomplish this, it was found advisable to give the League the technical right to use force, pacifists should not quibble.

The objections to a League of Nations, however, were by no means confined to religious pacifists. MacDonald wrote that the handing over of the issues of peace and war 'to an international committee of the governing classes gives no security to the people that the forces of the world will be used only in the causes of righteousness and liberty. . . .'[67] The only answer to the question of war was to put power in the hands of the people. The danger Bertrand Russell saw was that even supposing the League could prevent wars 'there was something in the very spirit and essence of it which was fundamentally opposed to the sort of world which I wish to see exist.' In contrast, J. A. Hobson stressed the need for an effective system of sanctions. He argued that if states could be restrained by others acting in concert 'we shall not merely have reduced the part which force plays in the general economy, but we shall have improved the direction of it.' The nations would have made all coercive force an instrument of justice; it would become, at last, moral. Against this, Ponsonby contended that 'Peace is not a set of circumstances, or the adjustment of material arrangement. If it were, it might be possible to enforce it. It is a condition of mind.' He rejected the notion that there were 'criminal nations' which could be coerced in the manner proposed. 'Peace-loving' and 'aggressive' nations did not exist; there were warlike and peaceful people in all countries. When the warmongers got the upper hand in any country it was not by punishing the people that the wrong thinking would be corrected. Lowes Dickinson agreed that in the sense of a moral and spiritual ideal, 'peace' could not be enforced, but the League to Enforce Peace did not have this sense in mind. It was concerned with specific acts of aggression. In that context, the use of force by the League would be force behind law.[68] Pethick Lawrence, on the other hand, directed his attack at another point. He doubted whether League supporters had really found a formula by which, if war broke out between nations, the innocent would be separated from the guilty. He believed that the diplomatists of the contending countries would be quite capable of obscuring the issue. Moreover, statesmen would interpret the 'facts' in a variety of ways. In this situation, it would be dangerous to promise in advance to use force. Hobson, however, thought this kind of criticism beside the point. Those who objected to sanctions should not imagine that their alternative was without a severe practical limitation. 'A League without a force sanction' he argued 'will cause each nation to rely as before entirely upon its own arms for defence, and it will evoke friendships for defensive or aggressive motives. There will be no possible check upon an early resumption of the competition in armaments.'[69]

The debate on the League, as on revolution and conscientious objection, revealed little unanimity. Ethel Snowden, the Secretary of the London Women's Peace Crusade agreed with Miss Tillard of the N.C.F. that it was 'a dreadful thing to have to confess so great a lack of the peace spirit in ourselves that we cannot meet and work together' but, she added with unconscious irony, 'it is no use forcing things.' They all ought to do their best to soften differences 'and gradually bring the various sections into a closer understanding of and sympathy with one another.' The only consolation for pacifists was that though they remained divided, the Government seemed no nearer winning the war.

CHAPTER SEVEN

The Era of Labour and Lansdowne, August 1917-November 1918

On 31 July, the third battle of Ypres—Passchendaele—began. The Prime Minister declined an invitation to witness the start of the offensive. He wanted military success but felt little confidence in this particular enterprise. Looking back over the year, he could rightly claim credit for having blunted the German submarine threat, but that merely prevented disaster; it did not open up the prospect of victory. Within a short time, however, it became clear that Haig's great campaign was not matching his expectations. The opposing armies became bogged down in the aptly named 'campaign of the mud'. Lloyd George's reservations had proved justified, yet he did not stop the slaughter. He allowed himself to be persuaded into continuing the offensive. He was assured that there would be good prospects in September; August had, after all, been an exceptionally rainy month.

The Prime Minister's compliance can largely be explained by the fact that, for domestic reasons, he needed a demonstration that the war could be won. After so many disappointments, the British public badly required reassurance. Not that the Cabinet was brimming with confidence. Hankey chose the morning of the renewed battle on 31 July to ask its members what they thought were the possibilities of peace. They professed to have confidence in a war *à outrance* for their objectives.[1] In reality, however, there were private doubts and anxieties. There was a strong possibility that President Wilson would exert some pressure on the Allies to moderate their war aims. He might well question the proposed territorial arrangements for Dalmatia, the Ottoman Empire and the German colonies. There could be difficulty about the vexed problem of the 'freedom of the seas'. Post-war economic policies could also prove a source of contention. It has been noted that as Britain's military prospects looked increasingly bleak, the idea of discriminating against Germany's post-war trade became increasingly attractive. It was once again felt that protectionist measures would be necessary in order to frustrate Germany's economic recovery and develop the relative strength of the Allies. Conscious of the possible domestic and international repercussions of discriminatory policies, the Cabinet trod warily, but the whole movement was an indication of deep anxiety.

In this situation, the Prime Minister was even prepared to authorize secret soundings on the possibility of reaching a separate peace with Austria or with Bulgaria. There was, however, little expectation that they would be successful. In undertaking this secret diplomacy, the Government of course retained the initiative and aroused no public expectations. It would be a different matter if the Government's stock sank so low that it was forced by public opinion to negotiate. In mid-summer, such were the unusual conditions in various parts of Europe that a development of this kind could not be altogether ruled out. On 19 July, even the Reichstag, on Erzberger's initiative, passed its famous resolution in favour of peace without annexations or indemnities. The British peace groups claimed that this was the start of a German campaign for a reasonable peace. The General Council of the U.D.C. welcomed the German action and urged British M.P.'s to do likewise. In the following week, taking up the challenge, Noel Buxton attacked the Government for contemplating the destruction of the Habsburgs. Besides prolonging the war for a cause which formed no part of the original occasion for going to war, it was an illusion to suppose that the Danubian states would be able to form a bulwark against Germany. Members were not moved when Ramsay MacDonald unfavourably compared their behaviour with that of the members of the Reichstag. Except as a demonstration by the minority of M.P.'s who had been critical of the Government throughout the war, the debate had no further significance. However, it did serve as a warning that there could be trouble ahead. Not all pacifists agreed with Bertrand Russell's contention that 'The chief obstacle to peace is now our own Government. Our Government has ceased to be representative of public opinion, and has begun to suspect that this is the case' but they were nevertheless highly critical.[2] The difficulty for the Cabinet was to oppose the idea of peace negotiations with Germany without thereby appearing to prolong the war for supposedly imperialist reasons.

Lloyd George might have been more impressed by the Reichstag resolution if it had not followed the fall of Bethmann Hollwegg. His successor as Chancellor, Michaelis, would not be bound by it, nor would the generals. The Prime Minister was resolved to fight on, hence Passchendaele, but there were enormous problems. Some of his colleagues feared that France and Italy could not be relied upon to continue the war beyond 1917. The main anxiety, however, was the situation in Russia. In an attempt to bolster morale there, it seemed a good idea to send Arthur Henderson, the representative of Labour in the War Cabinet, to establish personal contact with Kerensky. When Henderson returned to London towards the end of July, he was convinced of the need to hold an international Socialist conference, probably at Stockholm, as a means of keeping Kerensky in power. G. M. Young, who accompanied the minister to Russia, believed that his master's head had been turned by hearing 180 million Russians chant in chorus 'Peace without annexations or indemnities'. As a result, he predicted that Henderson would leave the Government and lead a great British labour-socialist peace movement. Arrangements were made for a special British Labour conference on 10 August to consider whether a British delegation should be sent to Stockholm. Before it was held, Henderson went to Paris with MacDonald and Wardle to discuss the question with French Socialists. It was the company he kept on this occasion which caused a storm. Wardle was 'pro-war', but MacDonald's recent speeches and increased activity had greatly annoyed the Cabinet. It seemed incongruous to Henderson's colleagues that at the height of the war he should go abroad with a pacifist. This displeasure resulted in the famous incident when Henderson was kept waiting outside the Cabinet room while the members within debated what to do. Although furious, Henderson did not resign on this occasion, but when he spoke at the special Labour conference in favour of sending delegates to Stockholm, his continuance in the Government was impossible. The Cabinet was suspicious of any international gathering which threatened the established position of governments and refused to allow British delegates to attend.

Henderson's resignation delighted pacifists and was, for them, a major turning point in the war. 'It was not *my* speech' wrote Henderson to Runciman 'what I said or omitted to say that made the little man angry, it was the vote. My Labour Colleagues had persuaded him *they* could defeat the Executive recommendation when it reached the Conference.' He had 'paid the penalty of trying to serve two Masters, the Government and the Labour Movement.' Now older and wiser, he regretted that he had not resigned earlier.[3] Henderson was now in a strong position to direct the party as he wanted. His resignation had not been primarily due to trade union pressure, though he was aware of growing discontent with the part played by patriotic Labour men in the Government. The Norwich trades council, for example, repudiated

G. H. Roberts as their candidate in August, though the National Executive refused to endorse any other candidate until late in 1918.[4] Henderson's personal relations with MacDonald, always delicate, were for the moment relatively good. The two men had never been as far apart in their view of the war as their popular labels might suggest. Together, they could help build up a powerful party which could challenge for power. Ponsonby wrote to Trevelyan that recruits would flow into such a revitalized party, and Henderson would be forced, more and more in their direction.[5] George Barnes, who replaced Henderson in the Cabinet, would not be an effective rival.

The resignation came just at the right time for the U.D.C. leadership. Their disillusionment with Liberalism was almost complete. 'I genuinely believed' wrote Morel in July 'Liberalism was a force, a real tangible force, making for righteousness in public affairs.' Since then he had discovered that it was a fraud and that his old interpretation was that of 'a tenderfoot, a greenhorn, an immature, inexperienced mind.' Nothing would now induce him to associate with any of the 'gang' which had brought the country to its present pass. He wanted instead to see a more catholic Social Democratic Party established with its external programme based on the principles of the U.D.C. The party would also have to face squarely the imperial responsibilities which had been incurred and which could not be dismissed or ignored by theorizing.[6] With their sights firmly fixed on a future Social Democratic Europe, the U.D.C. leaders were critical even of President Wilson. Deploring American hostility to the Stockholm Conference, MacDonald wrote to Buckler that he looked in vain 'for indications that Mr. Wilson thinks this war will have to be settled by political agreement, however long it is fought. . . .' He claimed that Europeans were being driven to the conclusion that America's entry into the war had set back the moral and political movements that had become so strong in consequence of the Russian revolution.[7]

Not all members of the U.D.C. shared these enthusiasms or believed that its aims were synonymous with social revolution. At the meeting of the U.D.C. Council in July it was agreed to co-operate with the proposed Soviets in Britain only 'so far as the U.D.C. programme is concerned.' Despite the fact that the leading members seemed to be advocating such a course, the Council refused to permit statements in the U.D.C.'s publications that the Union favoured peace by negotiation at the earliest possible moment.[8] At another level, there was sometimes considerable friction between local U.D.C. and I.L.P. branches. A notable quarrel had broken out in Cambridge. Palme Dutt complained to Bertrand Russell that the U.D.C. President there (Lowes Dickinson) and the Treasurer (Miss Eileen Power) had announced that they would resign if the I.L.P. were allowed to affiliate.[9] From another angle, the *Ploughshare* thought that pacifists deceived themselves about the real feelings of the majority of the working class. It was all very well to talk in raptures of the way in which the international proletariat would bring peace to the world but, it claimed, at their mass meetings in the Central Hall to discuss the proposed Stockholm conference 'the workers have shown for the hundredth time that they are conscious of no material solidarity.'[10]

Meanwhile, the battle of Passchendaele continued. Haig suggested to Robertson that an important reason for pressing on to victory was that, when it had been achieved, 'the chief people to suffer would be the socialists who are trying to rule us all at a time when the right-minded of the nation are so engaged on the country's battles that they are left free to work mischief.'[11] September passed into October without success for the right-minded: the continuing offensive in Flanders brought huge British losses with little tangible benefit in return. Still Lloyd George refused to stop it. Pacifists were critical of the fact that the British Government had not replied to the papal Peace Note addressed to the belligerents on 1 August. Charles Trevelyan, and other pacifists, pressed the Government on the matter in the House of Commons, though without success. The Foreign Secretary told them that the Government had nothing to add to the reply sent by the American Government.

Despite this appearance of intransigeance, Lloyd George was privately exploring alternatives to outright military victory. When the news from Russia became even more gloomy, he made it clear that the British people could not be expected to fight for the evacuation of occupied Russian territory if Russia herself gave up the struggle. In these circumstances he was prepared to contemplate a situation in which the two great Empires, the British and the German, reached an accommodation. Most of his colleagues, however, were not prepared to consider a settlement in which Germany gained in the East and lost in the West. They feared that Britain's Allies would reject it or be tempted to make their own terms. They pinned their hopes on a Russian recovery.

By early November, however, it was apparent that there was no chance of military success either on the Western or Eastern Fronts. The battle of Passchendaele ended, with the loss of 300,000 men and without any worthwhile gains. In addition, the Italians suffered a severe defeat at Caporetto and, although the line was held on the River Piave, it was a humiliating experience for them. The fact that the British were within four miles of Jerusalem, that the tanks had done well at Cambrai, that East Africa was being cleared and that at long last a Supreme Allied War Council was set up, seemed little compensation for the Bolshevik seizure of power in Russia. No further military assistance could be looked for from that quarter. There was now nobody in Russia with any legal right whatever to authority, wrote Lord Bryce in dismay, 'these Councils and Soviets are practically self-appointed. Half of them are said to be pro-Germans, mostly rogues—the rest crack-brained enthusiasts intoxicated with high-sounding phrases. . . .'[12]

On the whole, the revitalized Labour Movement rejoiced to hear of these developments. Henderson succeeded in pleasing both pacifists and supporters of the war by focussing attention on the need for social change at home. 'Henderson' reported Tom Jones, 'thought that it should be possible to run about 200 candidates and to steal the Government's reconstruction thunder.'[13] Although there was disappointment that the Stockholm Conference did not take place, Brailsford in the *Herald* rejoiced that the balance of the whole world was moving towards the Left. He believed that 'The growing demand for peace is not for *any* peace, but for peace on the basis of *the things for which British democracy took up arms*—disarmament, arbitration, the rights of small nations.' The war lords of all nations were incapable of concluding such a peace because they neither wanted nor understood it. If the people responded, however, peace might be possible by Christmas. There would have to be compromises. He agreed with Trevelyan that the mere replacement of German rule by French in Alsace-Lorraine, simply by act of conquest, would solve nothing. For their part, pacifists should also try to be realistic, 'total abolition of force is not conceivable tomorrow'. When it could not be eliminated, the next best thing was to ensure that force was under popular control. 'If the masses' he wrote at the end of October 'shrink from the slight burden of keeping the use of armed force in their own hands, they will be put under by those who will pay for it.'[14] The *Labour Leader* was equally anxious for the people to bestir themselves. 'The only hope for civilisation' it declared, was for the people in every country to 'take the work of making peace out of the hands of the power-drunk Imperialist few whose mad and conflicting ambitions made, and now prolong, the war.'[15] It believed that there was solid evidence of a change. Between March and September nearly fifty new branches of the I.L.P. had been started all over the country. The British middle and upper classes were well aware that the ferment of revolution was likely to spread from the continent to Britain.[16] What was needed was a great popular democratic party, combining 'all that is dynamic, social, revolutionary in the middle class, with all that is intelligent and public-spirited in the working class.'[17] Nevertheless, there was still some way to go, though many agreed with Snowden that the movement for democratic control had 'already advanced to a stage far beyond that reached by the British House of Commons.'[18]

It would have been surprising if the Government watched this resurgence with complete equanimity. The situation was indeed serious, but not yet dangerous. Two strategies were open to it. The Cabinet could use its powers under the Defence of the Realm Act to limit even further the circulation of pacifist propaganda. It could at the same time proceed against leading pacifists and thereby reduce the effectiveness of their societies. The danger of such a course was obvious. It might well have the consequence of strengthening the popularity of pacifists by providing them with martyrs. The alternative was simply to do nothing. This would demonstrate that the Government was calmly confident and in control. The difficulty with this course was that the Government was not in fact calmly confident. It is not therefore surprising that what emerged was a mixed policy of coercion and persuasion.[19]

The treatment of conscientious objectors provides a good illustration of this mixture. By the late summer, the press fury against slackers, so strident in the spring, seemed to have spent itself. There was an increasing public respect for those absolutist objectors who had shown the sincerity of their convictions by staying in prison. Admittedly under pressure, the Government was prepared to reconsider their position. The test case in this instance was not Clifford Allen but Stephen Hobhouse, a Quaker convert, whose father was a former M.P. and whose mother was one of the Potter sisters. Stephen and his wife had set up house before the war in the East End, where they amazed their friends by doing their own washing. It was a far cry from Balliol.[20] With her son in prison, Mrs. Hobhouse wrote a booklet, *I Appeal unto Caesar*, drawing attenion to the plight of the absolutists. She persuaded Gilbert Murray, a firm supporter of the war, to write an introduction deploring the treatment they had received. 'It is useless' Mrs. Hobhouse wrote 'to attempt any solution which involves a bargain, or acceptance of conditions on the part of these men.'[21] Their attitude to a State at war was such that they would feel the same objection to accepting conditions as the ordinary man would feel to compounding a felony. Some sympathisers felt that her picture of conscientious objectors as highthinking saints was exaggerated. From this standpoint, the Baptist leader, Dr. F. B. Meyer, author of the sympathetic booklet, *The Majesty of Conscience*, reported to Miss Marshall a conversation he had had with the military. General Childs held the view that some sixty per cent of conscientious objectors were 'more or less in general antagonism to ordered society'. It would, Meyer thought, be a pity to exasperate General

Childs who was the best, if not the only, friend they had in the War Office.[22] Whatever the truth of this contention, Hobhouse was released in November, after several months of pamphleteering, preaching and high-level intrigue.[23] A month later, despite his assertion that he would never accept special treatment, Clifford Allen was set free. Both men were in poor health, and it was on this ground that they were released. Other men, with the same principles, stayed in prison a lot longer.

Not surprisingly, the release of some of the absolutists was by no means popular with many Conservative supporters of the Government. They feared that the ex-prisoners would be paraded as heroes and encourage others in their obduracy. If the Government showed leniency then there was a danger that disaffection might spread, not only among conscientious objectors but also among serving soldiers. Pacifists did indeed welcome the stand of those few, like Siegfried Sassoon, who refused to go on fighting. Russell described Sassoon as 'altogether splendid, physically, mentally and spiritually. He has shown amazing courage in battle, and is now showing still greater courage by his defiance.'[24] It is, therefore probable that it was to meet these fears that the Government withdrew its objections to the disfranchisement of conscientious objectors in the same month as Hobhouse was released. This measure was passed despite objection from all parties and was seen as a deterrent to the growth of the absolutist movement.

The freeing of Hobhouse and Allen was undoubtedly a risk for the Government but it may also have calculated that for some pacifists such a vindication of the rights of conscience might be a magnificent victory but it was not peace. The spectacle of public support from pro-war intellectuals, churchmen and parliamentarians of all parties was rather an embarrassment in such circles. Even those like Miss Marshall who had worked hard to enlist this support were in two minds when it succeeded. Mrs. Hobhouse, in her view, had 'no sympathy with her son or appreciation for his fine disinterestedness.' She was 'simply anxious to make *her*self more comfortable by getting some of his discomforts and sufferings abated.'[25] Miss Marshall was also both glad, on personal grounds, that Allen was out of prison and yet not sure that it was the right step. Dr. Salter reiterated his opinion that the absolutists would do finer and more effective work for the cause by staying in prison.[26] Other pacifists, perhaps realizing the extent to which physical suffering was in considerable measure self-inflicted, thought that neither Allen nor Hobhouse should have accepted release on medical grounds. W. H. Ayles, himself a prisoner, had argued a few months previously that 'the bad health business does not exist to any appreciable extent and in 99 cases out of 100 the mind is more active and vigorous than it has ever been.' Indeed, he contended that 'The men who fail in mind or body *would have failed if they had been outside.*'[27]

In any case, by the end of 1917, the N.C.F. was a demoralized body. Russell was weary of the day to day burden of the Acting Chairmanship. He was also sure that the work for the better treatment of conscientious objectors was nearly at an end. 'The work for us now' he suggested to Miss Marshall 'is to direct peace work. France wants peace: Germany wants peace: England is the chief obstacle. We who are not liable to military service can share some of the sufferings of the C.O. by incurring imprisonment for peace agitation. I propose that the whole shadow organization shall begin at once to be used for this purpose.' He believed that their agitation could turn the scale. They should not take any steps to make sure that they remained within the law: indeed, if what they did was illegal it would only assist the cause.[28] Miss Marshall, however, was exhausted and on the verge of a nervous breakdown. Clifford Allen needed a long period of recuperation. Besides, he felt that the shaping of the future lay with the newly-organized Labour Movement, which would have to contend with violent elements in its midst. 'If we on our part' he concluded 'are so far removed from the life and thought of this vigorous new movement around us to refuse to distinguish the merits of wise aggressiveness from violence, when developing our own programme, then I fear lest, whilst we may succeed in keeping ourselves unsullied from the world, we may find the world pay little heed to our formulas and shibboleths.'[29] In effect, Allen recognized that the movement he had inspired with such high hopes at the beginning of the war had led nowhere.

Although the absolutist conscientious objectors were the most intransigent of pacifists, they were also, in a sense, the easiest for the government to handle. They at least usually claimed an objection in principle to all war. It was only to be expected that the majority of them would therefore favour peace at any price. More difficult to control were those pacifists who claimed that they were not peace at any price, but who nevertheless believed that peace was possible on reasonable terms. Freedom of the press in an absolute sense had not existed at all throughout the war. An official Press Bureau had been established at the outset, attempting to operate both by eliciting co-operation from the papers and by exercising control over the provision and use of news. Most of the press was prepared to accept the limitations the Bureau imposed, though editors did not always like the methods it employed. Various journals which could be described as pacifist did not co-operate, however. Under the various regulations of the Defence of the Realm Act, and the amendments to those regulations, the Government had power to prevent the spread of false reports or of reports likely to cause disaffection. It also had authority to enter premises used for publishing or distributing such literature. These powers were very wide but there was considerable reluctance in the early years of the war to use them to the full. It was not only that some Liberals felt unhappy about the regulations, but there was also considerable difficulty in securing convictions. In addition, both the Home Office and the Foreign Office spent a long time trying to saddle each other with the final responsibility for recommending prosecution. Views also differed as to whether the attempt to stir up peace feeling did constitute disaffection. Therefore, while there was a great deal of official discussion about banning pacifist propaganda, a wide range of pacifist literature continued to appear. The Government was, however, largely successful in preventing the circulation of this literature abroad. It was feared that in neutral countries especially, the Germans would make use of it to their advantage.

To some extent, this situation changed with Henderson's resignation in August. It was recognized, both at the Home Office and in the Cabinet that the *Labour Leader* had built up a far-reaching influence among the working class. Back in January 1917 the Home Office had decided, after lengthy consideration, to prosecute the paper. This was at a time when Lloyd George wanted Henderson in the Cabinet and it was largely this need which led to the decision being shelved. This situation no longer existed. There was renewed pressure to ban the *Labour Leader* and to restrict the liberty of expression which pacifists enjoyed. In an article, 'Licence for Pacifists', the *Morning Post* drew the attention of the Government, not for the first time, 'to the necessity of curbing the indefatigable and unscrupulous activities of the Pacifist conspiracy in this country—a conspiracy to undermine the nation's faith, to depress its spirits, to depress its cause, and to pervert its mind.' However, the *Labour Leader* and the *Herald* continued to appear. Partly it was felt that an attempt to suppress them altogether would draw more attention to the sentiments they expressed; partly, despite the sentiments of the *Morning Post,* the pro-war press was, on the whole, not anxious to see the Government intervene for fear that it might also be tempted to restrict the king-making activities of its own editors.[30]

It should not be thought, however, that there was excessive tenderness towards leading pacifists. E. D. Morel had been, for many months, the subject of unflattering official minutes. Towards the end of August, he was arrested and tried under the Defence of the Realm Act for soliciting a correspondent to send two of his publications to Romain Rolland, knowing him to be at the time in a neutral country, Switzerland. He was sentenced to six months imprisonment, from which he emerged, with remission for good conduct, at the end of January 1918. The experience shook Morel and it was not until some months afterwards that he was fit to resume work. He suffered, as it has been nicely put, from 'malnutrition of the ego'. For the U.D.C., the chief consolation was that the Government did not have evidence of serious treason by its secretary or it would surely have been used. In a special statement, the Union declared that the idea that Morel was in the pay of the Kaiser was contemptible. Scotland Yard had, in fact, done its best to discover more heinous activity. The accounts of the F.O.R., the N.C.C.L., the N.C.F., the U.D.C. and the Peace Negotiations Committee had all been seized and scrutinized for evidence of German money or influence. Nothing was found. Reluctantly, the War Cabinet had to accept that financial support from wealthy Quaker families largely accounted for the scale of U.D.C. activities. In view of the rumours which circulated, the Government was deeply disappointed not to be able to produce a British 'Bolo' to match the gentlemen discovered by Clemenceau.[31]

The decision actually to prosecute Morel was exceptional. It was more customary for the police to raid the offices of the various peace societies from time to time, taking away selected literature. These raids increased during November. Nor, apparently, were policemen unwilling in some instances to threaten printers with the destruction of their machinery if they continued to print pacifist publications. Also at this time the Government introduced the regulation that all pamphlets should be submitted to the Censor before publication. The U.D.C. agreed that any of its leaflets which had been sent to the Press Bureau and passed should be distributed, but those which had been rejected should be destroyed.[32] Any new leaflets were to be submitted to the Censor. This acquiescence contrasted with the spirited reaction of the Quakers. The Meeting for Sufferings passed a bold resolution stating that it was for Christians 'a paramount duty to be free to obey, and to act and speak in accord with, the law of God, a law higher than that of any State, and no government official can release men from this duty. . . .' Friends were fully aware of the gravity of such a decision, but they had no alternative but to continue to issue literature on war and peace without submitting it to the Censor.'[33] Even the General Committee of the F.O.R. protested strongly against this restriction on freedom of publication. These resolutions may have had some effect, for the wording of the regulation was changed. Pamphlets had to be submitted to the

Press Bureau for consideration rather than approval. The Home Secretary had been rather embarrassed to find certain U.D.C. and other pamphlets which had been passed by the Censor appearing in print with the addition of 'Passed by the Censor'. The impression this created was a trifle misleading.

Pacifists were right to suppose that in these months they were being subjected to greater controls than at any other point in the war. What is perhaps remarkable is that at such a time of crisis their liberty was not more restricted. Of course, at a local level, they were still harrassed by a miscellaneous collection of patriotic groups. Pacifists and patriots played cat and mouse with each other's meetings. It was not difficult to detect which side received the blessing of local authorities and police. In Bradford, it seems, pacifists were sufficiently wealthy to be able to purchase their own hall. In Leeds, however, as the organizers of the Convention had discovered, it was not easy to find a hall in which to hold large pacifist meetings. While it is true that the police usually took notes of pacifist speeches—at Southampton two detectives were discovered hiding under the grand piano at a Trades Council meeting—the number of prosecutions arising from such meetings dropped noticeably in 1917. As an example, the figures for Glamorgan have been cited.[34] It may well be that note was taken of the recommendation that in such potentially sensitive areas there should be full police protection for meetings of a pacifist character. The argument was that workers who were not themselves pacifists disliked petty prosecutions and the disturbance of meetings with official connivance.

There were also influential members of the War Cabinet who thought that, instead of trying to suppress pacifist propaganda, the Government should set its own propaganda in order. Probably significantly, it was after Henderson's resignation that Sir Edward Carson was given general supervision over domestic publicity. As a result of his investigations, he became convinced that the only really efficient system belonged to the pacifists. They seemed to have ample money and were conducting their campaign with great vigour. During a debate in the Commons in mid-November Carson told members that 'the amount of subterranean influence of a pernicious and pestilential character that has been developed, particularly within the last few months, goes far beyond anything that has been described in this House. . . .'[35] In order to counteract this tide, two separate bodies were encouraged. One, the British Workers League, was under the patronage of Lord Milner and was specifically designed to counter pacifism among the workers.[36] The other, the National War Aims Committee, had been launched on the third anniversary of Britain's entry into the war and was patronized by Lloyd George, Asquith, Bonar Law and Barnes. It was now given increased funds to try in particular to rival the U.D.C. Disappointingly in view of its title, the one thing the committee lacked was very definite information about war aims. When launching its activities, the Prime Minister had not stopped to elucidate. In the atmosphere of November 1917 this was no longer good enough. Pacifists were claiming that peace was possible on reasonable terms. Perhaps the Government would be good enough to throw a clearer light on its own objectives?

The Daily Telegraph was not normally required reading for pacifists. The issue of 29 November, however, was of exceptional interest. It contained a letter from the elder statesman, Lord Lansdowne, former Viceroy of India, Governor-General of Canada, Secretary of State for War, Foreign Secretary, defender of the House of Lords and opponent of Home Rule.[37] He shared the growing conservative fears for the established order if the war continued and wanted to explore the possibilities of peace before chaos ensued. He had not suddenly developed these anxieties. A year earlier he had expressed them to his then colleagues. On this occasion he first approached the Government with his anxieties and wondered whether the time was ripe to explore the possibilities of negotiation. Balfour thought that it was not. Since the Cabinet was not receptive, Lansdowne approached Dawson, editor of *The Times,* with a draft letter for publication in his columns. Dawson considered that the general effect of its publication would be 'thoroughly bad' and refused to publish. The Germans, he thought, would regard it as a tribute to their military superiority. Lansdowne would not be deterred. The Government should set out what were British war aims and find out whether it would be possible to reach agreement with Germany. The letter which *The Times* refused appeared in the *Daily Telegraph* on 29 November. It stressed the fact that the war had become so terrible in its consequences that no effort should be spared to find an end to the conflict. 'Some of the Allied claims for territory will probably become unattainable' he wrote 'others, again, notably the reparation due to Belgium remain, and must always remain, in the front rank; but when it comes to the wholesale rearrangements of the map of South-Eastern Europe, we may well ask for a suspension of judgment. . . .' If the war was to be brought to a close in time to avoid a world-wide catastrophe, 'it will be brought to a close because on both sides the people of the countries involved feel that it has already lasted too long.'

Every attempt was made to ridicule or ignore what *The Times* called an 'extraordinarily foolish and mischievous letter.' The popular pro-war press published pictures of Bowood, Lansdowne's seat in Wiltshire, and of Lansdowne House in Berkeley Square, to show that this elderly aristocrat was more concerned for the safety of his ample possessions than for a righteous victory. Dawson thought that for his action in publishing the letter, Lansdowne would shortly find himself the most popular man in Central Europe. 'What a gaffe of Lansdowne's' wrote Austen Chamberlain, 'how it came that he failed to see what an encouragement his letter would be to the Germans and to our own pacifists?' It was a mystery of the human mind which he could not fathom.[38] On 1 December, an official announcement appeared in the press claiming, incorrectly, that the Government had no foreknowledge of the intended publication of the letter. Lord Hardinge, the permanent secretary at the Foreign Office, who had seen a draft, wrote to offer his sympathy for the 'horrible attacks' which had been made on Lansdowne. Lloyd George seemed to be very angry. At the important Inter-Allied conference in Paris a few days later he claimed that he had been prepared to make a further statement about Allied war aims but that he now could not do so because it would be thought to be an endorsement of Lansdowne.[39]

If the reaction of the Northcliffe press and leading members of the Cabinet was unfavourable, Lansdowne also had considerable support. Provincial newspapers in Leeds, Liverpool, Birmingham, Sheffield, Glasgow, Manchester and Edinburgh all gave varying degrees of approval to Lansdowne's arguments. The metropolitan Liberal press was also sympathetic. The Marquess received support from Liberal politicians like Walter Runciman, who tried, not altogether successfully, to enlist the support of Lord Grey. Business and professional men wrote to express their appreciation of Lansdowne's courage. He had raised the issues which required discussion and debate. Lord Carnock, the former permanent under-secretary at the Foreign Office, wrote to say that he agreed with every word of the letter. The most ecstatic supporter of the initiative, however, was F. W. Hirst, now of *Common Sense*. For months his journal had been carrying on a campaign against the Government's handling of the war. He saw possibilities of realistic negotiations with the Central Powers but was dismayed to find no support from the Government. Now all had changed. 'Every man' he wrote 'whose moral and intellectual equipment is up to the average, whether he calls himself a Liberal or a Conservative or a Socialist—will feel on reading Lord Lansdowne's letter . . . that a way has at last been opened towards peace.'[40] At last, Lloyd George was doomed. The newspapers who had welcomed his arrival to power so enthusiastically in December 1916 now sounded half-hearted and flat in their comments. 'Nothing fails like failure' *Common Sense* claimed. 'He has not made good. . . . People have lost confidence in his promises and statements.'[41] Opponents of negotiation who would stake the national existence not for objects for which it was placed at risk, but for some future and ill-defined purpose, had been dealt a shattering blow. Hirst wrote to Lansdowne and speedily set himself up as secretary of a Lansdowne Committee with Earl Beauchamp as President.

'Lord Lansdowne's letter is thrilling' wrote Mrs. Swanwick to Miss Marshall. Bertrand Russell reported that he was 'immensely cheered up' by it.[42] Lady Courtney of Penwith described it as 'a veritable peace bomb'. Ponsonby considered it as the sanest and wisest pronouncement that had been delivered by a British statesman since August 1914. He promised Lansdowne the support of his associates, while at the same time agreeing to be restrained so that the initiative was not damned as 'pacifist'.[43] J. R. MacDonald also praised the Lansdowne letter as an example of how all thinking people were coming round to the I.L.P. view. 'Every day that passes' he concluded 'diminishes rather than increases the reasons why the I.L.P. should dissociate itself with the Labour party.'[44] For the *U.D.C.*, the difference between the Lansdowne and the Lloyd George policies represented the real cleavage in the nation. 'The moderate section of opinion in this country have at last found an expression of their secret longings.'[45]

This unanimity was impressive, but it was more the expression of pent-up frustration than a coherent response. The very fact that the supporters of an attempt to negotiate came from different political parties meant that it was impossible to tell how the Lansdowne movement would develop. 'The best way to peace' wrote Hirst 'would be to cut talk about liberty, democracy, League of Nations . . . and to get to business quickly to see what sort of territorial bargain can be struck. . . .'[46] Most pacifists agreed that the lack of an independent and clear-sighted press was a national disaster at this juncture but was Hirst also right to claim that 'the nation is beginning to look to Lord Lansdowne, and we believe it will not have to wait very long before his return to office and power'?[47] The editor of *Common Sense* organized the presentation of an Address of Thanks to Lansdowne in recognition of his lead in the cause of peace. Among the signatories were Lords Beauchamp, Buckmaster, Courtney, Farrer, Parmoor and Loreburn, together with Noel Buxton, Lowes Dickinson, J. A. Hobson, R. D. Holt, R. C. Lambert and George Lansbury. Great stress was placed upon Lord Lansdowne's honesty, courage and sagacity. Acknowledging the testimony, Lansdowne replied that an honourable peace could be obtained, and should be obtained. He trusted that there would be no 'unnecessary fencing' through an exaggerated fear of falling into peace traps, and exhorted the Government to leave no avenue unexplored, no matter how unpromising it might seem.[48]

The prospect of the seventy-two year old elder statesman as Prime Minister was one which even radicals like Arthur Ponsonby desired. However, the wisdom and sagacity which was now so widely esteemed in the noble Marquess had not often been noticed by radicals and Socialists in the past. Moreover, Lansdowne's support was least in his own party and he was perhaps regarded there as an aberrant Whig. Beneath the testimonies to his courage, therefore, there lay a contradiction. Lansdowne wanted peace to conserve the old order; radicals and Socialists wanted peace in order to change it. Both deplored the destruction and loss of life, but beyond this their vision of the new world was very different. No wide-ranging coalition of politicians, anxious to fall into line under Lansdowne, in fact existed.

Some Liberals saw the 'negotiated peace' controversy as an opportunity for Asquith to reassert himself as leader of the Liberal Party. Morale could be restored if the Liberals declared that they favoured a negotiated peace. Noel Buxton and Josiah Wedgwood drafted an appeal to him on these lines. However, they were forced to admit that Asquith's public commitment to such extravagant aims as the destruction of the Habsburg Monarchy hardly fitted him for the role they envisaged. Other Liberals whom they endeavoured to associate with the appeal were sceptical from the outset. E. T. John considered Asquith's position as infinitely less satisfactory than that of Lansdowne himself. He saw no possibility of an Asquithite peace group being formed. In contrast, others saw no benefit to Liberalism in the kind of peace Lansdowne seemed to be contemplating. They considered that the deliverance of Slavs from Austrian misgovernment would be a general benefit to humanity. Liberal war aims ought to stress the need for a conclusive and permanent peace, rather than a patched-up compromise. Noble aims should not be abandoned simply because of recent military disappointments. Despite this depressing reaction, for several months Buxton and others continued to envisage Asquith as the leader of a 'negotiated peace' party. They found it surprising that he did not seem prepared to be as equivocal as they were about the future status of Belgium, Alsace-Lorraine and Austria-Hungary.[49]

It was also difficult to envisage the Labour Movement agitating wholeheartedly for Lansdowne as Prime Minister. Arthur Henderson welcomed the letter in the *Daily Telegraph*, but was too deeply involved in his own preparations for a statement of Labour War Aims to be of much value to Hirst. For several months, a subcommittee of the Labour Party Executive and the T.U.C. Parliamentary Committee had been at work hammering out proposals.

The members took account of suggestions made by the U.D.C., the I.L.P., the Fabians and other bodies. Their own statement, which was ready a few weeks after the Lansdowne letter, demanded complete democratization, the abandonment of Imperialism, the suppression of secret diplomacy, the limitation of armaments and of national service, and the establishment of a League of Nations. The aim was to ensure, in a Wilsonian spirit, that there would be no more war on earth. The peoples would have lost the war unless some effective method of preventing any recurrence could be found. Nevertheless, despite critical references to Imperialist ambitions, Labour did insist on 'complete and untrammelled' independence for Belgium together with adequate reparation.[50] The Memorandum was presented to a special Labour conference on 28 December and accepted by 2,132,000 to 1,164,000 votes.

This statement was seen by the U.D.C. leaders, with considerable justification, as a vindication of their strategy. The Labour Movement had now come to adopt its broad objectives, though there might be details where agreement was not complete. Moreover, Trevelyan was very alive to the dramatic international situation. Negotiations had begun at Brest-Litovsk between the Bolsheviks and the Central Powers. Trotsky talked about the need for self-determination, open diplomacy, no annexations and no indemnities. The contrast between the Bolsheviks and the Allied Governments was believed to be proved by the fact that the Russians published the Allied secret treaties. Translations appeared in the *Manchester Guardian,* and the U.D.C. endeavoured to give them the widest possible circulation, publishing extracts in its monthly in January and February 1918. M. Philips Price, the *Manchester Guardian's* correspondent in Russia, was Trevelyan's cousin and a generous contributor to U.D.C. funds. There was, therefore, a touch of family pride in the U.D.C.'s appreciation of his work in Russia. The revelations, referring to Constantinople and the Ottoman Empire and to Italian aggrandisement, seemed to confirm that the original Allied intentions in the war had long been overtaken by more ambitious projects.[51]

The combination of the Lansdowne Letter, the Labour Statement on War Aims, and Bolshevik propaganda, led Lloyd George to feel that, after all, a comprehensive statement of Allied war aims was necessary. He had been receiving reports from the War Aims Committee stressing that allied objectives would have to be stated in a comprehensive and comprehensible fashion if the rank and file, at home and in the field, were to be saved from pacifist blandishments. The situation was more serious than it had ever been. Tom Jones found the atmosphere at the War Cabinet on 31 December 'completely changed'. Everybody was talking of peace. It was not only that Smuts and Kerr had just returned from their secret mission to meet Mensdorff, the former Austro-Hungarian Ambassador in London. The whole tone of the discussion was moderate. If the hope of destroying Prussian militarism had not completely disappeared, it was fully recognized that the Allies could not do it by themselves. Everything would depend upon the United States. The Cabinet therefore empowered the Prime Minister, Lord Robert Cecil and Smuts to provide drafts for a new declaration of war aims. The idea was to be 'Ultra-democratic'. The memoranda by Smuts and Cecil were considered by the War Cabinet on 3 January. Both contributions were quite conciliatory. Two days later, largely drawing upon their suggestions, Lloyd George made a comprehensive declaration before a trade union audience. He reiterated that the British Government demanded the restoration of Belgium together with an appropriate reparation. Serbia, Montenegro, the occupied parts of France, Italy and Roumania all had to be evacuated by alien armies. The provinces of Alsace and Lorraine should be restored to France and an ancient wrong thereby righted. Apart from the creation of an independent Poland, the destruction of Austria-Hungary was not an object of Allied policy. Nevertheless, the various nationalities should be granted genuine self-government on true democratic principles. Similarly with the Ottoman Empire. The homelands of the Turkish race with its capital at Constantinople would not be challenged, but Arabia, Armenia, Mesopotamia, Syria and Palestine were all entitled to a recognition of their separate national conditions. The future of the German colonies would be decided at a conference which would have as its primary consideration the wishes and interests of their native inhabitants. As for Germany herself, her disruption or destruction had never been a war aim.

The effect of his speech on British public opinion was all that the Prime Minister could have desired. It was firm without being extravagant. Three days later came President Wilson's 'Fourteen Points' speech. The two addresses provided comprehensive statements of British and American war aims and neither government wished to probe the areas where they diverged. It is not likely that the Prime Minister seriously supposed that Germany would respond. Since Germany was in the hour of military triumph she would not be in a conciliatory mood.

Pacifists were not impressed by these declarations, though they were somewhat embarrassed by them. 'We must put Mr. Lloyd George's points by the side of the declaration of the Central Powers' wrote Philip Snowden. 'We must show by that method that all the fundamentals of a just and lasting settlement are accepted by both sides.' Not everybody was so confident that this

was the case. Snowden also had to issue a warning against showing
enthusiasm for the 'Fourteen Points'. Especially with regard to
Austria-Hungary and Alsace-Lorraine, these were 'terms not for
negotiation but terms which would only be accepted by a nation
which had been completely defeated in the field.' Hirst, too,
lamented that 'our original war aims as stated to the public in the
autumn of 1914—the defence of Belgium and Northern France,
have altered out of all recognition. . . .'[52]

There was general agreement among pacifists that both the Prime
Minister and the President had been forced to make their declarations because of the Bolshevik challenge. 'Let the credit be given
to the men of faith and courage who lead Russia . . .' wrote
Trevelyan.[53] The problem, however, was to transform the separate
negotiations in which those men were perforce engaged into a
general peace conference. According to Charles Buxton, the brutal
fact was that, by refusing to join in the negotiations, the British
Government was leaving the Russian people in the lurch. In his
judgment, the aims which Labour had enunciated were now attain-
able. Allied statesmen would only take any practical steps if they
were compelled to do so by pressure from the working class. The
task of the British Labour Movement, he declared, was 'to compel
our Government to take part in the negotiations now proceeding.'
He hoped that the Labour Conference at Nottingham on 23
January would take the necessary steps.[54] The conference was an
emotional occasion, with the singing of the 'Red Flag', and cheers
for the International and the Russian Revolution. Among those
present were Huysmans, Vandervelde and Litvinvov. For one
observer it was a 'wonderful event', for the pro-war majority had
faded and the machine was now definitely in the hands of the
moderate peace people. The only thing that prevented the conference being definitely and publicly anti-war was that 'the anti-war
people were not quite strong enough to push their victory completely home.' It was, however, good to see that 'the Barnes-Hodge
crowd were on the carpet all the time!'[55] Despite this assessment,
other pacifists found the occasion rather disappointing. The *Herald*
thought that on the basis of his remarks Henderson was veering
away from them. According to Snowden in the *Labour Leader*,
the overwhelming majority of the Conference was of the I.L.P.
standpoint but he claimed that 'the restraining influence of the
Executive, and the weight of the block vote of two or three great
unions prevented the real opinions of the delegates from finding
expression. . . .'[56] The impact of Lloyd George's speech had been
considerable and the hope of pacifists that Labour would demand
an end to the war was disappointed. The trade unions pressed their
case for the conscription of wealth, but they did not block the

comb-out of labour which the Prime Minister desired in order to help win the war.

The peacemakers were now in a quandary. Dunnico and Buxton, on behalf of the Peace Negotiations Committee, addressed a letter to Trotsky in recognition of 'the brave and disinterested efforts that you and your Government have made to bring the war to an end, not only for Russia, but for Great Britain and the Allies also. . . .'[57] Snowden commented that the Bolshevik negotiators had amazed and completely confounded the German militarist authorities 'by completely ignoring the military position and taking their stand on enduring moral values. . . .'[58] Yet, they all knew that if Trotsky's strategy was to be successful, it would depend on the revolt of the working classes in all belligerent countries; in Britain as well as in Germany. There had, indeed, been some stirrings in Germany promoted by the Independent Socialists, but by the end of February the chances of a successful revolution seemed remote. In Britain, despite the undoubted change of mood, revolution was also not in prospect. The absolute pacifists in the I.L.P. remained opposed to all violence. In any case, Charles Roden Buxton had only just joined the I.L.P., to be followed by E. D. Morel when he came out of prison at the end of January. Pethick Lawrence had joined, but Ponsonby and Trevelyan were still Liberals, though in trouble with their constituencies. There was not a Marxist among them. *Justice* was quick to make the point. 'Are these gentlemen Socialists?' the paper wanted to know. 'Do they believe that the socialisation of the instruments of production and distribution are necessary to put an end to the economic chaos and clash of interests, and to ensure the emancipation of Labour from capitalist exploitation?'[59]

The only escape from the dilemma in which the Labour/Liberal pacifists found themselves was to enter the world of make-believe. Buxton congratulated Trotsky on the manner in which 'by the moral force of just and democratic ideas, you have succeeded in obtaining from the Central Powers the acceptance of those principles which form the only possible basis of a lasting peace.' Trevelyan wrote that '. . . the valiant Bolsheviks have made it certain that when the peace is made it will involve the evacuation of the German military conquests.'[60] A fortnight later, the German armies renewed their eastern offensive. The Bolsheviks were forced to sue for peace on humiliating terms. On 8 March, the Treaty of Brest-Litovsk was signed.

The withdrawal of Russia meant that Germany was in a position to concentrate her resources on attacking the Allies in the West. When at last victory was in prospect, it would be unlikely that the German High Command would forego the pleasure. The Allies had to brace themselves for what could prove the decisive encounter of the war. The alternative was to negotiate a peace which would recognize the German position in the East in return for concessions in the West. Such a policy seemed to have obvious attractions for Britain. It would both end the war and damage Bolshevism. There is little doubt that the Prime Minister himself was tempted by such a scheme. But neither his Allies nor most of his colleagues were convinced of its merits. It was pointed out that German consolidation in the East would threaten the British position in India. In the longer term, Germany might well be tempted to renew her attack in the West, strengthened by more men and resources. However serious this speculation on the subject of a peace at the expense of Russia, it gave way to the fight for survival. The Germans launched their western offensive on 21 March. They were determined to continue fighting unless they could obtain terms which would leave them territorially and economically better off than they had been at the beginning of the war. Through April, May and June, the situation for the Allies was critical. The possibility of collapse could not be discounted.

Although pacifists were despondent about the drift of events in Russia in February, they did not abate their criticisms of the British Government. The U.D.C. attacked the statement issued by the Supreme War Council at Versailles on 4 February. The General Council insisted that the time had come for a new Government which would enter into negotiations for a democratic peace. The need for such a change was common ground between all peace groups. Balfour's speech in the House of Commons on 27 February in which he stated that 'to begin negotiations unless you see your way to carrying them through successfully would be to commit the greatest crime against the future peace of the world', was itself called 'a crime against humanity' by Snowden. R. D. Holt in *Common Sense* called for a coalition of all who rejected the policy of the knock-out blow. To further this end, the Lansdowne Committee organized a conference on 25 February at the Essex Hall. A special attempt was made to cultivate Labour support by calling it a Lansdowne/Labour Conference. Speeches were made by the Liberal peers, Loreburn and Beauchamp. MacDonald, Smillie and Snowden spoke for Labour. MacDonald declared that for his part he would welcome a Lansdowne Government 'as an interregnum'. A Lansdowne peace-by-negotiation Government could not hold together for different purposes, but it could accomplish the main objective, at which point others would have to come in.[61] At Lansdowne House, the group of 'Lansdowne supporters' were not found altogether congenial. The Marquess wrote to his daughter that he was 'quite unrepentant about the original letter, which

has, I think, done good both at home and abroad.' If he had had
the wisdom of the serpent, however, he would have added 'a good
deal of padding as to my abhorrence of anything which could
be called a German peace.'[62] On 5 March, he sent another letter
to the *Daily Telegraph* drawing attention to the similarities between
the recent suggestion of Count Hertling for an 'intimate meeting'
and the ideas of President Wilson. *Common Sense* thought that the
impact would be even bigger than the first letter—and indeed its
circulation, both in Britain and abroad, was much wider. 'Clearly'
commented the paper 'the more enlightened leaders of the working-
classes have turned with a true instinct to Lord Lansdowne. He
could make an honourable peace. . . . The Lansdowne/Labour
Movement is now an accepted fact and a growing force, which will
ultimately save the country.'[63]

A second conference, again organized by Hirst, was held on 6
March. The speakers included those who had been pacifists
throughout the war and those who had held aloof from the Peace
Movement until a late stage: F. W. Hirst, F. W. Jowett, H. B.
Lees Smith, Mrs. Swanwick, Noel Buxton, J. A. Hobson, D. M.
Mason and P. A. Molteno. Their common theme was that the
militarists could never be trusted to make the peace, only Labour
could do that satisfactorily. It was claimed that the British failure
to 'diplomatise' had done more than anything else to maintain
militarism in Germany. In the House of Lords on 19 March, during
a debate on the League of Nations, Lansdowne brought his proposals before a less sympathetic audience. The precise kind of
peace he envisaged was not very clear. He was content to stress
that a great peace conference was needed which could then develop
into a League of Nations. In order to achieve such a meeting, a
crushing military victory was quite superfluous.

The U.D.C. had no formal connexion with the Lansdowne
movement. Nevertheless, its writers were scorching in their
condemnation of the Government and they equally desired its
replacement. Deeply disappointed though they were at the turn
of events in Russia, they were determined not to criticize Germany
for the terms of the Treaty of Brest-Litovsk. If German militarists
had used the opportunity of the weakness of Russia so would
their counterparts in the Allied countries in similar circumstances.
All its leading figures were anxious to insist that British objectives
be kept as limited as possible. Trevelyan, for example, insisted
that since some parts of Alsace and Lorraine were more French
than others, a compromise solution was both possible and just.
On the question of self-determination in general, J. A. Hobson
stressed that 'the liberty of one people must not interfere with the
effective liberty of other peoples.' Self-determination as a principle

was to be respected, but it was not an absolute and indefeasible right.[64] Others echoed their comments, but the note of optimism was no longer present. 'So long as Lloyd George is Prime Minister' wrote Ponsonby in the May issue of the *U.D.C.* 'this war will never end.' The Prime Minister sowed dissension among the military authorities, thrust upon the Army tasks beyond human endurance, did not use the diplomatic weapon and kept at his elbow an indolent Foreign Secretary. A private interview Ponsonby held with the Prime Minister in June confirmed this impression. 'There is very little hope' he noted 'of the diplomatic weapon being used while a dogged confidence in continuance is presumed to be the proper attitude for this country to adopt in the circumstances.' He did not say that the Government would actually turn down a favourable offer if it came along, but one would not be invited and it would not make an offer itself. However, he believed that ministers were 'in fact impressed far more than they admit publicly by our military failure and they feel that the position must to some extent be retrieved before any serious effort to stop can be made.'[65]

Although the relatively good percentage of the poll gained by a peace-by-negotiation candidate at Keighley in April was encouraging, the chances of replacing the Lloyd George coalition with one headed by Lansdowne were not very great. Hirst was despondent and blamed the press proprietors for not giving Lansdowne a fair hearing. The editor of *Common Sense* and his associates had hoped that their peace campaign would halt the disintegration of the Liberal Party. He now ruefully regretted that its leaders seemed to have little or nothing to say. Asquith was little better than Lloyd George. Trevelyan reproached the House of Commons for its insensitivity to the growing needs of democracy. In his view, it had abdicated its whole function of constructive statesmanship to the Government. There was, therefore, little chance of a parliamentary revolt to bring down the Government. In any case, even if Lloyd George was replaced, there were those who felt that the only conceivable alternative was no better. Explaining that he had now gravitated to some kind of Socialism, Morel declared that he 'could not serve under Asquith or Grey's banner, although I quite realise that the only alternative Govt. to L-G *at present* is a Grey-Asquith-Lansdowne-Henderson combination.'[66]

The troubles of the pacifists in these months, however, went even deeper. Frustration at the fact that the Government had regained some lost ground helped to renew old tensions. Relations between the I.L.P. and the Labour Party deteriorated. At the annual conference of the I.L.P. in Leicester during April, Snowden reacted angrily to the decision of the Labour Party not to allow the I.L.P. to be separately represented at a future Stockholm Conference. He denied that the Labour Party had the right to determine the British representation at such an assembly. Mac-Donald expressed disappointment with the Labour Party for 'despite its War Aims Memo., the Labour Party and its spokesmen have signally failed to show that they understand either the art or the science of a democratic war policy.'[67] The galling fact for pacifists was that in these critical months many Labour men were unwilling to be led further along the path to a negotiated peace. They did not find the prospect of German victory appealing.

Pacifists explained the German offensive in a variety of ways. For some, it represented the triumph of militarism over those liberal and moderate elements within the Central Powers of which Count Czernin was supposedly the chief spokesman and representative. *Common Sense* noted that the German action followed the Allied conference at Versailles in February which 'rejected any but a military decision. It followed also, upon the still more recent refusal of our Government to consider Count Hertling's proposals for peace conversations. . . .'[68] Pacifists were sure that the British Government should have given positive encouragement to the civilian authorities in Germany who were reputed to be struggling to obtain supremacy over the militarists. They could not always convince other observers that the situation was as simple. 'I wish I could see' wrote J. A. Spender to Noel Buxton 'any evidence that Germany is or was willing to conclude a peace on the basis of no annexations, and indemnities. No doubt a considerable number of the German people are, but to my mind all the evidence goes to show that the people in control always intended to get plunder in the East or the West, and preferably in both.'[69] A case in point was the speech in the Reichstag on 25 June by the Foreign Secretary, von Kühlmann, in which he appeared to offer the chance of genuine negotiation. The British Foreign Office interpreted it as a trap designed specially to weaken the will to victory of the Allied peoples and to aid the Lansdowne movement in particular. Pacifists, on the contrary, believed that it represented a genuine desire to reach a just settlement. Whichever interpretation was correct, the undoubted fact was that Kühlmann did not last long in office.

A month later, it was becoming clear that the tide had turned for the Allies. In the middle of July, Foch regained the initiative and the German onslaught had spent itself. Then, through August and September, the Allies counter-attacked. Ludendorff considered that the only way to save the situation was to ask for an armistice, on the supposition that Germany would live to fight another day. In order to give the right impression, Germany moved in a democratic direction. It was the new Liberal Chancellor, Prince Max of Baden, who made the formal request on 4 October to President Wilson. The German people took this as a sign of defeat and were surprised by the news. President Wilson, delighted that the Germans had apparently accepted the 'Fourteen Points', replied on 8 October pointing out that they would have to evacuate all occupied territory. On 12 October Prince Max confirmed his acceptance of the terms. Four days later Wilson made it clear that submarine warfare would also have to cease. The Germans now realized that they would have to make up their minds and end the war. At the end of October, the mutiny broke out at Kiel which touched off the German revolution. A republic was proclaimed in Berlin on 9 November. Two days later the armistice was signed. The war had at last come to an end.

In relation to these events, pacifists were no more influential from August to November than they had been from March until August. Only the reason for their ineffectiveness had changed. In the former period they had been open to the accusation that they were encouraging peace talks at a time of impending disaster; in the latter, they could be accused of urging peace talks when victory was in sight. As Snowden complained, the comments of pacifists were always deemed inappropriate. Hirst tried to keep the 'Lansdowne/Labour' campaign alive, but the combination proved increasingly difficult to keep in harness. Many Labour men agreed with him about Free Trade but felt that he was not sufficiently sympathetic to trade unions. Nor did they like his lack of utopian fervour. 'This is a world of ever-shifting ambitions and ideas' declared *Common Sense* in July. 'Its peace may be disturbed by republics as well as by empires. You may abolish Kings—you may abolish Premiers and Presidents—without abolishing wars.' Instead of advocating grandiose changes, pacifists would be more effective if they stressed the financial implications of the war. 'If the belligerent Governments of Europe could agree on a territorial compromise, the war would probably end, for the simple reason that the nations of Europe cannot afford to bleed to death. . . .'

A third Lansdowne/Labour conference was held on 31 July. Although the platform included Mrs. Snowden and Seymour Cocks, the majority represented the financial pacifists who backed *Common Sense*. The chairman, Earl Beauchamp, demanded the truth about both the financial situation and about secret diplomacy. It was an easy way of appealing to both sections of his audience. Lord Buckmaster declared that he was 'as resolute as he ever was in the prosecution of the aims for which we entered the war, but he was uneasy lest the aims for which we entered the war were not the aims with which we were continuing it.' Lansdowne himself sent his third and final letter to the conference. It was carefully phrased. He was not now prepared to 'affirm positively' that the stage had in fact been reached when there was a prospect of preliminary agreement upon essential policies. Germany, however, should be given a chance of demonstrating whether her overtures were sincere or not. He knew that they would be told that 'the moment when the Allied armies are achieving glorious success in the field is not the moment for even hinting at the possibility of peace' but he felt, on the contrary, that the time was ripe since recent events had shown that peace proposals were not the product of any doubt about the ability of the Allies to hold their own.[70] Unfortunately for Hirst, later in the summer Lansdowne decided that he no longer wanted to play an active part in the unusual movement his first letter had inspired. There were, in any case, many on the Left who shared Clifford Allen's suspicion of a coalition Government for peace making. He was 'sick and tired' of Labour not considering itself fit under its own auspices to carry schemes through. Hirst, however, did not give up. In September he was still urging the Liberal Party to shake off its Imperialist leaders and under Lords Beauchamp and Buckmaster, John Burns and R. D. Holt, form the centre of a powerful combination, with Lansdowne on one wing and Henderson on the other, which would restore peace abroad and freedom at home. The Lansdowne Committee did receive an approach from the U.D.C. Executive in October to co-operate in a series of peace demonstrations in big cities. Apart from gestures of this kind, *Common Sense* had to accept that its own plans for changing the Government and negotiating peace had not been successful.

'Labour' was more vigorous than 'Lansdowne', but the vigour was in part spent in internal debate. The summer witnessed a more sober assessment of the movement's growth and prospects. Friction between the I.L.P. and the Labour Party continued. Bruce Glasier felt compelled to issue a warning to I.L.P. members against disaffiliation. This would only mean that the movement would be paralysed in every constituency, to the joy of the capitalist. Pacifists, however, from July onwards, claimed to detect a muting of the peace theme by the Labour Party. This provoked fresh controversy about the best way to abolish war. The I.L.P. was anxious to stress that nothing could be achieved without the overthrow of capitalism and the effective functioning of the International. Many I.L.P. members felt that the Labour Party as a whole did not see the close connexion between these two potential developments. In August, Snowden wrote that if the Labour Party would help to fight Imperialists and Militarists at home, there would be a little more confidence in its profession of a desire to secure a common International Socialist policy. MacDonald stressed the need to show Russia that British Socialists were its disinterested friends who would help the regime to reorganize itself and build afresh. Yet, all the time, some members of the I.L.P. felt that it was wrong to give uncritical support to the Bolsheviks. 'Without being censorious or pharisaical' Dr. Salter wrote 'and with full allowance for the dangerous and isolated position in which the Bolshevik movement finds itself, we must definitely dissociate ourselves from its violence, its suppression of opposing criticism and its disregard of democracy.'[71] Letters in the *Labour Leader* revealed the anxiety in some quarters that the pacifism of some I.L.P. members was becoming merely tactical.

In this situation, MacDonald and Snowden were in a quandary. Snowden, in particular, used the language of the class struggle, but both men felt that it was too easy to suppose that war was simply caused by the desire for sordid economic advantage. They did not want to turn to Marxism or absolute pacifism. On the other hand, despite their membership of the U.D.C., they did not wish to see the ex-Liberal associates in the Union rise to prominence in their Labour Movement at their expense. Morel was back in action in the last few months of the war, condemning the feeble leadership of the Labour Party and claiming that it assisted the disastrous 'war at any price philosophy'. He urged British Labour to insist that the International should meet and force the governments to make peace. His exhortations do not seem to have been as effective as he had hoped. There was, indeed, a tendency for the U.D.C. leadership to exaggerate their influence. The impressive figures of the number of Labour bodies affiliated to the U.D.C. do not by any means imply that they were also controlled by it. In these circumstances, it is easy to understand why MacDonald was so reluctant to divulge his real convictions.

Throughout 1918, the N.C.F. continued to concern itself with the general cause of civil liberty, the particular cause of the conscientious objector and the political situation as a whole. Nevertheless, the spirit had gone out of the leadership. Since Allen was still too weak and Miss Marshall was exhausted, the responsibility for formulating policy fell upon Bertrand Russell. He was depressed both by the continual quarrels within the Fellowship and by the course of the war. The terms Lloyd George had announced in January had secured the support of Labour and it therefore seemed to Russell likely that the war would continue until both sides were destroyed by starvation and western civilization with them. The chances of the N.C.F. saving that civilization were remote and he was disinclined to go on serving it. If Russell resigned there was a possibility that the whole organization would disintegrate. Allen had no intention of resuming, believing that the men in prison would be watched over more effectively by an informal group. This, he thought, 'would leave me and others free to do through Labour channels the much more important things that we all want done—but can never be carried out either through the C.O.'s in prison or through the F.S.C. or the N.C.F.'[72]

In an article in the *Tribunal* on 3 January, Russell wrote a piece on the latest proposals to be put forward by Germany. He included the sentence, 'The American garrison which will . . . be occupying England and France, whether or not they will prove efficient against the Germans, will no doubt be capable of intimidating strikers, an occupation to which the American army is accustomed when at home.' It was this remark which led to his arrest and a prison sentence of six months. Russell admitted that if he had known the blaze of publicity that was going to be directed upon that one sentence he would have phrased it very much more carefully, in such a way as to prevent a misunderstanding by a public not used to the tone of exasperated and pugnacious pacifists.[73] His own opinion was that he had been prosecuted because it was known that he intended to withdraw from N.C.F. work. Allen, Grubb and the *Tribunal* wanted to turn Russell's trial in early February into an onslaught on the Defence of the Realm Act. 'Our fore-fathers went to prison again and again' the journal declared 'were outlawed and banished in order to hand on to their successors the right of free-born men to speak freely. In our day and generation, we must keep inviolate the principles they have established.'[74] After the trial was over he received many letters congratulating him on making the Government look asinine. Russell himself, however, was rather anxious to arrange for his release so that he could settle down to a book on modern logic. Lowes Dickinson was not very optimistic. 'We are governed by men as base as they are incompetent,' he wrote to Russell 'and the country maddened by fear and hate, continues to will it so.' He found himself blushing all over to be English, yet he knew that the individual Englishman was a decent and well-meaning chap; 'It's the pack and its leaders that are so vile.' Allen tried to console the prisoner by arguing that his sentence would strengthen his position immeasurably for the time when he started to spread his views again. It was a fact that 'so many people seem more easily moved by practical demonstrations of sincerity than the truth of what is said.'[75]

However much Russell might be storing up future credit in this fashion, his arrest was not the only incidence of police attention. Following an issue in April in which people were urged to stop the war, the *Tribunal's* printer received a visit from the police who smashed his machinery. Even this visitation, however, did not stop the journal from appearing, though in reduced size. It was produced at this time in circumstances of great secrecy by skilful ladies. Official attention of this kind added to the excitement of the C.O. cause for some of its supporters. Others, however, were drifting away from the N.C.F. because they now considered it had outlived its usefulness. Allen noted with regret that Morgan Jones, previously one of the most ardent of conscientious objectors, was now very much engrossed in planning his adoption as a parliamentary candidate, and had little interest left in the N.C.F. In the prevailing military situation, even the resolution of the I.L.P. conference at Leicester calling for the release of conscientious objectors had a rather formal ring.

Whatever the attitude of those outside, however, the conscientious objectors themselves were not prepared simply to wait until the war danger eased and public opinion became more sympathetic. 'I have opposed this war' C. H. Norman declared 'from a hatred of the principle of killing men in the furtherance of the scheme of ambitious cliques; therefore I am compelled to continue my refusal to submit to military authority.'[76] The attitude of such men and their supporters became increasingly visionary. Dr. Salter professed to see victory ahead, 'and by victory, I mean not the release of our prisoners, not absolute exemption for conscientious objectors, not partial and personal relief for those who go before tribunals, but the downfall of conscription and militarism itself.'[77] Such rhetoric was necessary to keep up flagging spirits. Salter, Grubb and Hunter urged members of the N.C.F. not to fret about exemptions, absolute or otherwise. The whole subject had generated too much controversy and members had neglected the fact that their message was essentially one of love.

The Home Office made one final attempt to deal with the absolutists, short of actually releasing them. It was advised, wrongly as events turned out, that if they were transferred to a special establishment and given as much freedom as possible, they would accept their position. However, within a month, it became clear that they had no such intention. Under the leadership of W. H. Ayles, a very early member of the N.C.F., the absolutists issued a statement of protest. It stated that they wanted to serve the community, but not in any way which would help the war effort. They were therefore not willing to accept any scheme of work which implied acceptance of such a purpose. Finally, they claimed to stand for the inviolable rights of conscience in the affairs of life. 'We ask for liberty to serve, and if necessary to suffer for the community and its well-being. As long as the Government denies us this right, we can only take with cheerful-

ness and unmistakeable determination, whatever penalties are
imposed upon us.'[78] The Home Office abandoned the scheme and
the men were returned to normal prison life.

Russell was released from prison in September. However, he
had no intention of resuming active political work, claiming that
'since Brest Litovsk our duty to preach has ceased because our
chance of success has ceased'. Allen thought this pessimism un-
warranted and believed that the effect of the writings and speeches
of men like Brailsford and Snowden was invaluable. He admitted,
however, that there was 'precious little good to be gained by
preaching extreme non-resistance.' Allen added that he hated 'all
the rubbish a good many of our own young people talk about the
resistance of a handful of young pacifists being the way to prevent
war. . . .' He was also 'sick to death with endless discussion about
drawing lines between different kinds of national service and keep
a very open mind upon so-called bargains of that kind, but that's
because my resistance is far less directed against war than it is
to preserving liberty.'[79] Another man who was weary of controversy
was the hard-working Political Secretary of the N.C.F., C. G.
Ammon. He announced his resignation in August. When, therefore,
the armistice arrived, that total victory over all militarism envisaged
by Dr. Salter still seemed as far away as ever. The bizarre situation
seemed also to have arrived in which Russell and Allen were
talking of the folly of the young. They seemed to be claiming that
they had not even set out to abolish war but, all along, had been
concerned with liberty.

Shortly after the end of the war, Allen wrote that the Quakers
'had been to a very large extent responsible for the gradual break
up of the N.C.F. His intention throughout had been to engage in
a fierce fight with conscription, whereas the Quaker attitude was
'more in the nature of a testimony to certain accepted and traditional opinions about war.'[80] The interpretation Allen placed upon
his activities implied that, after all, it was the religious pacifists
whose objection to war was dogmatic and fundamental. His contention was, of course, an oversimplification. The antithesis between
'Quakers' in the N.C.F. and 'us' was false. The N.C.F. lost its
way because there were almost as many opinions as there were
members. It was an organization which knew how to say 'no'
stridently but not how to say 'yes'. Certainly, tension between
'religious' and 'secular' objectors did develop in 1918, but a
distinction between 'concern for liberty' marking the political wing
and 'concern for a historical tradition about war' marking the
religious, does not do justice to the complexity of the situation.

Allen's distinction might have had more validity if the religious
groups had taken a narrow definition of religion. On the contrary,

many wanted to stretch the term as much as possible. The F.O.R., for example, held a special conference in June 1918 on the relationship between their religious beliefs and political action. The members decided that it was part of their religious duty to remember pacifists in prison or suffering social ostracism, other peace societies, the churches, the Labour movement and, lastly, the work of national reconstruction.[81] Of course, such resolutions did not necessarily resolve the problem and, as before, individuals went their own way. There was, however, a widespread hope for the emergence of a new man, 'a type of man in whom the religious and social sense will be united as rarely before.'[82] The Christian would lose his other worldliness and the Socialist would acknowledge 'spiritual values'. The same vision also moved many Friends. Religious and social ideals should so intermingle that it would be impossible to distinguish the one from the other. To some extent, this had already happened. Charles Roden Buxton, for example, joined the Society of Friends during the war because he was impressed by its attempt to put the teachings of the gospels into practice. On the other hand, there were many Friends who found in the U.D.C., the N.C.C.L. or the N.C.F. the political expression of their religious beliefs. Quakers were no less concerned with liberty than was the N.C.F., but both groups were divided on the extent to which they should submit their publications to the Censor as required by the regulations. This issue led to at least one resignation from the Peace Committee and produced a vigorous correspondence in the columns of the *Friend*. It was also true that the 'accepted and traditional opinions about war' were in fact considerably questioned. According to the *Ploughshare* the standard of the old Peace Movement was almost entirely one of middle-classness. Most of its members lived in an atmosphere of comfortable security. Its morality was bourgeois and rather crudely dogmatic. In future, however, Quakers would have to identify themselves with the emerging Labour Movement if their message was to be effective. Others, however, felt that this group of Quaker Socialists placed too much stress on the importance of the economic factor as the cause of war.[83]

There was, therefore, tension between some 'religious' and some 'non-religious' pacifists—indeed it continued into the post-war period when the balance of J. W. Graham's history, *Conscription and Conscience* was questioned—but it was not upon this rock that the Fellowship sank. The real problem was that its leaders had never been certain, despite the rhetoric and emotion, what its real purpose was. By the end of 1918 they had even ceased to pretend otherwise.

The Peace Movement had not defeated conscription, either for military or industrial purposes, nor had it forced the Government to make a negotiated peace. The only consolaton which 1918 seemed to offer was the progress made by the League of Nations idea. It would be mistaken, however, to see even this as a simple response to pacifist agitation. There was indeed a relationship between the debate on the League in the country and Government policy, but it was not a direct one.

In his speech of 5 January, Lloyd George had mentioned the need to reduce the crushing weight of modern armaments and he declared that a great attempt should also be made to establish some kind of international organization to prevent war. It has been supposed that, in making this reference, the Prime Minister and his Cabinet were 'reluctantly making a few verbal concessions to the new Zeitgeist.' In fact, as has been observed, these remarks did not represent either a concession to President Wilson, the British Labour Movement or the Bolsheviks. They were the result of a combination of the Prime Minister's previously expressed interest in disarmament and the recommendation which a committee of the Imperial War Cabinet had already made.[84]

After the speech, a new Committee, the Phillimore Committee, started work considering the various proposals for a League in detail. Nevertheless, despite the fact that the members began work at the end of January, outside supporters of the League were concerned that both the British and American Governments expressed general interest, but, seemingly, would not make a comprehensive proposal. 'If the Governments don't take action' wrote Lord Bryce to A. L. Lowell in February, 'could a small committee of a few skilled and eminent Americans and Englishmen be found to work out the matter together, and work out the best practicable scheme?'[85] It was, however, extremely difficult to make much Anglo-American progress on the matter at governmental level. Since President Wilson did not want to take on any commitments beyond those entailed by fighting the war, 'there was no way in which the British Government could bring up the League question so as to compel discussion on it.'[86] Wilson's vague support for the idea in his public speeches was therefore irritating. It encouraged British advocates of the League to demand clarification of their own Government's policy. The Government, however, was unwilling to make too definite a stand before it had a further report on the American position. The discussion of the League idea was also hindered by the fact that the question straddled government departments.

There was little further progress until the Phillimore Committee presented its report to the Foreign Secretary on 20 March. Its proceedings had, to some extent, been characterized by a difference of approach between the historians, Holland Rose and Corbett, and the Foreign Office representatives, Crowe and Tyrrell. Nevertheless, they were agreed on their recommendations. Recognizing that nations would not forego their independence, either legally, politically or economically, their proposals were essentially designed to find a way in which states could be helped to avoid conflict by a period of delay and by resort to a conference. The function of the conference would be to investigate the facts and make a recommendation to the parties concerned. The suggestion would not be binding and force would not be used to ensure that it was accepted. Where various forms of coercion—military, naval, financial and economic—might be used would be to compel the disputants to bring their problem to the conference in the first place. The Committee was interested in the management of crises within the existing order of states rather than any attempt to reconstruct the international order itself.

The report was presented at an unfortunate time. The Germans launched their spring offensive on the following day. As Curzon remarked in the Cabinet, 'It all depends how the war is going to end. The League of Nations assumes we are victorious.'[87] In the ensuing months, when it was far from clear that this would be the case, the Cabinet was not disposed to exert itself unduly on the project. Besides, President Wilson made it quite clear that he still refused to draw up even a provisional constitution for the new organization.

At the end of April, however, a new figure appeared among the public supporters of the League of Nations. David Davies, wealthy Welshman and formerly one of the Prime Minister's private secretaries, held a 'League of Nations lunch' at the Carlton. For some weeks, Davies had been scouting round for ways in which he could involve himself in the question. He did have strong personal convictions on the need for an international organization and also an immediate concern for the future of Free Trade. He wanted to mount a big propaganda campaign to stimulate public enthusiasm, but he was by no means sure that the L.N.S. was the right body to benefit from his bounty. At the lunch were, amongst others, Wickham Steed of *The Times,* J. A. Spender of the *Westminster Gazette,* J. L. Garvin of the *Observer,* Arthur Henderson and J. H. Thomas, C. A. McCurdy and Sir Willoughby Dickinson. Thomas, the General Secretary of the National Union of Railwaymen, stated that if a German peace offensive started he feared that many of the members of his union would favour coming to terms. It was therefore important to counter such tendencies by putting the League of Nations in the forefront.[88] It is possible that in this matter Davies was acting for the most well-known Welshman of all.

The existing members of the L.N.S. were not altogether pleased by this offer of support. Lowes Dickinson felt certain that Spender and others would press for the immediate establishment of a League by the Allied Governments. He felt certain that such a move would lose the idea a great deal of support. He had been present at a meeting of the Labour Party Advisory Committee on International Affairs and, when such a proposal had been made there, it was 'treated by everybody as destroying the very idea of a true league, and as practically substituting for it an alliance against the central powers.' Willoughby Dickinson tried to reassure his namesake. 'The main idea of some of our new friends' he wrote 'is that we should set up a policy that might have its effect on the war inasmuch as it would provide a solution towards which both belligerents and neutrals would turn as being an acceptable outcome of the war.' He thought that if the matter were presented in this way, it would attract the masses of the people more effectively than would be the case if the L.N.S. posed as the society which attached so much importance to getting Germany into the League that it would not take any steps to advance until it was sure of this result.[89]

At this point, however, Davies decided to form his own organization rather than wait for the L.N.S. to make up its mind about his plans. At a meeting on 24 June, Gilbert Murray, C. A. McCurdy, J. A. Spender, H. G. Wells and Davies himself constituted themselves the provisional executive of the League of Free Nations Association. Professor Murray was the Chairman of the new body. Yet, no sooner had it been established, than fresh talks took place to try to bring about a merger with the L.N.S. On 26 July, representatives from both societies, Willoughby Dickinson, Spender, McCurdy, H. N. Spalding, R. Unwin, L. S. Woolf and A. Williams agreed in principle that amalgamation was desirable. The formula which both sides accepted was that 'a League of Nations in the full acceptance of the term cannot be founded until after the war, inasmuch as no league formed now could include nations fighting against each other. But that need not prevent the Allies from formulating their ideas.' Davies was pleased with this outcome. The patriotic sections of the community, he argued, would only be interested in a League of *Free* Nations. The L.N.S. had become identified in some minds with pacifist leanings, and partly for this reason it had been difficult to popularise the League. He stressed that he was not concerned with making peace, but with making sure that British war aims were pure and honest. The L.N.S. had only about twelve hundred members and no funds worth speaking of. He was aiming at a membership of several thousands within a few months. Now that the war was going better, he anticipated that the public would be more sympathetic.[90]

Meanwhile, within the official sphere, the Phillimore Committee produced its final report on 3 July.[91] It consisted largely of an examination of the various schemes for a League which had been put forward both since the war and over the centuries. The authors concluded that there was substantial reason to hope that the growth of popular government, together with the gruesome experience of war, would offer the League a good chance of success. Attached to the report was a most interesting appendix drawn up by the Chairman specifically commenting on the proposals made by the L.N.S., the Fabians, the Bryce group, Brailsford, Hobson and Lowes Dickinson among others. Whatever the nature of its own proposals, the committee had at least given careful consideration to those of others. Once again, however, despite the willingness of Cecil and Balfour, there was no definite follow-up to the Phillimore proposals. The major obstacle was again President Wilson. He remained resolved to be silent. If the Phillimore Report was published he would be forced to make some kind of comment probably to the effect that the proposals 'lacked teeth'. He therefore remained opposed to the idea of setting up some kind of League during the war since that would make it appear too exclusively an Allied affair. Those who wanted to see something started argued that it could be made quite clear to the Germans that they could join the League subsequently if they agreed to abide by its rules. Therefore, despite the fact that the Foreign Office set up a League of Nations section under Eustace Percy, nothing definite could be done and for several months the League idea lay dormant. In this respect, to a considerable degree. 'official' thought on the League paralleled 'unofficial'.

If the League scheme ran into difficulties within the civil service, it did not prove easy to accomplish the amalgamation which the two League societies had agreed in principle. Some in both camps remained suspicious. Willoughby Dickinson was particularly anxious to rebut suggestions that the L.N.S. was pacifist. Aneurin Williams was not a 'pacifist' and, although this might not be said of Noel Buxton and Lowes Dickinson, neither of them, he claimed, were among the 'Stop-the-War' crowd. It might be truer of Brailsford and Hobson, but 'neither . . . had been in any sense prominent in our affairs.'[92] After further bickering, it was agreed as a condition of the amalgamation that Lord Grey of Fallodon, the former Foreign Secretary, should be President of the new combined body. Grey was initially reluctant, but agreed because of his interest in the League. When in office he had given encouragement to the idea and it now became his chief interest in politics. He had published a pamphlet urging that Heads of

States should not merely pay lip-service to the idea. All states had to be prepared to forego the right to use force in any dispute before the matter had gone to a conference, or before some kind of conciliation or arbitration had been tried. In his judgment 'the establishment and maintenance of a League of Nations . . . is more important and essential to secure peace than any of the actual terms that may conclude the war . . .'[93] Grey took the chair at a joint meeting of the two societies in the Central Hall, Westminster and a few days later, on 10 October, the League of Nations Union was born. It described itself as a British organization founded to promote the formation of a World League of Free Peoples for the securing of international justice, mutual defence and permanent peace. The members of such a League would agree to submit all disputes arising between themselves to methods of peaceful settlement. They would suppress jointly 'by the use of all means at their disposal' any attempt by any state to disturb the peace of the world. They would create a Supreme Court and respect and enforce its decisions. They would establish a permanent Council to develop international law, to settle differences not suitable for submission to the Supreme Court, to supervise and control armaments, and to act jointly in matters of common concern. The League would also act as trustee and guardian of undeveloped territories. Finally, it would substitute international order for the conflict of nations 'and thus finally liberate man from the curse of war.'[94] Bryce was not alone in thinking that a general regulation of all international questions by a Council was quite utopian. 'Those who know how great the jealousies are,' he wrote to C. W. Eliot 'and the incompatibilities also of temper and ideas between the existing nations of Europe, cannot believe that any such scheme would work. We shall have done very well for the present if we set up machinery for preserving peace.'[95] The great danger, as far as he was concerned, was that once Germany had been completely defeated—and he and most of the other L.N.U. leaders wanted victory—the question of forming a League might get postponed and forgotten. They had to act vigorously to make sure that this did not happen.

However, while the L.N.U. was afraid that the Government might renege on the great project, other pacifists were not sure that this would be a disaster. They felt that in order to make their schemes at all palatable to the Government the League supporters had disastrously compromised their pacifism. In all sections of the Peace Movement, the League continued to excite acute controversy. Among Friends, an unofficial group formed themselves into a League of Nations Committee which they invited all in the Society to support. They declared their approval of the proposals put forward by President Wilson. Their claim was that over three thousand adult Quakers—approximately one sixth of the total membership—had already promised support to the Committee. 'We agree that good will and moral influence are the essential bases of a league of nations' they stated 'but we cannot exclude the possible need for the exercise of economic pressure, and even, in the last resort, the use of such force as may become necessary to restrain the evil doer and to uphold the authority of the League.'[96] A conference of Friends in November failed to produce agreement. Many felt that, once any kind of compromise was made with the ancient and living testimony of the Society, its vitality would be destroyed. The letters of the subject in the *Friend* during September and October were fairly evenly divided. The same division of opinion is to be found among the other Christian peace groups.

Opinion in the Labour Movement, too, was strongly critical of the kind of League that was being contemplated. To Snowden it was a waste of time to talk about a League unless it was accompanied by a declaration from the Great Powers favouring economic equality and disarmament. He was particularly critical of Grey's proposals, writing that, incredibly, the former Foreign Secretary appeared to believe that a League of Nations which had armaments at its command to enforce peace would prevent war. The only real guarantee of peace was disarmament.[97] A writer in the *Tribunal* went further. However 'futile' it might be to hope for a total abolition by the Great Powers of their military forces, nothing short of such a step would ensure the foundation of a League of (really) Free Nations. Force and Freedom could never exist together. An armed League, with or without conscription, might turn out to be nothing more than a Holy Alliance of capitalistic states,[98] *Common Sense* was also suspicious.

The problem was partly that Grey's prominent association with the League movement made it virtually certain that E. D. Morel and the U.D.C. group would be conspicuously unenthusiastic. This was also true of many in the Labour movement who were strongly critical of the former Foreign Secretary's pre-war diplomacy. Nor was the reputation of the supposed transatlantic champion of the League, President Wilson, altogether secure. Snowden and MacDonald could not make up their minds about him. The behaviour of Sam Gompers and a group of his American Federation of Labour colleagues at the September Inter-Allied Labour and Socialist Conference in London, caused general suspicion of American intentions. Apparently, Gompers was complete master of the occasion, blocking any amendment or resolution which did not meet with his approval. He implied that I.L.P. delegates expressing pacifist sentiments were either stupid, criminal or merely deaf. Snowden was furious at the way in which the bourgeois imperialist

Governments received such support at a Socialist and Labour Conference. MacDonald, too, was scornful of the backwardness of American Labour in these matters. Nevertheless, he continued to profess great hopes in the American democracy. President Wilson's policy was the one which he and others had been pressing since May 1915. He was not carrying the policy of the Allied Governments but was running contrary to it. The Allies had not even accepted his 'Fourteen Points'.[99] Others had nagging doubts both about the President and his League—and it is difficult to tell how far one sprang from the other. Mrs. Swanwick, for example, was very critical of the American crusader who talked about 'the common will of mankind' in a censored, regulation-ridden, and conscripted world. Morel hedged, writing 'We have not always agreed with the *methods* by which President Wilson hopes to achieve his policy. We shall not always agree with them . . . But his POLICY is ours. The forces which oppose him are the forces which oppose us. . . .'[100] Others were not convinced that it was possible to draw this distinction between methods and aims.

The effect of these doubts was to place Labour supporters of the League on the defensive. Arthur Henderson—under suspicion in some circles for not standing up to Gompers—was forced to stress that Labour placed more faith in the solidarity of peoples than in the machinery of judicial conciliation and arbitration, however impressive such machinery might be. The League had to be something bigger than simply an organisation to prevent war. Its ultimate purpose had to be to create a common mind in the world. It would be quite insufficient for it to be merely an agreement between governments. The League would have to bring foreign policy under the control of popularly elected assemblies which would guard the sovereign rights of the people. It implied the end of secret diplomacy and the development of parliamentary control over Cabinets. Foreign Ministers, agents of international finance and diplomatists would all have to be kept under vigilant scrutiny. Finally, he believed, the League would render powerless 'the evil influence of the armament trusts which are so largely responsible for the awful tragedy in which the world is at present involved.' J. A. Hobson joined him in stressing that the kind of League which emerged would depend upon the strength of the democratic forces in the countries concerned. He urged pacifists, particularly in the ranks of Labour, not to despair of the League prematurely. 'If democracy wins through in most of the great nations so that their national Governments are democratically controlled, there is every hope that the League of Nations would be animated by the same spirit.'[101]

When peace came, therefore, the precise form of the League of

Nations was a matter for conjecture. The Government had plans, but these were by no means complete and had not been disclosed. Hobson might well be right; the eventual framework might indeed depend upon the views of the democracy.

CHAPTER EIGHT

The Peace Movement and the Peace Settlement

The assumption behind the Peace Movement throughout the war and the spur to its efforts to ensure a just peace was that pacifists were speaking in the name of the people. The General Election of 1918 gave an opportunity for testing the truth of this claim. The electorate had been more than doubled by the extension of the franchise to all adult males and many women. For this reason, it could then be regarded as the most democratic election in British history. Its outcome would help to determine the government's stand during the peace negotiations. The Prime Minister was anxious to remain in office at the head of as wide a coalition of national opinion as was possible. However, Asquith refused his invitation, as did the Labour Party. The issue before the electorate was therefore whether or not the victorious coalition should be given a fresh mandate under the man who had won the war. The nature of the forthcoming peace was of course extensively discussed and few politicians doubted the strength of anti-German sentiment. It was a feeling which Lloyd George both encouraged and deplored according to circumstance.

In this atmosphere, pacifists could hardly be expected to do well. They did not attempt to apologize for their war-time convictions. In his election address, Snowden reiterated that wars were in the main due to the intrigues of financiers and capitalists. He declared that he had worked to make this impossible in the future and that was why he had been attacked and abused. Similarly, Trevelyan claimed that he had 'refused to be silenced when I preached exactly those principles which the great President now is making universal. I regret that the British Government did nothing to lead the world in this direction.'[1]

In contrast to the fate of a patriotic Labour man like George

Barnes, whose constituency, Glasgow Gorbals, refused to readopt him, the sitting Labour pacifists had little difficulty with their associations. Their fate at the polls, however, was very different. Snowden came bottom at Blackburn with one fifth of the total; MacDonald lost at Leicester in a straight fight with a third; Jowett came second at Bradford East with over a third; Anderson lost at Sheffield Attercliffe in a straight fight with a third. Other prominent peace figures who fought as I.L.P. candidates did no better. Charles Roden Buxton came third at Accrington with just over a fifth of the total; C. G. Ammon came bottom at Camberwell North with a fifth; H. N. Brailsford lost in a straight fight at Montrose with a quarter. Others fared similarly, losing either to Coalition Unionists, Coalition Liberals or to the British Workers League.

Other prominent pacifists were forced by circumstances to fight as Independents. Trevelyan stood as such at Elland, the constituency he had represented as a Liberal, because the Labour candidate would not stand down. Trevelyan came bottom, preceded by a Coalition Unionist, Liberal and Labour, with only a tenth of the poll. A similar situation occurred in the contest for Dumbarton Burghs. The Scottish Miners had already adopted a candidate when the I.L.P. put Ponsonby's name forward. MacDonald even went to Dunfermline in an attempt to persuade the Miners to withdraw. They refused. MacDonald was furious at what he regarded as their narrow-minded behaviour. Henderson, on the other hand, considered that MacDonald had no business to interfere at all. In the event, Ponsonby came third, after the Labour candidate with over a fifth of the poll.

Others still thought of themselves as primarily Liberals, even if, like Noel Buxton at Norfolk North, they described themselves as Liberal/Labour. He lost by 200 votes. On the other hand, in the Don Valley, H. B. Lees Smith, fighting as a Liberal, pushed Labour into bottom place and came second to a Coalition British Workers League candidate. At Penistone, S. Arnold, a prominent anti-conscriptionist, stood as a Liberal, defeated the Coalition Unionist and pushed Labour into bottom place. At Frome in Somerset, however, the sitting Liberal, Sir John Barlow, who was of a similar disposition, again stood as a Liberal but lost the seat to a Coalition Unionist. Both the winner and the Labour candidate polled five times more votes than he did. There are, therefore, individual variations which make it difficult to say precisely how damaging 'pacifism' was to a candidate. It is certainly not possible to say that the more extreme the pacifist the more dismal his performance. Asquith, Runciman, Sir John Simon and other non-Coalition Liberals all lost their seats, as did Arthur Henderson.

M

However much there might be some consolation in the details of individual results, the general verdict of the electorate was devastating. All those who had voted, wrote Snowden, had been 'swayed by unreasoning passion, by the determination to carry into the political settlement of the war the same spirit which prompted its military continuation to the knock-out blow.'[2] In explaining his own defeat, MacDonald blamed 'the unregenerated villadom and the darkened slumdom' which were always boon companions on these occasions. The only hope for the future lay in the 'intelligent artisan and the intellectual well-to-do'.[3] In the immediate aftermath, the defeated tried to console themselves. Trevelyan thought that he and Ponsonby could have won if they had been the official Labour candidates. Seymour Cocks professed to have no regrets for his own defeat, but was 'heartily glad to see Asquith, Simon and all their gang out of it.' The whole situation was, in his opinion, quite ludicrous. He might have been a little surprised to learn that King George agreed. 'What is one to think of people who kick out Asquith and elect Billing?' he remarked to his private secretary, who happened to be Arthur Ponsonby's brother. Snowden professed to be 'very well satisfied with the general results much as I deplore the fate of particular candidates.' Lloyd George, he claimed, had signally failed to sweep the country.[4] Clifford Allen was glad that Labour had not been returned in triumph without him. Less selfishly, he was glad that the party had been forced into a thoroughly unrepresentative position. The swing back of the reaction would, in time, be that much stronger. Miss Marshall thought the election result would prevent that softening of the edges of controversy 'so dear to those of good will but timid heart and woolly brain.' However, she feared that Lloyd George would become more autocratic and 'we may yet have revolution by violence in this country. In any case the character of the new House of Commons is bound to turn more and more people's hopes towards direct action. . . .'[5]

These reactions illustrate the dilemma in which pacifists found themselves. They were committed, for the most part, to the acceptance of the electoral system and to the principles of British parliamentary government. They believed, of course, that the result had been manipulated by politicians and press. Yet to believe this was to admit something potentially frightening about the behaviour of mass publics. Some pacifists were already disturbed by that school of social psychology which stressed the instinctive reactions of man in the mass. Pacifists condemned the excitement of war as 'irrational', but it might be impossible for men to behave socially in any other fashion. They assumed both that peace was in itself desirable and that, once shown the way, men would obediently walk in it. Both of these assumptions now seemed questionable. Hence the interest in 'direct action' to which Miss Marshall referred. By using violence, pacifists might be able to persuade people to desire that peace which pacifists said they ought to desire!

The psychological, sociological and philosophical problems posed by this situation were profound. They needed careful and mature consideration. In the short term, however, pacifists had to accept that the General Election had left them with little scope for influencing the Peace settlement. A swing back in their favour might well occur in the future, but it was hardly likely to happen quickly. The Peace Movement was therefore engaged in two tasks during 1919. Firstly, it provided a commentary, and a very vocal one at times, on the territorial, political and economic aspects of peacemaking. Secondly, it was reflecting on its experience during the war and considering what future, if any, it should have with the return of peace.

The negotiations in Paris began in January and took place against a background of a Europe still in turmoil. The notion that the Allies would prepare a preliminary peace between themselves which would then be open to discussion with Germany soon had to be abandoned. Time passed more quickly than had been anticipated and it became more and more important to have some kind of settlement which would introduce a note of stability in a disordered world. Whatever the fanfare beforehand, open diplomacy did not long survive the pressures of negotiation. In the end, the treaty with Germany was signed on 28 June, though the settlements with Austria, Hungary, Bulgaria and Turkey still had to be reached. The details of the process by which the final settlement was reached cannot concern us here. The irony was that Lloyd George found himself prisoner of his own previous rhetoric. He came to see that the expectation of enormous reparations from Germany was extravagant. It was equally undesirable to impose a vicious territorial settlement on the defeated states because that would only deepen German hostility and engender demands for revenge in the future. It might also lead to co-operation between Germany and Russia against the West. Yet, while he perceived the need for greater moderation, he could only manoeuvre within narrow limits. The final result was a settlement which neither conciliated nor coerced the defeated states effectively, though whether any alternative was possible remains an open question.

Germany was indeed deprived of territory. Alsace and Lorraine returned to France, Eupen and Malmedy went to Belgium, Slesvig to Denmark and extensive areas in the east were incorporated in the new state of Poland. Lloyd George, however, secured a plebiscite in Silesia and the port of Danzig was created a free city under the League of Nations. In the west, France had at one stage demanded that the left bank of the Rhine be permanently detached from Germany, but Lloyd George successfully resisted the proposal on the grounds that another Alsace-Lorraine situation would be created. The French had to be content with a neutralised Rhineland under Allied occupation and with the Saar valley placed under the League of Nations—both for a period of fifteen years. As a result of these decisions, despite losing some territory, Germany continued to be a most powerful state. The Allies also decided that German Austria should be established as an independent state which could not be linked with Germany without the permission of the League of Nations. The Germans of former Austrian Bohemia and Moravia were included in the new state of Czechoslovakia without their wishes being taken into account. Both of these decisions may have been justifiable on other grounds, but they clearly ran contrary to the strict application of the doctrine of national self-determination. Overseas, Germany's colonies were not returned to her. They were administered by Britain and the Empire 'under mandate' from the League of Nations. An attempt was also made to prevent the revival of 'militarism' by forbidding Germany to manufacture heavy weapons and relieving her of most of those she still possessed. The new German army was not to excede 100,000 men. The Allies stated that this action could be regarded as a preliminary to a general disarmament. The British had the particular satisfaction of knowing that the German Fleet had scuttled itself in captivity at Scapa Flow.

Pacifists watched these proceedings with dismay and the final result with disgust. In February, Ponsonby wrote that the difficulty in Paris was not to discover 'what the Allied nations and their recent enemies will agree to, but to find a solution of the conflicting claims of the friends who have collared such a colossal bit of "swag".'[6] The *Labour Leader* saw the French claims as 'a revelation of the militarist and imperialist character of the French Government.' They threw an illuminating light on the origin and nature of the war, showing that 'the rulers of France are, as the rulers of France always have been, the most militarist and most imperialist class in Europe.'[7] The *U.D.C.* was also extremely critical of the claims of the new Poland, describing them as extravagant. The whole pattern of the settlement in Central Europe it found most disturbing. In the latter stages of the war most of its writers had resisted the break-up of the Habsburg Empire. Their judgment of the consequences of such action was being vindicated by events. As the shape of the settlement became clear, Ponsonby and Kneeshaw were vehement in their denunciation. The peace was not being openly arrived at, the economic barriers had not been removed, Germany alone was to be disarmed, Germany's colonies were taken over by the British Empire, Russian territory had not been completely evacuated, Belgium had taken Eupen and Malmedy to which she had no title, the Saar seemed likely to be consigned to France, Italian claims went far beyond those of nationality, and German territory had been seized to compose Poland. It was a formidable list.[8] Norman Angell prophesied that 'If the price of this peace is the maintenance during thirty years of great military establishments throughout Europe—and that admittedly is the price of it—then the price must also include the abandonment of Socialism and the failure of the fight for a more complete industrial democracy.'[9]

Pacifists found no more consolation in the economic aspects of the settlement. Lloyd George had managed to include the cost of war pensions in the bill for civilian damages. At the same time, however, he realized that the capacity of Germany to pay was being greatly exaggerated. He achieved a compromise whereby Germany had to recognize her full liability, but the actual amount to be paid was left for an expert commission to determine at a later date when, supposedly, the atmosphere would be calmer. This result did not mollify his critics. Indeed, it was perhaps the punishment of reparations which angered pacifists most of all in the settlement. This was partly because reparations was closely linked to the clause in the peace treaty whereby Germany accepted responsibility for the war. Many British pacifists, after all, had spent the war attempting to rebut the view that Germany was solely, or even primarily, responsible. It is not, therefore, surprising to find that it was Norman Angell who published the first detailed attack on the economic aspects of the settlement. He held that it was quite evident that countries like Germany and Austria, in a condition of starvation, bankruptcy and internal disorder, could not pay what was expected. If they were to be restored to a position in which they could pay, then food and work was an immediate necessity. Unless this was done, out of hunger, hopelessness, anger, lack of work and industrial chaos would come Bolshevism. The Treaty was trying to do two mutually exclusive things—reduce the economic power of Germany and find funds for reparations. He was also very dissatisfied with the general situation in Central and Eastern Europe. A settlement based on absolute sovereignty and 'ownership' of the soil would inevitably conflict with the vital need to promote economic co-operation in Europe. The solution he proposed was a European Economic Council, responsible to the League of Nations, which would arrange German reparation payments, but which would also make sure that countries gained access to the raw materials they would need. Angell's attack gained in force when, at the end of the year, J. M. Keynes published his brilliant critique, *The Economic Consequences of the Peace*. Although personally friendly with 'pacifists', he had nevertheless served at the peace conference in an official capacity. It was partly for this reason that his acrid descriptions of the proceedings, as well as his economic reasoning, soon began to have a devastating effect upon informed opinion. For pacifists, Keynes's contentions seemed to confirm the wisdom of what they had been saying for months.[10]

As far as the general political aspects of the Treaty were concerned, even some supporters of the Government had doubts, at least privately, about the outcome. For many of them, however, the creation of the League of Nations offered great hope, both for a lasting peace and for removing some aspects of the settlement to which they objected. For others, the League was both disappointing and dangerous and the divisions on the subject during the war were not resolved at the peace.

After the armistice, the Executive of the newly formed L.N.U. had been quick to prepare a memorandum on the place of the League at the peace conference. It was sent to the Government. 'The acceptance in principle of a League of Nations', it urged, 'is not to be regarded as one of the items of the Peace Settlement, but it is the foundation on which the whole settlement must rest; consequently it should form the first act of the Congress.' The great danger was that, without a League, individual governments might feel compelled by the need for security to insist on strategic frontiers, irrespective of the rights of others. In addition, the League would provide the only safe way to secure the abolition of secret diplomacy.[11] On 16 December, a more important memorandum was submitted to the War Cabinet. General Smuts advocated a League of Nations which would settle disputes and impose sanctions on an aggressor, but he believed that it would have to be accompanied by an inner transformation of international conditions and institutions. The League could then become an ever visible, living, working organ of the polity of civilization. A. E. Zimmern, who was at this time working in the Foreign Office, wrote to Murray that these proposals went further towards giving a positive function to the League than any of the other suggestions that had been officially considered. It would be impossible to tell what their reception would be in the conference room. Zimmern's chief concern was 'to avoid any suggestion that the Allies are not strictly bound by the terms of their memorandum to Wilson prior to the Armistice.' He admitted that 'we have lost our moral standing on this matter in the last six weeks, but we must try to pretend we have not.'[12]

The L.N.U. placed a great deal of hope in the efforts of Lord Robert Cecil. His support for the League idea was well known, and it was supposed that his advocacy would be invaluable. When in office, he had kept in touch with the leaders of the old L.N.S. and read their publications. Nevertheless, in April 1918, he had felt bound to decline an invitation to join the Society. He felt that to do so would be to appear to commit himself publicly to its proposals. His colleagues would not think this appropriate.[13] This reply illustrates the awkwardness of Cecil's position. He wanted outside support, yet at the same time found it rather embarrassing. His enthusiasm for the League in Cabinet was not as great an advantage for the project as might be supposed. His personal relations with the Prime Minister were not very good, and there was also a tendency for others to feel that his zeal for the League was somewhat unbalanced. The quirkiness about Cecil seemed to be confirmed by his resignation from the Government at the end of the war over the question of the Disestablishment of the Welsh Church. Lord Robert himself then claimed that he could do more for the League outside the Government than as a minister.

Despite his resignation, when he came back to the Commons after the General Election, he was offered, on Smuts' prompting, the position of special adviser to the Government on the question of the League. In this new capacity, he wrote to Gilbert Murray on 20 December that the atmosphere in Paris was not likely to be suited to the quiet working out of proposals, but he would do his best. In the meantime, the subject would continue to be studied in the Foreign Office by Philip Baker. His aim, he wrote early in January, was to bring about the 'closest possible association between the official and unofficial exponents of the League of Nations idea. . . .'[14] Partly as a result of Cecil's prompting, on 25 January, it was agreed in Paris to set up a League of Nations to promote international co-operation. The institution would be an integral part of the general treaty of peace. On 3 February, a committee was established charged with the task of drawing up the Covenant of this new organization. Within eleven days, a first draft was completed and sent to the various governments for further consideration. The next stage in its progress, however, led to fierce debate. Worried about the opposition which he might encounter in the United States, President Wilson wanted to include a specific reference to the Monroe Doctrine. The French, on the other hand, feared that the League would come to rest on vague idealistic appeals for international co-operation and would offer no real guarantee against a revived Germany. Cecil's role in these negotiations was important, though it would be wrong to suppose that the Prime Minister invariably kept him in his confidence. 'I feel rather uncomfortable' wrote Cecil plaintively to Lloyd George in early April 'partly because like the British public I don't know what is going on.' He urged the need for a speedy conclusion to the negotiations, though he felt that the idea of leaving unstated the amount of reparation to be made by Germany was unwise because it would perpetuate uncertainty when the general economic position in Europe was already alarming enough.[15]

Despite the knowledge that Cecil had been working hard for the League, the publication of the Draft Covenant caused its unofficial supporters considerable alarm. Willoughby Dickinson admitted that it was by no means perfect, but thought that if it was criticized too sharply 'we may find ourselves classed among its opponents, and it will have quite enough of that ilk without us. . . .' In detail, the L.N.U. Research Committee did not like a number of the proposals. It deplored the absence of a representative assembly. It objected to the fact that in the Body of Delegates, as in the Executive Council, the voting would be by states, leaving no room for other than national expressions of opinion. Even worse, the draft Article 12 seemed to leave a loophole which permitted war. The Committee 'doubted whether it will be found possible to stop at making war improbable. The only way to make it improbable is to make it impossible. . . .'[16] From another standpoint, however, Bryce saw difficulty in trying to make member states take action irrespective of their own views on a particular question. He thought, revealingly, that the difficulty might disappear in practice 'because the League would not, in its own interests, think of forcing upon such a country as the United States or Great Britain, any course to which either was opposed. . . .' This remark reflects the growing concern, not so much with the details of the League, as with the possibility that the United States might not join. 'The work on this side of the Atlantic' warned Lord Grey towards the end of March 'is done for the present. It is in the United States that the danger to the League of Nations now lies. If the draft is to be altered at all, it should be solely to meet the objection of the Senate of the U.S.A.' American support was essential for, wrote Bryce 'without the co-operation of America the whole thing will fail. . . .'[17]

On 28 April, the Covenant of the League was adopted. France was also given a guarantee by the United States and Britain that they would come to her assistance if Germany attacked. President

Wilson had succeeded in incorporating Article 10 into the Covenant under which the members agreed to preserve the territorial integrity and political independence of all member states. Even so, the members of the L.N.U. were a little disappointed with the final result. In March, Gilbert Murray had been envisaging an international Congress which would be deliberative and to some extent legislative, a committee of which should form a kind of executive government. Now, he had to confess that the League which had emerged was less an international body and more an intergovernmental institution. Nevertheless, he was convinced that 'in each case the Covenant has gone just about as far as it was wise to go, stopping short at the point at which either some great nation would have refused to join the League, or else where the present state of Europe made impartial action impossible.' It would be fatal, he believed, for men of goodwill to quibble at this point over details; it was enough to know that a start in an international adventure had been made.[18]

An appeal of this kind was even more necessary after the full peace treaty had been signed. It then became increasingly important to clarify the relationship between the provisions of the Covenant on the one hand, and the territorial and economic provisions of the treaty on the other. As far as many L.N.U. members were concerned, their early optimism turned sour as the summer progressed. Cecil himself thought that the Pime Minister would be interested in a long letter pointing out his feeling that 'in these negotiations our moral prestige has greatly suffered.' It would be a disastrous consequence of the peace conference if the 'moral leadership of the nations passes from us to the United States.' Some of the criticisms of the Treaty were, he admitted, extreme, but he was disturbed to find that all impartial opinion in neutral countries was now against the Entente Powers for the peace they had made. The whole situation did not augur well for the future of the League.[19] Lord Bryce, too, writing to Sir Eric Drummond, the newly appointed Secretary-General of the League, described his fear that the territorial settlement might jeopardize the League experiment. Drummond was not so gloomy, but he felt that future disputes could only be avoided if the Council of the League really developed into a satisfactory working institution. It would be hopeless to expect any further modification in the terms of the Covenant. Cecil decided that it would be vital to insist that 'in no sense can the League be made responsible for the terms of the Treaty.' Others were less sanguine. They feared that people would be bound to lump the Covenant and the Peace Treaty together. The danger was particularly acute in the United States.[20]

When the news came through in November that the United States

Senate had indeed refused to ratify the Treaty, there was deep depression in British League circles. Lord Grey had accepted a futile special mission to Washington with the main object of trying to persuade President Wilson to be more flexible in the hope that the Treaty might then be accepted. Failure made him despondent. Bryce too was inclined to blame the President for not consulting the Senators at an earlier stage. He greatly regretted that 'the Paris Conference should have sanctioned many injustices, because this makes it easier to say "why should we bind ourselves now to a guarantee to territories the frontiers of which have been unjustly drawn?" '[21] Cecil was also afraid that all he had worked for was now in serious danger. In November 1919 he had already come to the conclusion that it was the first duty of the League to admit Germany to its membership. In January 1920, under the impact of reading Keynes's book he was quite clear that 'we shall have to begin a campaign for the revision of the Treaty as soon as possible.'[22] Unless something drastic was done to attract public support, the L.N.U. would fail. To their dismay, the leaders found that, with the war over, people were not prepared to wax enthusiastic about such terms as 'the enforcement of sanctions' or 'economic boycott'. Nor, regrettably, was it even possible for the various bodies supporting the League in Europe to agree. Willoughby Dickinson returned from a meeting in Brussels with the news that the French and Belgians were adamantly against admitting Germany to the League. It was abundantly clear, both at home and abroad, that the success of the great experiment could not be confidently anticipated, even by its most ardent supporters.

Many other war-time pacifists, not members of the L.N.U., watched these developments with a mixture of wry amusement and dismay. They were not very inclined to assist in the propagation of the League gospel. For them, both the League that was created and the general peace settlement were the consequence of the attitude towards the war adopted by Lord Bryce, Gilbert Murray, Lord Robert Cecil and their friends. It was all very well for them to regret the inadequacies of the peace, but it was the logical outcome of the 'fight to the finish' which they had supported. 'They are objecting' wrote the *Socialist Review* 'to the inevitable result of their own conduct.'[23] How naive, absolute pacifists argued, to suppose that once public opinion had been stimulated to the task of winning the war, it could be diverted, at will, to produce a reconciling peace. Criticism of the League was therefore to be found in all pacifist circles. While some considered that it was better than nothing, others considered it a dangerous menace in need of drastic revision before it could become at all acceptable.

The Christian societies contained members of both these opinions. At the Annual General Meeting of the Peace Society in May 1919, it seemed to be the general view that although the Covenant did not embody all the society's principles, it nevertheless offered the possibility of an international system which avoided war. One speaker, on the other hand, felt that 'if the Kingdom of Christ were to be established at any given point or at any given moment, the inevitable consequence would be that the League of Nations would proclaim war against it.'[24] The Fellowship of Reconciliation, too, felt that the League did not represent a sharp enough break with the past.[25] There was general agreement with the criticism of sanctions advanced by Carl Heath, the secretary of the National Peace Council. If a state intended to treat the result of arbitration as a mere scrap of paper he could see a case for the use of military force. What was not explained, however, was how the agreement to use military force would be protected from similar contemptuous treatment. There was also agreement with the argument that no small state would ever be likely to attempt a war alone, so it would either be one of the larger states or a combination of states which would confront the international force. This meant that 'in any case in which the international force would come into use it would be faced with military strength comparable with its own.' Quite apart from more fundamental objections which some Christians might have, the plain fact was that the League was fraudulent as a system of peacemaking and would never achieve the results which its supporters anticipated. The National Peace Council, now with Trevelyan as its President, considered that the League had to be radically revised 'to meet the essential demand for a world society of the peoples.' No League which was 'inter-government only, no League which is merely the fruit of diplomatic compromise at a Peace Congress of the Powers, will be rooted enough to withstand the sedulous fostering of misunderstanding among the peoples by sectional interests.'[26]

The Society of Friends was no more satisfied with the outcome than the other bodies. Friends had felt the full weight of public disapproval in the General Election of 1918 and only one from their number had been returned to the Commons. The *Friend* likened the situation to the plight of Cobden and Bright after the Crimean War.[27] In view of the long controversy over the League idea it was hardly surprising that the reality provoked equal disagreement. Three Quakers had been elected to the Council of the L.N.U., but Edward Grubb told the Yearly Meeting that he hoped Friends would be careful to distinguish between a real League of Nations and the body which was in process of formation. The Covenant, in his view, was a mockery of a glorious concept.[28]

The Quaker Socialists of the *Ploughshare* were even more critical. In a letter in its columns, Lady Barlow declared that she had joined the Society of Friends 'believing that I was joining the only religious community in the country which is opposed to the use of armed force.' She was now astonished to hear some Friends openly supporting sanctions. 'The League of Nations is a great step forward,' she admitted, but only 'for those who have hitherto believed in unlimited armaments. But Friends, reinforced by the experience of centuries, have a higher ethic to hold before the world. . . .'[29]

The members of the U.D.C., particularly those like Hobson and Brailsford, who had written books on the idea of the League were all disappointed. Initially, the U.D.C. had been reluctant to antagonize prospective supporters by attacking the League prematurely. When he saw the Draft Covenant, however, Hobson could no longer restrain himself. 'A careful reading of the document' he declared 'shows the whole scheme poisoned by the vices of autocracy, chauvinism, conservatism and futility. The structure and composition of the League are thoroughly bad. The breath of democracy is nowhere to be found. Nations do not meet at all, only States, and States do not meet as equals.' The only consolation to be derived from this scheme of tyranny was its complete futility. Clemenceau, he thought, must have laughed with delight when he saw the proposals.[30] 'Our cheers have helped to spread the idea of the League' wrote Brailsford ruefully but unless it could be shaped in a democratic mould it might prove a 'curse to Labour and a fetter on liberty.'[31]

The U.D.C. Council debated the Draft at a lively meeting on 8 March. A resolution was passed welcoming the League in principle but describing the Draft as 'undemocratic and inequitable'. It stressed the need for popular representation and control, the general abolition of conscription, the right of all civilized states to join on equal terms, the necessity of a general reduction of armaments and the abolition of all private arms manufacture. It also wanted to see the mandatory principle extended and the 'Open Door' policy applied to all dependent colonies and protectorates. In order to make the new organization democratic, it advocated majority voting in all legislative and administrative decisions.[32] The peacemakers in Paris did not find themselves able to agree to all these suggestions and U.D.C. condemnation mounted. In an article entitled 'The Lion's Share', Ponsonby remarked ironically that 'the British Empire is not going to come out a loser.' The business of 'mandates' was only a twentieth century device for annexation. The Executive could not resist observing that far from making the world safe for democracy the peace was a betrayal of democracy. 'For our part' it continued 'we do not recognise it as having any moral validity and regard as our chief task the substitution for it of a Peace which will correspond with President Wilson's Fourteen Points and the aspirations and ideals of the common people everywhere.'[33] By the autumn, every possible opportunity was taken to protest against the existing League in favour of the 'real' League. It had to be made clear that as it stood, the League offered no effective security for international peace. Hobson was anxious that the noble concept should not be rejected out of hand 'because of its terrible defects of form and spirit'. Pacifists should, instead, 'concentrate upon thinking out the ways in which it could be reformed if the persons who met to bring it into active life were no longer the representatives of an obsolete and sceptical diplomacy, but the forward-looking and courageous representatives of the creative will of peoples, with a faith in the saving power of international co-operation.'[34]

The *International Review*, successor to *War and Peace*, took a similarly critical view of the settlement as a whole. It too regretted the fact that no place was being provided for 'delegates of the people' which it contrasted with 'representatives of the government'. The view was expressed in April that either the Conference could rely on force, break Germany up and deny the Germans the right of self-determination or it could establish a League of Nations and offer fair and equal treatment with all other states to Germany. A month later, it felt that the 'principle' of the League had indeed been accepted, but it was being accompanied by a vindictive imperialist peace which in practice would make a real League impossible. The new frontiers were not being drawn in accordance with right and nationality but with reference to military considerations. There was no justification for the annexation of German territory and population by Poland, or for the cutting away of the Saar. It looked, in fact, as though the Allies were preparing to use the League as a new Holy Alliance against Communism. The instability of the governments in the newly created states was a threat to peace and proof of the failure of the Allied policy. The American withdrawal was disappointing, but it was 'an illusion for statesmen to believe that a nation like the U.S.A. will guarantee (the peace of Paris) or join any League for its guarantee.' Those who had sown injustices reaped their reward.[35]

'Pacifists' in the Labour Movement were no less critical. Joseph King, a recent recruit from Liberalism, attacked the 'Political Crooks at the Peace Conference' who had set up a League of Nations to enslave the vanquished and menace the world. Only

Labour, organized and united in each European land, could defeat this wicked League of Victors. The *Labour Leader* found it odd that the League which should be the very essence of impartiality would carry out the orders of the nations who were allied during the war. MacDonald agreed. The peace was one by which 'officialdom, diplomacy, governmental executives, discredited by the war and weakened in their own nation in consequence of the war, are to entrench themselves behind the walls of an international authority which will be in a position to impose its will upon the representative assemblies of the nation.' Once again, MacDonald reiterated that the League could never succeed in preventing war by using force. 'That has never been done' he wrote 'and never can be done. The only problem of war is the causes of war.'[36] Amongst the conscientious objectors, it was agreed that the League of Nations was the greatest fraud in history. The noble vision had been degraded into a mere League of the most powerful Allies. The old enemy, the Balance of Power, had reappeared. There was no point in limiting the German army to a hundred thousand men if a British army of conscripts was to be maintained.[37] Snowden described the Peace Treaty as 'a war to extermination upon the German Democracy.' If the Allies insisted upon its terms, then the wars to which it would inevitably give rise would be revolts and revolutions of democracies. A declaration by prominent Trade Unionists and Labour politicians also stressed the likelihood of future wars arising from the settlement. It created a condition of 'unrest and injustice which must make the League of Nations, if it survives at all, merely the instrument of Imperialist domination.' The germ of good which the League undoubtedly contained would be rendered sterile by the circumstances of its creation.[38] C. D. Burns urged Labour not to neglect the possibilities of the newly formed International Labour Office but even that would require the constant support of an enlightened and vigilant public opinion.[39]

By the end of 1919, therefore, a comprehensive 'revisionist' programme was in existence. The peace to end peace had to be changed. Campaigners were urged in the Labour Party publication *Labour and the Peace Treaty* to concentrate their efforts on revising the settlement in its entirety. Among the specific points where action was demanded were the admission of Germany and Austria to the League, a fixed sum for reparation payments, a guarantee that Germany would have adequate access to raw materials and economic opportunities, the cancellation of the temporary cession of the Saar Valley, and permission for the Germans of Austria, Czechoslovakia and the Tyrol to determine their own political future. The rejection of the Treaty and the League was complete. It was time for the Peace Movement to wage peace all over again.[40]

CHAPTER NINE

The Peace Movement in Perspective

The issues with which this book has been concerned—war and peace, violence and non-violence, freedom and obligation—have not disappeared from the contemporary world. Full consideration of them would involve a detailed discussion of current thought in many fields of enquiry from biology to philosophy. It is not, however, the purpose of this conclusion to undertake such a task; the objective is much more limited. It is to assess the significance of war-time pacifism for British politics between the wars. The insights and shortcomings of the opinions that have been presented must, in large measure, be left to speak for themselves.

The Peace Movement of 1919 was very different from the Peace Movement of 1914. At the end of the war, each different section had to take stock and decide what pacifism involved in the post-war world. The Peace Society was the oldest organized Christian expression of concern for peace. In 1919, however, it could not altogether disguise the fact that it had lost both prestige and support. Its income declined and its journal, *The Herald of Peace* appeared somewhat erratically. Nevertheless, its Secretary, the Rev. Herbert Dunnico, was determined that it should not die. He stood unsuccessfully as Labour candidate for Ilford in the 1918 General Election and clearly hoped to see the Society prosper by bringing together its traditional Nonconformist support and the Labour Movement. He sat as Labour M.P. for Consett, Co. Durham from 1922 to 1931. Throughout the inter-war period, the Peace Society continued to provide a forum for Labour and Liberal M.P.s, holding discussions on disarmament, the League of Nations and related questions. However, it could never become a very influential body. Lack of finance was crippling. 'When we remember' commented an editorial in 1928 'that there is hardly one of the ten or twelve peace organisations in Britain (excepting the League of Nations Union) whose net income exceeds £2,000 per annum the amount of work achieved is really surprising.'[1]

The fate of the Peace Society represented a humiliating decline from the period when it had exercised unchallenged supremacy in the Peace Movement. The Fellowship of Reconciliation, by contrast, had only been formed in response to the war. To some extent, it had replaced the Peace Society. A correspondence between Dunnico and C. J. Cadoux, a Congregationalist pacifist theologian, in December 1916 reveals some of the tension. Cadoux had evidently cast aspersions on the pacifism of the Peace Society. 'To suggest that the FoR was the first Society to take a thorough-going and uncompromising stand against the present war is moonshine' Dunnico replied '. . . if one wanted to be hypercritical, one could easily retort by saying that even now the FoR is making no organised stand against the war. . . .' The Peace Society had stood firm and he had welcomed the FoR when it was founded. Nevertheless, he disliked very much 'the pharisaical attitude adopted by some of its members towards other organisations' and intended to make his views on the subject very clear.[2] However, the FoR survived such exchanges and grew slowly and steadily throughout the war. Its leaders were intellectually and spiritually sensitive Christians whose very sensitivity perhaps made them imprecise about their objectives. In September 1919, a motion was put to its General Committee urging that the Fellowship should disband on the grounds that its witness was no longer needed. The war spirit which had brought it into existence was, for the moment, quiescent. The motion was defeated.[3] The FoR remained in existence as a specifically Christian pacifist society. During the twenties its membership remained roughly seven thousand. A pruning of membership lists then halved that number. In the middle thirties, however, fresh recruits began to join in increasing numbers. The extreme hostility with which it was regarded immediately after the war did not take long to disappear. One of its most important members, G. M. Ll. Davies was elected as an M.P. for the University of Wales in 1923, specifically as a Christian Pacifist. However, on the whole, the Fellowship did not seek direct political influence and Davies himself found membership of the House of Commons uncongenial. It retained a basic individualism which saw the remedy for war in terms of personal goodwill. The FoR liked to appeal for a 'moral miracle' and saw the life of Christ as an example of heroism and adventure. For many members the Cross became a symbol of pacifist endurance rather than of redemption.[4]

The Society of Friends was not, of course, specifically a peace society in the sense either of the Peace Society or the Fellowship of Reconciliation. There was no question of it dissolving when the war ended. Quakers took part in the activities of many groups, but they did not neglect the discussion of peace in their own Society. The war had, in fact, severely tested the nature of the peace testimony. One school of Quaker thought saw the pacifist position as essentially a-political. Friends were committed absolutely to an ethic of non-violent resistance. The political consequences of this stand were irrelevant to its merits. A second school was equally committed to an absolutist ethic, but supposed that its political consequences would be invariably beneficial. They therefore advocated Christian pacifism on pragmatic as well as on absolutist grounds. A third school was prepared to adjust the testimony to the political realities of the moment. Such people were prepared to tolerate, in the last resort, the use of armed force by the League of Nations. A final school broke away from the individualism of the traditional peace testimony, and stressed that war had to be seen in its full social and economic context. In their view, only when powerful economic forces had been overcome could the world be made free from war. This made it seem more necessary than ever to unite even with those who believed in using violence, provided that they were 'sincere anti-militarists'. They found it impossible to distinguish between 'violent' and 'non-violent' movements of social protest. The only important question was whether or not the protest was justified. Their attitude, however, was by no means acceptable to all. There were complaints about Quaker apologists who seemed to have the business of running Bolshevik propaganda in England and who overlooked the fact that Lenin and his friends both predicted and prepared for the civil war in Russia. This debate between various schools of Quaker thought continued for many years. It was, therefore, not easy to spell out the implications of the peace testimony in a way which would command universal assent within the Society. Nevertheless, nearly all agreed that 'The Christian way of life revealed in the New Testament, the voice of conscience, revealed in the soul, the preciousness of personality revealed by the transfiguring force of love, and the irrationality revealed in modern warfare, either together or singly, present grounds which for those who feel them make participation in war under any conditions impossible.'[5]

The activity of British Christian Pacifists during the First World War highlights the tensions of Christian existence. They recognized that they were in a small minority in the churches—though they were uncertain whether to be proud or ashamed of this fact. They constituted *ecclesiola in ecclesia*, seeking a higher level of perfection than that which most other Christians seemed prepared to accept. They were critical of the churches for compromising with the world and, in their eyes, betraying the gospel. They wanted Christians of the world to unite, finding it intolerable that the body of Christ should be so divided that its members were fighting and killing each other on the battle-field. They watched with dismay as, in country after country, religion was pressed into the service of the State.

They were, of course, quite correct to observe that the Church of England was the national established church, so closely linked to the State as to make withdrawal of support for the war impossible. Even supposing that the Archbishop of Canterbury had wanted to, he would not have been able to carry the rest of the church with him. The boundary between Church and State, Christian and non-Christian, was bewilderingly confused. The essence of the matter was that it was impossible for the church to behave like a sect. The penalty of establishment was an inevitable fuzziness on public issues; the advantage was in the diffuseness of its influence. A survey of Anglican attitudes to the First World War is beyond the scope of this study. Naturally, most churchmen accepted the justice of their country's cause; yet at the same time they tried to temper the more extravagant aims and promises. To pacifists, however, this was not enough.

The position of the Free Churches was rather different. Their very title indicates a desire to be free from state control. The historic ethos of Baptist and Congregationalists, Quakers and, to a lesser extent, Methodists, was 'dissenting', their membership largely drawn from those without power in the State. It was, therefore, psychologically easier for many Free Churchmen to take an attitude which set them at variance with the majority of their fellow countrymen. The court testimony of Walter Ayles of the N.C.F. was not uncommon. He declared that his parents were both Nonconformists and he had been brought up on the stories of his ancestors who had been evicted from their chapels, evicted from their homes, beggared and imprisoned—all because they refused to be disloyal to conscience. In being a conscientious objector against war he was following in their tradition.[6] Nevertheless, however much such an appeal might have stirred Free Churchmen, the majority of them supported the war—though there were more pacifists in proportion to their total numbers than there were in the Church of England. Leading theologians argued powerfully and acutely against pacifism, while often at the same time conducting a vigorous campaign for the rights of the conscientious objectors.[7]

In all the churches, sensitive minds as well as crude ones supported the war, aware of the emotional and intellectual challenges it presented, yet conscious that there was no escaping the central dilemmas of Christian life; in the world yet not of the world, *simul justus et peccator*.

The faithfulness of Christian pacifists was, to some extent, rewarded in the post-war world. All the churches became more interested in the problem of peace, feeling in retrospect rather embarrassed by their support for the war. There was a growing attempt to cultivate a 'Christian International'. During the latter stages of the war, the Archbishop of Uppsala, Nathan Soderblom had attempted to promote a Christian Stockholm Conference, but it ran into substantially the same difficulties as the Labour one. After 1919, however, both institutional and personal contacts between Christians in Britain and in Europe were strengthened. Church leaders were aware that the war had shaken Christian belief. If they could show concen for peace they might demonstrate that relevance which the institutional churches seemed in danger of losing. It is significant that as early as 1924 the membership of an influential ecumenical commission on 'Christianity and War' contained a majority of absolute pacifists. All sorts of inter-denominational peace propaganda was undertaken—notably by the 'Christ and Peace' Council launched in 1929. Wartime pacifists took a prominent part in this kind of activity. The most well-known Christian pacifist of the inter-war period was, however, the Rev. Dick Sheppard, whose Peace Pledge Union, with its declaration 'I renounce war and never again, directly or indirectly, will I support or sanction another' attracted some 150,000 signatures. The P.P.U. was supported by many who had been active in the Peace Movement during the war, but also included many who had no such connexion. It seemed for a time in the middle thirties that absolute pacifism was growing strongly. The peace groups within the various churches reported increased membership and activity. When pacifism became fashionable, the atmosphere seemed far removed from the First World War. Yet, despite this success, the ambiguities of the Christian pacifist strategy remained what they had been then. It was fundamentally unclear whether Christian pacifism was political or a-political, whether it repre-sented an attempt to mobilize the churches as pressure groups against war, or a personal decision by individuals never to fight.[8]

In any case, the intellectual traffic in the thirties was not all one way. The kind of Liberal Protestantism which had formed the basis of much Christian pacifism was itself under attack. Con-temporary political and theological developments in Germany led to a reconsideration of the whole problem of war. Also influential were the writings of the American theologian and commentator, Reinhold Niebuhr, himself a former member of the American Fellowship of Reconciliation. In his wake, Christian 'realists' began to stress that pacifists had no understanding of political problems from the inside, and hence no understanding of the demands of power. Pacifists wrongly supposed that the Sermon on the Mount could be taken as a simple blueprint for society and that 'love' was an immediately applicable possibility in social action. Niebuhr also argued that the condemnation of violence came loudest from middle-class Christians who had enough economic and other forms of covert power for their views to be heard and wishes met without violence. Pacifists were right to urge that naked self-interest had to be transcended, they were wrong to assume that human beings, either individually or in groups, could ever do so completely. They too easily accepted the notion that human history could evolve in such a way that conflict and violence could be eliminated. They were wrong to despise the structures and conventions by which the terrifying possibilities of power had been controlled in the past. Niebuhr's powerful arguments, if not his tortuous prose, found many English admirers. Partly under his influence, a number of Christians who had been active pacifists in the First World War changed their minds. Among them, for example, were two prominent Free Churchmen, Hugh Martin and Nathaniel Micklem, authors respectively of *The Christian as Soldier* and *May God Defend the Right*. Despite these defections, however, it is probable that most Christian pacifists who had adhered to their beliefs through the First World War did so again, if they were still alive, in the Second. The converts to pacifism in the thirties, however, were more fickle in their allegiance. The war against Hitler seemed to demonstrate to many of them that, after all, war could be the lesser of two evils.[9]

The contribution of the U.D.C. to the Peace Movement was of a very different order. The Christian societies spent much of their time discussing ethical questions, puzzling over the psychological nature of the peace they sought. Their attitude to politics was ambiguous and uncertain. In the last resort, their outlook depended on an act of faith. The tone of the U.D.C. leadership was, by contrast, mainly secular. They had little time for metaphysical meditation. They all abhorred war but, at least in theory, did not rule out the possibility that there might be one in which they would be prepared to fight for their beliefs. They were, for the most part, active politicians caught in a confused party situation. They claimed to have discovered the solution to the problem of war in the democratic control of foreign policy.

It is obvious why the idea should have been so attractive. The fact that war had broken out in 1914 discredited the existing system of conducting foreign policy. It was, the U.D.C. believed, only reasonable to assume that an alternative system would be more successful. It could not be seriously claimed that, before 1914, 'democratic control' of foreign policy existed. The people had been kept in ignorance concerning the precise state of Anglo-French relations. Sir Edward Grey had been particularly reticent in his general comments. At one point, even the Cabinet was kept in ignorance. Yet, whatever the truth of these contentions, Grey always acknowledged that in the last resort the opinion of the public was vital, even though policy was formulated by a relatively small group of men. If it was believed that public opinion would not accept a particular policy, there was little future for it. No doubt, this was in some measure merely a conventional expression, since little attempt was made to discover what public opinion on specific questions actually was. In a system of representative government, the only way in which opinion could be tested was in the House of Commons. And, in the summer of 1914, the Foreign Secretary carried the Commons with him in the decision to go to war. It was also abundantly clear that in 1919 the House of Commons welcomed the peace that had been made. The U.D.C. was unwilling to accept these facts. It rightly observed that while the House of Commons could exercise final control, it could only do so at a very late stage in the policy-making process when, perhaps, no alternative course was feasible.

The problem was to reverse this situation. It was easier to condemn the existing arrangements and declaim the need for 'democratic control' than to see how such control could be implemented. The leaders of the U.D.C. were in a quandary. They professed to believe that the 'people' had been opposed to the war, had desired a negotiated peace and had disliked the peace settlement. The prevailing system of parliamentary government seemed to show otherwise. It might, therefore, have been logical to challenge the basic assumptions of such a system, and to argue that the real wishes of the population could be accurately and meaningfully obtained in some other way. On the whole, however, although the idea of a referendum was mentioned, the U.D.C. leaders were wedded to the notion of parliamentary government. The various proposals they advocated—more information for the House, scrutiny of Treaties, close questioning of the Foreign Secretary, the possible establishment of a Foreign Affairs Committee—were all supposed to strengthen the power of the House of Commons.

Ponsonby's proposals received a general welcome even from those who did not agree with him about the war. A reviewer in the *Nation* considered that some measure of secrecy in dealings between governments would have to remain, but executives would soon discover that they would not again be trusted as they had been trusted in the past. Their constituents would want time to consider not only their acts, but the general tendencies of their policy.[10] Others, however, were more critical. Gilbert Murray wrote that '. . . the vital issue at stake in foreign politics is much more an issue between reason and unreason, between prudence and recklessness, between moderation and chauvinism, than, as Mr. Ponsonby insists on regarding it, between democratic and oligarchic sentiment'.[11] It was absurd to suppose that the people of any one country was disinterested. He happened to believe that British foreign policy was conducted above the average standard of the nation not below it. Philip Kerr made a different point in a letter to Morel. He thought that a foreign affairs committee would not be of much assistance. In the United States, it meant that 'the President is in a despotic condition even greater than that of Sir Edward Grey.' He believed that 'if democracy is really to have control of foreign affairs, the electors must be able to *vote* on foreign issues and I don't see how these are to be presented to them except at a general election at which domestic policy is not in question and when two parties representing conflicting policies, compete for their suffrages.'[12] The difficulty with Kerr's suggestion is that such an election is inconceivable. At general elections, domestic and foreign issues are hopelessly intermingled, no more so than in 1918. It was, indeed, precisely this impasse which tempted some U.D.C. members to flirt with the idea of 'direct action'. They demanded that the workers should close ranks to end British intervention in Russia and to alter the Versailles Treaty. But was 'direct action' to be equated with 'democratic control'? At the Labour Party Conference in June 1919, the Chairman considered it 'both unwise and undemocratic, because we fail to get a majority at the polls, to turn round and demand that we should substitute industrial action.' J. H. Thomas also pointed out that Labour had made its case to the electorate and, sad though it was, 'our people believed them and not us. We ought clearly to recognise that, if Labour is going to govern, we can't have some outside body attempting to rebel against parliamentary institutions without it recoiling on our own heads.'[13]

The only way for the U.D.C. to resolve its problem was to hasten the day when the members of the House of Commons actually held the views which the people were supposed to hold. It was not easy to see how this could be done. The moment the war ended, the U.D.C. as a body was in difficulties. No one could see the way forward very clearly. Writers have stressed that its influence on the formulation of Labour foreign policy at this time would be 'difficult to exaggerate' but this is itself an exaggeration. The U.D.C. was only a collection of individuals. It had been formed by dissident Liberals and Labour men whose disaffection from their parties had given the Union what cohesion it possessed. In the post-war world, the situation was different. The chief Labour members—MacDonald, Snowden and Jowett—were now primarily concerned with advancing their own positions in the Labour Movement rather than with their membership of the U.D.C. The ex-Liberals now had to make their own way in their new party without the support of a U.D.C. 'bloc'. It is true that Roden Buxton, Ponsonby, Brailsford, Trevelyan, Angell and others did sit on the Labour Advisory Committee on Foreign Affairs set up in 1917, but they did so as individuals, not as a U.D.C. delegation. The discussions of the committee were no doubt admirable, but it would be unwise to assume that these gentlemen swiftly gained influence over the Labour Movement. The crucial debate on 'direct action' against intervention in Russia took place among the Trade Unionists of the Triple Alliance, not in a U.D.C. committee room.

It is true that Morel was anxious to perpetuate the U.D.C. and he had an ambitious scheme for some kind of international counterpart. Probably for financial reasons, this latter project did not come off. As a journalist and pamphleteer, his energy was as prodigious as ever. He continued to attack British pre-war diplomacy, the secret history of a great betrayal as he called his exposure. He believed that the public life of Europe, and British public life, was 'poisoned by this colossal falsehood of a German war "plot", of Germany the "criminal nation" to justify the Great Iniquity which is termed the Versailles "Peace".' He was incensed by the degrading use by the French of black African troops in Europe. Yet, despite the constant onslaught maintained by Morel, the U.D.C. journal, now called *Foreign Affairs*, noted gloomily in December 1920. 'We can never, in this generation, hope to touch the mob which is in regular attendance at football matches or fills the cinemas. Our appeal can only, as ever, be to the thinking minority.'[14] It was a curious commentary on democratic control.

It did not take long for the defeated parliamentary candidates of 1918 to gain some favour with the electorate. Some thirty members of the Union, including Ponsonby and Trevelyan were returned to the House of Commons in 1922, though it would be difficult to establish either that their membership had played a significant part in their election or determined their subsequent political behaviour. Morel's defeat of Churchill at Dundee was spectacular and a notable political career was confidently forecast for him. MacDonald, of course, was elected Leader of the Labour Party.[15] A year later, at the end of 1923, the first Labour Government was formed and there were, apparently, nine members of the U.D.C. in the Cabinet. This fact, however, seems to have little significance. Despite his membership of the U.D.C., it would appear that MacDonald had little time for some of its principles. Schemes for tinkering with the structure of the House of Commons had little relevance to the problem of war and peace. The only real possibility of preventing war would be if the Labour Movements in the major European countries developed a common conscious- ✓ ness and a common interest. The splits and divisions in the Labour Movement made this a very difficult task, but only a solid community of sentiment and interest could withstand the emotional and economic pressures that led to war. He believed himself to be equipped to tackle the problem and took personal charge of the Foreign Office.

Morel also believed himself to be the ideal Foreign Secretary for the hour. Not surprisingly, he then became critical of the government's foreign policy, making little allowance for its difficult situation in the House of Commons. The label 'U.D.C.' now became an embarrassment rather than an occasion for camaraderie. Ponsonby, Under-Secretary of State for Foreign Affairs, told Morel that after one of his outbursts a statement had had to be issued to the effect that the U.D.C. was an entirely private body 'in no way connected with the Government'. Trevelyan, Thomson and Attlee had been asked to withdraw their acceptance of Vice-Presidencies of the Union. Ponsonby admitted that their previous connection with the U.D.C. made things 'exceedingly awkward'.[16] Morel was also critical of the way the Government had handled the negotiation of the Anglo-Soviet Treaty—though not, interestingly, of the secrecy involved. After the Treaty had been signed, Ponsonby implored Morel to use his influence 'to make our people . . . turn their attention to converting Liberals and controverting Tories and leave off disparaging MacDonald, distrusting me, and abusing the F.O.'[17] The Prime Minister also expressed himself forcefully. 'What so many people do not understand' he wrote to Morel in March 1924 'is that it is quite impossible for any Foreign Secretary to start by saying—"Now I begin everything afresh". One has steadily to transform the methods and position which one inherited, and that is being done . . . I really cannot straighten up the mess of Europe in six or seven weeks. . . .'[18] An 'Old Diplomat' could not have done better. Ponsonby was similarly cautious about his central dogma. 'With regard to the vexed question of parliamentary control' he wrote 'it is very difficult to see what the next step should be and you yourself are not quite

clear on the subject . . . *The test of time* appears to be the only
one that can really place this whole matter on permanently
satisfactory lines. No spectacular demonstration or resolution can
really help . . . As to the U.D.C., surely it does not exist merely
for the establishment of this one reform. . . .?'[19]

The Labour Government came to an end in November 1924. As
though symbolically, in the same month E. D. Morel died, a
disappointed and exhausted man. 'You know that I never trusted
J.R.' wrote Snowden at the end of the Government 'but he has
added to the attributes I knew, during the last nine months, an
incapacity I never thought him capable of.' It was a sad commentary on the dreams of a decade earlier. After the death of
Morel, the U.D.C. continued in existence but it was never again
quite the body it had once been. In the ten years it could claim
some credit for the fact that the 'old diplomacy' it had so bitterly
attacked had lost ground. There were, of course, other reasons for
this development. It was one of the ironies of the situation that
the man the U.D.C. most detested, Lloyd George, shared many
of their opinions and prejudices about the Foreign Office and
operated with little regard for its susceptibilities.

After 1924, most of the U.D.C. figures of the First World War
went their separate ways. Charles Roden Buxton had to be content
with a vigorous interest in international and colonial questions in
an advisory capacity outside the House of Commons. He lost his
seat at Accrington in December 1923, entered parliament again in
1929, only to be defeated in 1931. His book *The Alternative to War*,
published in 1936, demonstrates that his interest in the problem
of peace continued unabated. His consistent opposition to the
Treaty of Versailles, and the evils that he believed flowed from it,
placed him in an embarrassing position in the later thirties. Like
his brother Noel, Minister of Agriculture in both Labour Governments, he believed that appeasement was necessary. Mindful of
their experience in the First World War, much as they detested
Nazism, they believed that it was necessary to explore the possibility of reaching a negotiated peace with Germany.

Ponsonby's service in the first Labour Government reminded
him of the practical difficulties involved in conducting foreign
affairs, but it did not alter his pacifist convictions. In 1927 he was
responsible for drawing up a peace letter urging disarmament by
example. He claimed 150,000 signatures. 'I share your longing for
peace' the Prime Minister replied, 'God forbid that it should be
again disturbed. . . .' However, Baldwin did not believe that the
cause of peace would be served by making Britain impotent.[20] In
1928 Ponsonby published *Falsehood in War-Time*, 'an amazing
collection of carefully documented lies' and it had wide influence,

reaching a ninth impression by 1940. It had a consequence which he neither anticipated nor liked; it conditioned many in the thirties to be sceptical about the alleged atrocities taking place in Germany. In the second Labour Government, he first served as Under-Secretary at the Dominions Office, but later took a peerage in order to reinforce the Labour Party in the House of Lords. Despite an appeal from MacDonald, he refused to support the National Government in 1931, accepting instead Henderson's offer of the Opposition leadership in the Lords. However, Ponsonby did not abandon his quest for unilateral disarmament and this inevitably led him into difficulties with Henderson who was both Chairman of the Labour Party and Chairman of the Disarmament Conference at Geneva. A speech Ponsonby made in the House of Lords on 10 May 1932 brought the issue into the open. He wrote to George Lansbury, the acting Leader of the party—Henderson lost his seat in 1931—that he considered his position impossible. People urged him 'not to embarrass Henderson' but disarmament was so vital that he could not accept a restriction on his freedom of speech. Lansbury succeeded in smoothing things over—his own position on the question of pacifism was hardly comfortable. However, in November 1935 Ponsonby did resign in strong disagreement with the policy of trying to enforce sanctions against Italy. Leaving aside pure pacifist objections on grounds of war resistance or disarmament by example, he believed that all he had said about sanctions over twenty years had been proved true even beyond his expectation. Sanctions could neither be complete nor drastic and to stand any chance they needed some display of force behind them. As it was, they had greatly helped Mussolini in rallying public opinion in Italy and had done nothing to stop the war. Nobody detested Fascism or Nazism more than he did, but so long as external grievances remained, the dictators would be able to dominate their people. Thereafter Ponsonby continued to be critical of Labour Party policy and the advent of the Second World War did not cause him to change his pacifist convictions.

In both Labour Governments Charles Trevelyan had ministerial responsibility for education. This did not, however, prevent him from maintaining a strong interest in foreign affairs. He too strongly favoured disarmament, though not with quite the unilateral emphasis of Ponsonby. After the ignominious end of the second Labour Government, his views moved steadily to the left. At the Hastings Labour Party Conference in 1933 he sponsored a resolution pledging opposition to any war 'by organised working class action, including a general strike.' It was carried with acclamation. At the same time, however, support was also expressed for Henderson's advocacy of the League of Nations and 'collective security'. Trevelyan's own sympathies were with the Socialist League. In the month after Munich, Mrs. Swanwick passed on a report to Ponsonby that Charles was now the only 'militarist' in the Trevelyan family.[21] He had the rare distinction of beginning the Second World War at loggerheads with the Labour Party as he had begun the First in disagreement with the Liberal Party.

In the same letter, Mrs. Swanwick reflected 'Surely we cannot complain of lack of variety in our associates from time to time. I often wonder where E.D.M. would have stood, if he had lived till now. Would his French sense of "justesse" have held? or would his Communist leanings have dragged him over to the war-side?' Mrs. Swanwick herself continued to play an active part in many peace activities. She was very prominent in the Women's International League for Peace and Freedom. She was a member of the British Empire Delegation to the Fifth Assembly of the League of Nations in 1924. Between 1924 and 1928 she was the editor of *Foreign Affairs*. The organization of a 'Peace Pilgrimage' in 1926 urging the Foreign Secretary to accelerate disarmament was largely her work. Passionately opposed to what she termed 'incantations', she was happy in the occasion of her death in 1939.[22]

Reflecting on other early members of the U.D.C., she described Norman Angell as 'a sad case'. Angell records receiving blistering letters from her complaining of his 'betrayal of pacifism'. After the war, he entertained parliamentary ambitions, while still keeping up a formidable output of writing. His extended examination of the peace settlement, *The Fruits of Victory* gained high praise from Keynes—which was hardly surprising since its contentions were similar to his own. It was not until 1929, however, that his attempt to become a Labour M.P. was successful. At the next election two years later, he refused to stand again, having decided that the House of Commons was not for him. It was better to pursue his vocation as a writer and publicist. After 1931 he retained a certain sympathy for MacDonald and honours and books flowed thick and fast; a knighthood, the Nobel Peace Prize, *Preface to Peace, The Unseen Assassins, This Have and Have Not Business* and many other articles and essays. He was, however, no longer regarded by his erstwhile associates as a 'pacifist'. As to some extent had always been true from the early days of *The Great Illusion,* he remained an individualist amongst pacifists.[23]

Angell's position, both as regards politics and economics, was akin to that of J. A. Hobson. Although Hobson did stand as an Independent candidate in the General Election of 1918 he never seriously wanted a political career. His sympathies after the war were clearly with Labour, though he described himself as feeling a little uncomfortable in a body governed by trade union members and their finance on the one hand, and what he described as 'full-blooded Socialists', on the other. He believed that the great lesson of the war was that justice as well as charity began at home. It was impracticable to hope for peace and justice in international affairs when the conditions for peace and justice within the nations had not been obtained. He therefore associated himself prominently with the 'Living Wage' campaign. The weakness of the Peace Movement was, he felt, still what it had always been. Pacifism was a negative concept—'don't fight'—whereas there was always a positive dramatic concept associated with the call to arms. Reflection, he thought, undoubtedly disclosed the benefits of peace, but most people found mere reflection uninteresting. Disorder, insecurity, irregularity, 'the exciting', 'the unpredictable' were what touched the imagination. Above all, however, he told an audience at the South Place Ethical Society in 1932, 'we are brought up eventually against the barrier of sovereign nationality. So long as the process of social self-government is confined within this barrier, wars will remain not merely possible but inevitable.' How the barrier was to be removed, however, he never made clear. Looking at the continent of Europe at this time he deplored the 'facile acquiescence of whole people in the absolute dominion of self-appointed Masters.' When the people seemed so spineless in this situation, it seemed rather futile to talk about democratic control. He died in 1940 before it was clear just how absolute the dominion of the self-appointed Masters would become. He believed, however, that they had to be resisted.[24]

Brailsford was closely associated with Hobson on economic and other questions in the period between the wars. He also was an unsuccessful candidate in 1918. Thereafter, his efforts were mainly devoted to journalism. He edited the *New Leader* in the twenties and wrote numerous books, pamphlets and articles on international questions. His articles also appeared in the United States, often in the *New Republic*. In the twenties he constantly reiterated his contempt for the Treaty of Versailles and virtually held it responsible for all Europe's ills. He recognized that the dread of German militarism was sincere, but the French desire to dominate the continent was even more sinister. He lamented that the 'semi-Socialists' of 'half-starved Germany' had been given little chance.[25] His fiercest criticisms, however, were reserved for the peace settlement in Central Europe. The dismemberment of the Habsburg Monarchy was a tragedy and it was no answer to say that at the moment of the armistice it was inevitable. It had only become so because the nationalist extremists of these countries, encouraged by the secret treaties made by the Allies, had frustrated 'all the efforts of Viennese statesmanship to arrive at a federal solution.' National self-determination produced egotism and a damaging political and economic isolation. Whatever its faults, German culture had maintained a high level of attainment throughout the old Empire, and this level would now collapse. It was not even as though self-determination had been applied fairly, the worst case being the subjection of over three millions of Germans to Czech rule.'[26] By the later twenties, he became somewhat resigned to the fact that the frontiers could not be changed. The task therefore became to make them unimportant. While national cultures were to be respected he wrote that 'Socialist morality insists on rejecting or transforming the whole state of mind which one associates with nationalism.' Russia, he thought, had led the way by transforming the old Tsarist Empire into a Socialist Federation.

The political developments of the thirties pulled Brailsford in different directions. He continued to stress the folly of 'Balkanising' Europe and maltreating Germany. At the same time, he had to confess that the German nation, which in his view possessed the most highly trained intelligence in Europe, seemed to find democracy unworkable. National sovereignty was a piece of barbarism, but since it persisted, Germany was right to recover hers in the only possible way, 'by asserting it'. Hitler was right to smash the fetters of Versailles.[27] This sympathy did not mean that Brailsford had abandoned his underlying interpretation of the international situation. 'War in the modern world' he wrote in *Property or Peace?* (1934) 'is an outgrowth of the system of property. When men will to banish war, they must abandon the exclusive and monopolist institution of property. . . .'[28] However, the immediate problem was that the revival of Germany threatened the Soviet Union. A Liberal might still plead for conciliation, but a Socialist perceived the digging of the trenches in an international class war. Socialists all over Europe would have to defend the Soviet Union. Stalin's show trials, however, came as a severe shock to Brailsford. No path now ran clearly through the debris and 'after this bloodbath one has to realize that in a land where loyal opposition is impossible there can be neither stability nor health.'[29] Stalin was now a 'barbarian' who shot men on fantastic charges. He found Hitler equally brutal, yet in a crisis like that of September 1938 it was impossible to erase his strongly expressed support for the Sudeten Germans. Those who had known Brailsford in the First World War might have been surprised to find him writing an Open Letter to readers of the *New Republic* in June 1940 urging them to 'Banish from your daily lives the values and psychology of peace. Train your young men in the whole accursed art of war. Postpone . . . every civilized purpose, every humane ambition.'[30]

Lowes Dickinson died in 1932 and did not have to face the political dilemmas of the thirties. Not by temperament an organizer or politician, he devoted himself after the war to writing a fair account of the origins of the conflict. He had been shocked by what he regarded as the prejudices of academic historians in universities. In 1926, when he was quite optimistic about the international situation, he published *The International Anarchy*. 'I know that this is a good book' he recorded privately. 'I believe it to be possibly the best book on the subject, because it is the only one I know which stresses the only important fact, that it is not this or that nation nor its policy, but the anarchy that causes wars.' The book was widely and favourably reviewed, but Dickinson found its sales disappointing. This was, he thought, 'another testimony to the general truth that truth is the last thing people care about. . . .' In this verdict he was too pessimistic. His book became, for a time, the standard interpretation of the origins of the war and a generation of undergraduates was raised upon it. For better or worse, it constituted his lasting legacy to the study of war and peace.[31]

No simple conclusion emerges from this brief examination of the subsequent careers of some leading U.D.C. figures. 'Even the most perfectly organised society' wrote Reinhold Niebuhr 'must seek for a decent equilibrium of the vitalities and powers under its organisation. If this is not done, strong disproportions of power develop, and whenever power is inordinate, injustice develops.'[32] The U.D.C. writers correctly diagnosed some of the evils of their world, yet in their pursuit of peace they underestimated the fundamental problems of power. They insisted that there was a particular point in time when it would be possible to banish war. That point of time would be, variously, when domestic grievances were removed, when capitalism was destroyed or when nationalism was overcome. MacDonald tried in vain to keep this optimism in check. 'Do remember that this is going to be a pretty long game' he warned J. A. Hobson in 1924 'and that reserves will have to be poured in at the right point and at the right time. To destroy the militarist spirit of France is my first object.'[33] If the object is no longer the same, the game is still being played.

The nature of the N.C.F.'s pacifism was even more unclear at the end of the war than it had been at the beginning. Naturally, with the signing of the armistice, there were renewed calls for the release of conscientious objectors. However, it was difficult for the Government to take such a step ahead of men who had actually fought. Supporters of the conscientious objectors expressed dark fears that conscription would continue to disfigure British life for many years. As for the objectors themselves, the delay led to hunger strikes and organized attempts to disrupt prison life. The most conspicuous example of this latter policy was at Wandsworth prison. As a result the Governor was 'sent on leave' and his successor found conditions in a state of near anarchy. Some of the absolutists tried to restrain their colleagues from their physical and verbal assaults on the prison authorities, but with scant success. As has been observed, those who advocated restraint soon discovered that 'in an open conflict with authority, the anarchists were contemptuous of the convictions that motivated the majority of conscientious objectors.'[34] Order was restored, but there was now, ironically, strong pressure from the War Office to release conscientious objectors as soon as possible. In the succeeding months, they were released in stages and the last batch, in January, was drawn from the Non-Combatant Corps.

While the men were still detained, the N.C.F. kept up a campaign for their release. Apart from this activity, however, many doubted whether the N.C.F. could survive merely on the legacy of its war-time experiences. Some argued that it was composed of men and women holding such divergent views that combination for more than one temporary object during the war would prove impossible. Christians should return to their churches and chapels and Socialists should devote their energies to the Labour Movement. Initially, Fenner Brockway argued against this advice. He thought that conscription would be retained and therefore the banding together of men and women who would refuse to take part in, or prepare for, war was necessary and important. While he naturally supported the I.L.P., it would be unlikely to become a party whose membership was limited to those who would pledge themselves to refuse any kind of war service. He therefore urged that the N.C.F. should be 'a great missionary body inside the Socialist and Christian movements, and be recognised as a Peace Society which would be counted on retaining its Pacifism in times of war.'[35] This appeal was too emotional for the ever-critical C. H. Norman. Talk of a great missionary movement was all very well, but it had to be recognized that most of the financial subsidies came from one side of the movement. The inevitable result, he considered, was that an anti-militarist organization, founded on pacifist principles, had been transformed into a non-resistance organization inspired by passivism and submissiveness. In peacetime he believed that the temperamental differences between the anti-militarist section and the passivist section of the N.C.F. would become much more accentuated. In his opinion, the activism of the general strike was the true method of preventing war and the passivism of mere resistance to military service was quite futile.[36]

Edward Grubb, Quaker treasurer of the Fellowship since July

1915, was well aware of Norman's target. 'Never once within my remembrance' he countered 'has any subscriber not in membership with us attempted to control or influence the decisions of the committee in any way.' From the very beginning the committee was itself divided along the lines that Norman had outlined and 'outside control' was a myth.[37] On the other hand, W. J. Chamberlain did not think that Norman's division of the membership into 'anti-militarists' and 'passivists' was accurate. It did not correspond to his own experience. Norman wrongly implied that anyone who did not happen to agree with one or other of the methods adopted by the 'activists' was not 'anti-militarist'. The real division, he considered, was between 'anti-militarists' and 'anti-capitalist-militarists'. The N.C.F. would have to make up its mind on this issue. Personally, he would rather have a thousand members who were against the militarism of the capitalist.[38]

The question was not entirely academic. The members had before them the example of the Bolsheviks, and the figure of Lenin produced strong reactions. His form of society might be ideal, but because of the way he had set about organizing it, Aylmer Rose called him 'the most dangerous and undesirable man in Europe, and the sooner we all set to work to combat his ideas the better, lest our country follow Russia into an anarchy of bloodshed, the end of which no one can even guess.'[39] Others were ardent defenders of Russia. W. J. Chamberlain thought that just as pacifism should not be simply equated with anti-capitalism, so it should not be identified with anti-Socialism. Dr. Salter, on the other hand, argued in favour of a body which stressed pacifism, pure and simple. He recognized that probably three quarters of the N.C.F. membership were convinced Socialists, partly I.L.P. and partly from the extreme left. There had been lately a landslide towards the left and he doubted whether a third of the membership now believed all war to be wrong. He contended that in the post-war world there would be a need for a coherent body of firm pacifists. Such would never result from a temporary alliance of Tolstoyan pacifists, physical force anarchists and anti-capitalist-militarists. The only way to get a coherent body was to draw up an agreed statement of belief.[40] However, a special conference in August 1919 recognized the impossibility of reaching such an agreed position. It was therefore decided to disband the Fellowship. Clifford Allen, at the closing meeting, praised the N.C.F. for keeping alive the spirit of international goodwill and uniting men and women in personal testimony to their pacifist faith. The dissolution of the N.C.F. in 1919 was testimony to the fact that the tension in which it had constantly lived was insupportable. Its members stressed the absolute right of the individual, yet at the same time as Socialists, condemned individualism.

Although the N.C.F. died, it was not long before some of its former members started their own organization, the No More War Movement. It developed out of a conference in London during February 1921 presided over by W. J. Chamberlain. Soon afterwards, a member of its committee, Wilfrid Wellock, attended an Anti-Militarist Congress at The Hague. From this meeting emerged the War Resisters' International. 'War Resistance' was the keynote of this post-war pacifism. Its outlook was 'active' rather than 'passive' The leading members of the two bodies worked in close collaboration with the I.L.P. of which they were also members. In 1926, Walter Ayles, formerly a member of the N.C.F. committee, was appointed Organizing Secretary. Branches were established all over the country, the Chairman, Fenner Brockway, making good use of the contacts built up during the war. Propaganda campaigns and public meetings were held in large cities and the notion of 'resistance to war' was attractive. In 1926 the I.L.P. Annual Conference passed a resolution stressing the need for immediate disarmament and war resistance—any threat of war would be met by refusal to bear arms, make them, or in any way assist the war effort. Moved and seconded by Brockway and Ponsonby, the same proposal was also accepted by the Labour Conference of that year. The resolution seemed to be a vindication of the N.C.F. outlook. A surprising number of its members and supporters were already in parliament: Morgan Jones for Caerphilly in 1921, C. G. Ammon for Camberwell North in 1922, J. H. Hudson for Huddersfield in 1923, C. H. Wilson for Sheffield, Attercliffe in 1922, A. Salter for Bermondsey West in 1922 and W. H. Ayles for Bristol North in 1923.

Despite the 1926 Conference victory, 'war resistance' did not become the dominant outlook in the Labour Party. The ex-N.C.F. men were not strong enough in number to dominate party policy on the question of war and peace. There was a great deal of sympathy for their position, but not enough intellectual agreement with it. Despite the fact that the 1926 resolution was moved by Brockway and Ponsonby, the N.C.F. and U.D.C. streams in the Labour Party did not really join forces. There was a little in Brockway's contention that the U.D.C. was for gentlemen and the N.C.F. for players. It was also the case that junior office in the Labour Governments tempered the pacifism of men like Ammon and Jones. Some pacifists found it a little surprising that Ammon followed up his post as Parliamentary Secretary to the N.C.F. by serving as Parliamentary Secretary to the First Lord of the Admiralty in the two Labour Governments. The arrival of Wellock, Sorensen and Brockway to the Commons in 1929 was not sufficient reinforcement to the ranks of 'No More War'. MacDonald and Henderson disliked each other's approaches to foreign policy but they both had little time for absolute pacifism.

The impotence of the No More War Movement was closely connected with the squabbles which led to the break between the I.L.P. and the Labour Party. It could not bridge the gap between those who wanted the I.L.P. to stick to 'Socialism' and those who felt that the party had no future on its own. Once again, at the heart of the matter was the tension between adherence to a supposed principle and the practical need for influence. 'The impression was being created' said a speaker at the 1929 conference 'that the I.L.P. was a small self-righteous sect. . . . It was looked upon as sectarian and its effort to make Socialists was weakened rather than strengthened.' There is some irony in the fact that the speaker was C. R. Buxton. The sectarian impulse was, however, too strong for many to resist it, at least temporarily. Separation from the Labour Party may have preserved the purity of the I.L.P. but its effect was to heighten the tension between pacifism and revolution. When Fenner Brockway realized that he wanted the anarchists to win the Spanish Civil War, he concluded that it was 'not the amount of violence used which determined good or evil results, but the ideas, the sense of human values.' Apparently, when he came to this discovery, the basis of his old pacifist philosophy disappeared. Every day that capitalism lasted, he wrote, the principle of pacifism was being denied as surely as when war was actually taking place. The resentment of the working class against 'bourgeois capitalism' was fully justified. Alfred Salter of Bermondsey, on the other hand, remained a convinced Christian pacifist until the end of his life. He regarded willingness to be conquered by Nazi Germany and the martyrdom which would follow as the test of pacifism.[41]

Allen, Russell and Miss Marshall all followed different paths in the post-war world. The effect of their war-time experiences on their public and personal lives was immense. Clifford Allen's health, always delicate, never fully recovered from his imprisonment. He did try to re-enter politics, becoming Chairman of the I.L.P. for a short while. He resigned in 1925 after a clash with Maxton and it seemed that his political career was over. In 1931, however, he emerged as a defender of MacDonald in the great crisis of the second Labour Government. He supported the National Labour Party and received a peerage. He was regarded by many of his erstwhile colleagues in the N.C.F. as a complete turncoat, although he naturally saw his conduct in a different light. His personal belief in unilateral disarmament was unchanged but he realized that the country would not accept such a course. 'I therefore consider it to be my duty' he wrote in 1935 'not merely to protect the integrity of my own conscience, but to make what contribution I can to urging a world, which adheres to a belief in force, to use it collectively for the sake of peace through the process of law.'[42] At the height of the crisis of September 1938 he pleaded for restraint and understanding. His final efforts to promote peace drained his feeble strength. Six months after war was averted, Allen was dead.

During the war, and immediately afterwards, Allen considered himself a disciple of Bertrand Russell. The two men, together with Charles Roden Buxton, went to Russia in 1920 as members of a British Labour delegation. Russell and Allen did not interpret what they saw in the same light and their personal and political relations sharply deteriorated. The intensively subjective nature of Russell's 'pacifism' became clear from his subsequent comments and actions. Despite the prominent part he had played in the N.C.F. he had always stated that his view of pacifism was never quite the same as anyone else's. This truth was amply confirmed between the wars. In 1936, after some hesitation, he wrote to Ponsonby that he was prepared to sign the P.P.U. pledge to renounce war and never support another.[43] It seemed, therefore, that he had become an absolutist. However, when war broke out in 1939 he decided that it was necessary to defeat Hitler because there could not be any lasting peace in the world while the German dictator prospered. The course of world history in the next thirty years was to give him ample opportunity for further oscillation.

Miss Marshall's subsequent career was a sad one. She never recovered her health fully and her personal hopes were dashed. Some of her female associates had never been happy about her brilliant excursion into the world of the N.C.F. and they, at least, were pleased when she concentrated her peace work in the Women's International League for Peace and Freedom. When the Second World War came she too believed that Hitler had to be defeated.

The refusal of the N.C.F. and of many Quakers to be compelled to fight raised in acute form the problem of obligation in society. Until the First World War, it was an issue which, in this particular form, the British had largely been able to avoid. In the last resort, the objection of the pacifist to fighting was not one which could be touched by rational discussion. The spectacle of the Tribunals set up by the Government to assess 'conscience' therefore has its ludicrous aspects. There was ample room for conflict and mis-understanding between the Government and the objector. It is arguable, however, that in time of war a Government is entitled to restrict activity which might jeopardize the survival of the majority. A philosopher has taken an imaginary example of a country attacked by a barbaric enemy. The country contained a minority of Quakers so large that their exemption would ensure its military defeat. 'It would seem that in that case' he argues 'the government should introduce conscription without exemptions. This would force those of weaker faith to fight. The government would have to punish those whose faith held out, though it would admire them more. . . .'[44] This is, however, very much a philosopher's example. It was indeed precisely the aim of the absolutist pacifist in the First World War to create such a large minority that no nation would ever contemplate going to war. The difficulty with the example lies in the idea of 'punishing' a large faithful minority in war-time. Such an act would not, in a mysterious way, render the nation more effective as a fighting unit. The organizational problems would be such that it would be easier to leave the minority alone—supposing that the minority was not actively subversive and seeking the victory of the enemy. It is probably the case that during the First World War the imprison-ment of the absolutists and the whole system of Tribunals led to a greater waste of time and resources than if absolute exemption had been granted at the outset. Whatever the force of this sug-gestion, the members of the old N.C.F. could subsequently claim with justice that they had established their principle firmly. Opposition to conscription in peacetime remained a principle which no British politician could afford to ignore.

The League of Nations Union, the last to be formed, was the most influential body in post-war British politics of all the peace organizations which have so far been considered. Until the disillusionment of the later thirties, no other pressure group could rival its influence on the conduct of foreign affairs. Yet, despite the appearance of prestige and influence, the Union's supporters were by no means in full agreement on the role it should play. Some considered that it was primarily an educational body, disseminating information about the League and building up a body of informed opinion in its support. Others believed that the L.N.U. was a political body, influencing the policy of the Government of the day on League matters. Throughout the inter-war period, the leaders wavered uneasily between these two objectives. On the one hand, it was a non-party organization sup-ported by the three main parties; on the other, the fact was that its leaders were all prominently associated with particular parties.

It was also well known that the bland assertions of support for the League made by successive governments did not necessarily correspond with the private sentiments of ministers.

Partly for these reasons, the relation of the L.N.U. to the 'Peace Movement' was highly ambiguous. Personal animosities complicated the situation. Many of the pacifists of the First World War felt that Gilbert Murray, David Davies and Lord Robert Cecil, to name but three, who had keenly supported the war, could hardly be called pacifists. E. D. Morel and Gilbert Murray, for example, engaged in a furious correspondence in August 1919 concerning their views on the war. Murray concluded from this exchange that the subject was still too raw to permit much co-operation.[45] In 1922, Morel was still writing that so long as the L.N.U.'s leaders insisted on Germany's sole responsibility for the war 'what real contribution can the Union, or the League itself for that matter, make to the healing of the world. . . .'[46] MacDonald, too, privately expressed contempt for Murray's wartime attitude. In 1923, he had his opportunity for revenge. He refused an honorary position in the L.N.U. on the grounds that he had been slighted by members of the Union who disapproved of his wartime 'pacifism'. 'The views I hold today' he told Murray grandly 'are the views I held from 1914 onwards and those who objected to them then, must object to them still. . . .' J. A. Hobson was somewhat more conciliatory. 'Bad as I hold the present form of the League to be' he wrote '. . . I have always argued both in America and here in favour of seeking to amend the present League rather than trying to set up another.' Ponsonby was temperate but thought that on the whole he was better out of the Union. 'They may be able to do good work with jingos and moderates' he wrote 'but in order to free the League of Nations and to make it a real force we must denounce the Peace Treaties and get rid of the myth of Germany's sole responsibility.' He regretted to have to say that some L.N.U. people he had met were very far from adopting this standpoint.[47]

The leaders of the Union were therefore in a constant quandary. Individuals and groups tried to push it in opposite directions. Someone like David Davies was constantly pressing for a more ambitious scheme than the existing League. Having pointed out the 'Flaw in the Covenant' he moved on to remedy it with a proposal for a Tribunal for the compulsory settlement of international disputes and an international police force to carry out its decisions. He worked uneasily within the L.N.U., chiefly in Wales. He founded the Chair of International Politics at University College, Aberystwyth, though its first occupant, A. E. Zimmern, was anxious not to be regarded as simply a propagandist for the League. Davies poured money into the Welsh Council of the L.N.U. and was encouraged by a memorial from the women of Wales to the United States urging it to join the League. Even so, he was not satisfied. At one time, he bought the moribund *Review of Reviews* and tried to run it as a vehicle for his ideas, though unsuccessfully. He wrote books of very considerable length and finally set up an organization, the *New Commonwealth* to propagate their message. Davies' ideas caused the L.N.U. hierarchy some embarrassment, though the loss of his money threatened to cause even more. So long as he confined his activities to the astonishingly peaceful principality, conflict could be avoided.

Davies was a man of strong personal views and the capacity to give them publicity. Ever since his intervention in 1918 he had been regarded with some suspicion by what might be termed the soft centre of the L.N.U. membership. Given the attitude adopted by prominent Labour 'pacifists' in the twenties it seemed tempting to many not to talk of international police forces but to underplay the possible use of force in carrying out collective security altogether. Writing to Cecil in 1939, Murray admitted that in the early years the Union had 'talked too much pacifism and did not sufficiently insist on the reign of law.'[48] This policy was to some extent successful in softening Labour objections, but there were obvious limits beyond which the policy could not be followed without jeopardizing the whole framework of the Covenant. In December 1926, for example, the Executive Committee of the L.N.U. refused to accept an advertisement for a big meeting in the Albert Hall organized by Ponsonby in favour of unilateral disarmament. It was felt that to accept such a notice would be to appear to support Ponsonby's position. Subsequently, Philip Noel-Baker complained that while previously Labour was coming round to the League 'in the last six months they have *positively moved away* and they are in great danger of becoming actively and universally hostile.'[49]

However, unless attempts were made to distinguish the L.N.U.'s position on collective security and disarmament from that of absolute pacifists, any pretence that it could also claim to speak for Conservatives would collapse completely. In the twenties there were many complaints that at the local level, L.N.U. branches were dominated by members of the Liberal and Labour parties, some of whom were in fact virtually absolute pacifists. Writing in the journal of the No More War Movement about the L.N.U., Walter Ayles put the relationship between 'absolutes' and 'moderates' rather neatly. He claimed that the members of the L.N.U. accepted no obligations as to their actions in an international crisis. It therefore included absolute pacifists like himself and 'militarists like Lord Cushendun'. Obviously, he continued, if war broke out the L.N.U. would dissolve, and even in a crisis its action would be equivocal. Nevertheless, the Union was 'a necessary part of our tactic for peace. The L.N.U. doesn't officially like the N.M.W.M. because we are too thorough. The N.M.W.M. however, does like the L.N.U., but we do not think it very courageous.'[50]

The difficulty was that there was no Conservative politician in good standing with his party who played a prominent part in the L.N.U.'s activities. Here again, as to some extent had been true during the war, Lord Robert Cecil's single-minded devotion to the League was a doubtful asset. His activities in the early twenties, trying to form a Centre Party with Grey as a possible Prime Minister, had not gone unnoticed. In November 1922 he wrote to Murray that he would 'rather see a League Government in power than an anti-League Conservative one, and I shall not hesitate to act on that opinion. I will do what I can to keep the Conservatives straight.'[51] Not all Conservatives liked being kept straight by Cecil. When he joined the Conservative Government in 1925, he was constantly at loggerheads with some of his colleagues on League of Nations and disarmament matters. In 1927 he at last resigned. In a letter to the Foreign Secretary, Sir Austen Chamberlain, he explained that his difficulty was not that his colleagues had behaved badly towards him. It was more simple. They did not agree with him. He believed that a world congress for disarmament was the most important step in the pacification of the world. They did not.[52]

The alienation of the L.N.U. from the National Governments of the thirties became more and more pronounced. Its relationship to the upsurge of absolute pacifism associated with the Peace Pledge Union became increasingly confused. Cecil's decision to press for a National Declaration—what later became known as the Peace Ballot, caused much anger among Conservatives. Sir Austen Chamberlain declared that his sleeping partnership in the Union had become a shirt of nessus which he could no longer endure.[53] The National Declaration was by no means a 'pacifist' document, yet the notion that it was a 'Peace' Ballot was confusing. When the results were made public, there can be little doubt that the Government was compelled to pay more formal respect to the League than would otherwise have been the case. Yet, despite this impressive result, the influence of the L.N.U. steadily declined after 1935. There were policy differences, personal difficulties and problems of organization. Resignations multiplied. Many former supporters now declared that the European situation was so different from that imagined by those who had framed the League that the Covenant was no longer relevant. New times produced new allies. In 1927 Cecil lamented that Churchill was out of sympathy with the whole conception of disarmament. 'War' he commented 'is the only thing that interests him in politics.'[54] In 1932 he wrote to Ponsonby: 'I often wonder what Party I belong to, but it certainly is not that which owns Winston Churchill—if there is such a party.'[55] Four years later Churchill and Cecil corresponded on apparently friendly terms and both agreed on the necessity for 'Arms and the Covenant'. Writing to Ponsonby a fortnight after Munich, Mrs. Swanwick excoriated what she termed 'the whole L.N.U. crowd'. What incalculable harm they had done to the English conception of a useful League! By 1939, many absolutists found a certain malicious delight in the fact that the League of Nations Union, the great exponent of 'realism' had conspicuously failed.

The pacifists of the First World War did little to influence the course of the fighting. Only at particular moments did their activities assume fleeting importance. They did, however, leave their mark on Britain between the wars. After 1919, victory did not bring a brave new world and there was an understandable inclination to remember only the horrors of war. In this situation, to a deserved reputation for courage and independence of thought, pacifists added an undeserved claim to wisdom. Perhaps the greatest testimony to the inadequacy of its ideology lay in the Peace Movement itself. The peace societies preached the possibility of permanent unity and concord on a universal scale, yet on their own small scale exhibited few signs of co-operation between themselves. New societies were formed supposedly to develop slight shades of conviction on a particular problem. Existing societies became jealous and manoeuvred to maintain their status. Pacifists constantly condemned 'power politics', yet, within the Peace Movement the struggle for mastery constantly showed itself both between individuals and groups. They ostracized their opponents as fiercely as they were themselves ostracized. The danger to good government, wrote Lord Acton in his sweeping fashion, 'is not that a particular class is unfit to govern. Every class is unfit to govern.' It was a truth which the Peace Movement only slowly accepted.

THE END

References

CHAPTER ONE

1. *The Herald of Peace*, April 1912.
2. *The Herald of Peace*, July 1912.
3. *The Herald of Peace*, October 1912; W. E. Darby, *The Claims of the 'New Pacifism'* (London, 1913).
4. D. James, *Lord Roberts* (London, 1954); D. Newsome, *Godliness and Good Learning* (London, 1961); T. Ropp, 'Conscription in Great Britain, 1900-1914: A Failure in Civil-Military Communications?', *Military Affairs*, 20 (1956).
5. N. Angell, *The Great Illusion* (London, 1910) pp. 26-8, 242, 280, 297.
6. Angell MS, Angell to MacDonald, 8 and 13 June 1912.
7. Cited in E. B. and P. J. Noel Baker, *J. Allen Baker, M.P. A Memoir* (London, 1927) pp. 161-3; H. C. White, *Willoughby Hyett Dickinson, A Memoir* (Gloucester, 1956).
8. *The Peacemaker*, July 1911.
9. *The Peacemaker*, February 1912, March 1913, June 1913, June 1914.
10. *The Peace Year Book 1914* (London, 1914).
11. *Peace Committee Minutes*, May 1912, April 1913, October 1913.
12. M. Anderson, *Noel Buxton. A Life* (London, 1952 p. 46.
13. A. Ponsonby, *Democracy and the Control of Foreign Affairs* (London, 1912) p. 29.
14. Cited in K. G. Robbins, 'British Diplomacy and Bulgaria, 1914-1915', *Slavonic and East European Review*, October 1971, 567.
15. *Monthly Circular of the National Peace Council*, Special Supplement, June 1912.
16. *The Socialist Review*, January 1913.
17. N. Angell, *War and the Workers* (London, n.d., 1913?) pp. 16, 37-8.
18. *The Socialist Review*, March 1913.
19. J. R. MacDonald, *Labour and War* (London, 1912).
20. J. A. Hobson, *Imperialism. A Study* (London, 1938 ed.) pp. 47, 93, 171; *The Crisis of Liberalism* (London, 1909) p. x.
21. H. N. Brailsford, *The War of Steel and Gold* (London, 1914) pp. 27, 35.
22. *The Herald of Peace*, June 1914.
23. C. Trebilcock, 'Legends of the British Armaments Industry, 1890-1914: A Revision', *Journal of Contemporary History*, 5, 4 (1970) p. 7.

CHAPTER TWO

1. Ponsonby MS, Ponsonby to Lloyd George, September 1912.
2. Ponsonby MS, Letter to Grey and notes of a conversation with him, 29 July 1914; Ponsonby to Asquith, 30 July 1914.

3. Asquith, *Memories and Reflections* (London, 1928) Vol. II, p. 7.
4. T. E. Harvey to W. Harvey, 30 July 1914 cited in C. Hazlehurst, *Politicians at War* (London, 1971) p. 39.
5. Ponsonby MS, Churchill to Ponsonby, 31 July 1914.
6. Ponsonby MS, Resolution of a meeting of Liberal members held during the adjournment of the House 3 August 1914.
7. Scott to Angell, 5 August 1914 in N. Angell, *After All* (London, 1951) p. 185.
8. *Proceedings of the International Polity Summer School, July 1914* (London, 1915) p. 30; R. O. Kapp, *The Failure of Sociology* (London, 1914) pp. 31-2; *War and Peace,* August 1914.
9. *The Herald of Peace,* October 1914.
10. J. Clifford, *The War and the Churches* (London, 1914) p. 8.
11. A. R. Fry, *A Quaker Adventure* (London, 1926) p. xix; *Report of the London Yearly Meeting of Friends, 1915* (London, 1915) p. 99; J. Dudley, *The Life of Edward Grubb, 1854-1939* (London, 1946) pp. 104-5.
12. M. E. Hirst, *The Quakers in Peace and War* (London, 1923) p. 538.
13. G. D. H. Cole, *Labour in War Time* (London, 1915) pp. 24-5.
14. Cited in P. Stansky, *The Left and War* (London, 1969) pp. 57-8; *The Socialist Review,* October-December 1914.
15. Cole, *Labour in War Time,* p. 32.
16. W. Kendall, *The Revolutionary Movement in Britain, 1900-21* (London, 1969) pp. 87-9.
17. J. Marlowe, *Late Victorian, The Life of Sir Arnold Wilson* (London, 1967) p. 76.
18. Burns MS, Diary 27 July 1914; E. Hobhouse to Burns, 4 August 1914.
19. Trevelyan MS, Trevelyan to Runciman, 1 August 1900.
20. Morel MS, Ponsonby to Morel, n.d. ? September 1914.
21. Trevelyan MS, 'The Question of Belgian Neutrality' P. J. Baker.
22. Runciman MS, Trevelyan to Runciman, 4 August 1914.
23. Trevelyan MS, Memorandum 'British Democratic League or a British League for uniting the democracies of Europe' n.d.
24. Morel MS, Trevelyan to Morel, 5 August 1914.
25. Morel MS, Trevelyan to Morel, 20 February 1913.
26. Trevelyan MS, G. M. Trevelyan to C. P. Trevelyan, 8 August 1914.
27. Murray MS, B. Hammond to Lady M. Murray, 19 August 1914.
28. Burns MS, L. T. Hobhouse to Burns, 6 August 1914.
29. For further details see M. Swartz, *The Union of Democratic Control in British Politics during the First World War* (Oxford, 1971) pp. 28-33.
30. Bryce MS, Trevelyan to Bryce, 2 September 1914. See also K. G. Robbins, 'Lord Bryce and the First World War' *The Historical Journal,* X, 2 (1967).
31. Scott MS, Memoranda 3 and 4 September 1914.
32. Morel MS, Birkenhead Liberal Association to Morel 28 September 1914.
33. Ponsonby MS, Trevelyan to Ponsonby 14 September 1914.
34. Morel MS, Scott to Morel, 10 September 1914.
35. Scott MS, Trevelyan to Scott, 13 September 1914.
36. Morel MS, Scott to Morel, 24 September 1914.
37. Morel MS, Rowntree to Morel, 5 October 1914. Rowntree offered to resign his parliamentary seat, but his constituency association asked him to stay. E. Vipont, *Arnold Rowntree. A Life* (London, 1955) p. 66.
38. Ponsonby MS, Morrell to Ponsonby, 1 September 1914.
39. Trevelyan MS, Trevelyan to H. Samuel, 31 January 1905.

40. Murray MS, MacDonald to Murray, 28 August 1914 and 2 September 1914.
41. Republished in G. Murray, *Faith, War and Policy* (London, 1917) p. 7.
42. U.D.C. Collection.
43. Bryce MS, Trevelyan to Bryce, 28 September 1914.
44. Morel MS, MacDonald to Morel, 8 September 1914.
45. Murray MS, MacDonald to Murray, 6 October 1914; Lord Elton, *The Life of James Ramsay MacDonald* (London, 1939) p. 263.
46. Morel MS, MacDonald to Morel, 24 August 1914.
47. Personal information; Lady K. Courtney, *Extracts from a Diary during the War* (Privately published, 1927) p. 12.
48. A. D. Lindsay, 'The Political Theory of Mr. Norman Angell', *The Political Quarterly,* December 1914.
49. Morel MS, Morel to Trevelyan, 6 November 1914.
50. Lansbury MS, Trevelyan to Lansbury, 7 August 1914.
51. *The Herald,* 26 September 1914.
52. Lansbury MS, Salter to Lansbury, 27 September 1914.
53. *The Socialist Review,* October-December 1914, Editorial; 'Secret Diplomacy' F. W. Jowett; 'Socialism during the War' J. R. MacDonald.
54. *The Labour Leader,* 12 November 1914.
55. *The Socialist Review,* October-December 1914 'History Repeats Itself' Keir Hardie; W. Stewart, *J. Keir Hardie* (London, 1921) pp. 316-17).
56. H. G. Wood, *H. T. Hodgkin. A Memoir* (London, 1937) pp. 152-3.
57. For further information see W. E. Orchard, *From Faith to Faith* (London, 1933); M. Royden, *A Threefold Cord* (London, 1948); G. Lansbury, *My Life* (London, 1928) p. 211; ed. J. M. Fry, *Christ and Peace.* (London, 1915).
58. H. M. Swanwick, *I Have Been Young* (London, 1935) pp. 245-7.
59. Morel MS, Morel to Royden, 9 September 1914; Swanwick to Morel, 21 September 1914.
60. Marshall MS, Miss I. O. Ford to Marshall, 25 October 1914; Ethel N. Williams to Marshall, 31 December 1914.
61. Morel MS, Swanwick to Morel, 21 September 1914.
62. J. A. Hobson, *Confessions of an Economic Heretic* (London, 1938) p. 93.

CHAPTER THREE

1. E. M. Forster, *Goldsworthy Lowes Dickinson* (London 1934); Ashbee MS, Dickinson to Mrs. C. R. Ashbee, 15 August 1914; *War and Peace,* September 1914; C. R. Ashbee, Diary 4 November 1914.
2. Ashbee MS, Dickinson to Mrs. C. R. Ashbee, 4 November 1914; Bryce MS, Dickinson to Bryce, 20 October 1914.
3. Ashbee MS, Dickinson to Ashbee, n.d. November 1914; H. R. Winkler, *The League of Nations Movement in Great Britain, 1914-1919* (New Brunswick, N.J., 1952) now needs to be supplemented by M. D. Dubin, 'Toward the Concept of Collective Security: The Bryce Group's "Proposals for the Avoidance of War" 1914-1917', *International Organization,* xxiv, 2, 1970 and W. F. Kuehl, *Seeking World Order, The United States and International Organization to 1920* (Nashville, 1969) pp. 186ff.
4. Ed. M. Cole, *Beatrice Webb's Diaries, 1912-24* (London, 1952) p. 30.
5. L. S. Woolf, *Beginning Again. An Autobiography of the Years 1911-18* (London, 1964) pp 177-191.
6. *War and Peace,* January 1915.

7. *War and Peace,* February 1915.
8. J. A. Hobson, *Towards International Government* (London, 1915) pp. 21-2, 37, 89, 95-6, 183; *A League of Nations,* U.D.C. Pamphlet No. 15A.
9. The League of Nations Society, *Explanation of the Objects of the Society* (Letchworth, 1916).
10. Dickinson to Ponsonby, 2 April 1915 in Forster, *Dickinson,* p. 165.
11. G. L. Dickinson, *The Foundations of a League of Peace* (Boston, 1915).
12. G. L. Dickinson, *After the War* (London, 1915) p. 13.
13. Ashbee MS, Dickinson to Ashbee, January 1915.
14. Marshall MS, Dickinson to Marshall, April 1915.
15. W. H. Dickinson MS, Lowell to G. L. Dickinson, 17 August 1915.
16. *War and Peace,* March 1915.
17. U.D.C. Pamphlet No. 1 *The Morrow of the War.*
18. U.D.C. Pamphlet No. 2 *Shall this war end German militarism?* N. Angell.
19. Trevelyan MS, Denman to Trevelyan, 28 May 1915; Ponsonby to Trevelyan, 22 May 1915; Ponsonby MS, Trevelyan to Ponsonby, 27 May 1915; Morel MS, Morel to Trevelyan, June 1915.
20. C. R. Buxton MS, Buxton to V. de Bunsen, 21 August 1914; to his wife, 5 October 1914. See also Robbins 'British Diplomacy and Bulgaria'.
21. C. R. Buxton MS, Buxton to Bryce, 10 June 1915; Bryce to Buxton, 25 June 1915; Buxton to Bryce, 30 June 1915.
22. C. R. Buxton MS, 'The Case for Negotiation' September 1915.
23. C. R. Buxton MS, Bryce to Buxton, 17 September 1915; Morley to Buxton, 27 September 1915; Courtney of Penwith to Buxton, 14 September 1915; Archbishop of Canterbury to Buxton, 30 September 1915; MacDonald to Buxton, 8 October 1915.
24. C. R. Buxton MS, Loreburn to Buxton, 23 September 1915; Denman to Buxton, 12 October 1915; Burns MS, Loreburn to Burns, 26 July 1915.
25. C. R. Buxton MS, Private information; Buxton to his wife, 15 May 1917; C. G. Coulton, *Pacificist Illusions* (Cambridge, 1915).
26. Trevelyan MS, Wedgwood to Morel, 18 September 1915.
27. *Report of the London Yearly Meeting of Friends, 1915* (London, 1915) pp. 97-8.
28. *The Friend,* 16 and 23 April 1915.
29. *The Friend,* 28 May 1915.
30. *The Friend,* 26 February, 1915.
31. *Peace Comittee and Meeting for Sufferings Minutes,* July-August 1915.
32. *Meeting for Sufferings Minutes,* June 1915.
33. *Report of the London Yearly Meeting, 1915* pp. 143-4.
34. *F.O.R. General Committee Minutes,* 28 January and 8 February, 1915; *U.D.C. Executive Minutes,* 21 September 1915.
35. I.L.P. City of London Branch MS, Annual Report, 4 March 1915; Letters to the Secretary from Angell, 20 November 1914; Russell 6 July 1915; Morel, 8 July 1915; Pethick Lawrence, 13 July 1915; Swanwick, 11 December 1915; Morel MS, Trevelyan to Morel, July 1915.
36. Morel MS, Trevelyan to Morel, 23 September 1914.
37. U.D.C. Leaflet No. 5 *Crushing Germany;* No. 8 *Our Soldiers and the Union of Democratic Control;* No. 10 *Why we should think about peace.* A. Ponsonby; No. 11 *War and Diplomacy.* E. D. Morel.

38. Ashbee MS, Dickinson to Ashbee, 26 March 1915; *War and Peace,* May 1915.
39. *War and Peace,* June 1915, Editorial; August 1915, Mrs. Swanwick; October 1915, C. R. Buxton.
40. U.D.C. Pamphlet No. 6 *The National Policy,* pp. 12-13.
41. U.D.C. Pamphlet No. 9 *Why we should state terms of settlement.*
42. U.D.C. Pamphlet No. 8 *The War and the Workers.*
43. *The Labour Leader,* 26 August 1915.
44. *The Labour Leader,* 9 September 1915.
45. *The Labour Leader,* 23 September 1915.
46. *The Labour Leader,* 25 November 1915.
47. Angell MS, Morel to Angell, 25 March 1915.
48. *U.D.C. General Council,* 22 June 1915.
49. U.D.C. MS, Confidential Memorandum by E. D. Morel, November 1915.
50. *U.D.C. Executive Committee Minutes.*
51. *U.D.C. General Council,* 22 June 1915.
52. *War and Peace,* July 1915.
53. A. F. Brockway, *The Life of Alfred Salter; Bermondsey Story* (London, 1949).
54. *The Socialist Review,* August-September, 1915; Labour and War Pamphlets No. 2 *Militarism.* J. B. Glasier.
55. *Report of the Annual Conference of the Independent Labour Party . . . Norwich, April 5-6, 1915* (London, 1915); A. F. Brockway, *Socialism over Sixty Years,* (London, 1946).
56. A. J. B. Marwick, *Clifford Allen, The Open Conspirator* (Edinburgh, 1964); M. Gilbert, *Plough My Own Furrow: The Life of Lord Allen of Hurtwood* (London, 1965); A. M. McBriar, *Fabian Socialism and British Politics* (Cambridge, 1962) pp. 140-1; *The Labour Leader,* 27 May 1915.
57. *The Labour Leader,* 3 June 1915.
58. *The Labour Leader,* 6 May 1915.
59. R. Harrison, 'The War Emergency Workers' National Committee, 1914-1920' in ed. A. Briggs and J. Saville, *Essays in Labour History, 1886-1923* (London, 1971) pp. 211-259.
60. Marshall MS, B. Webb to Marshall, 15 September 1915.
61. Swartz, *The Union of Democratic Control,* pp. 107-10; Trevelyan MS, Trevelyan to Simon, 22 August 1915.
62. Walter Runciman wrote that in his personal view 'the worst cases of injury to national interest by newspapers have been ignored, and the least pernicious has been chosen by our Coalition colleagues.' Trevelyan MS, Runciman to Trevelyan, 23 August 1915: Ponsonby MS, Murray to Ponsonby, 22 July 1915; Trevelyan to Ponsonby, 24 July 1915.

CHAPTER FOUR

1. R. S. Churchill, *Lord Derby* (London, 1959).
2. D. Hayes, *Conscription Conflict* (London, 1949); Both here and elsewhere the exposition of government policy is greatly indebted to J. Rae, *Conscience and Politics, The British Government and the Conscientious Objector to Military Service, 1916-1919* (London, 1970).
3. *The Herald of Peace,* January 1916.

4. *War and Peace,* November 1915.
5. *The U.D.C.,* January 1916.
6. *The Socialist Review,* November 1915.
7. *The Socialist Review,* January 1916.
8. *The Nation,* 26 February 1916.
9. *F.O.R. General Committee Minutes,* 7 January 1916.
10. *Meeting for Sufferings Minutes,* September 1915.
11. *Meeting for Sufferings Minutes,* January 1916.
12. Morel MS, Hirst to Morel, 19 August 1914.
13. Russell MS, Dickinson to Russell, 17 and 19 June 1915; Morel MS, U.D.C. Executive resolution.
14. Morel MS, Morel to Trevelyan, 9 June 1915.
15. *U.D.C. General Council,* 29 October 1915.
16. J. H. Thomas, *My Life* (London, 1937) pp. 39-41; M. I. Thomis 'The Labour Movement and Compulsory Military Service, 1914-16' London M. A Thesis, 1959.
17. D. Kirkwood, *My Life of Revolt* (London, 1935) p. 116; The whole subject is discussed by J. Hinton 'The Clyde Workers' Committee and the Dilution Struggle' in eds. A. Briggs and J. Saville, *Essays in Labour History* . . . (London, 1971) pp. 152-84.
18. A. F. Brockway, *Inside the Left* (London, 1947).
19. Allen MS, Transcript of the speech. Quoted with slight variation in J. W Graham, *Conscription and Conscience. A History 1916-19* (London, 1922) pp. 174-182.
20. R. C. Lambert, *The Parliamentary History of Conscription in Great Britain* (London, 1917) pp. 77-9.
21. *The Herald of Peace,* February 1916.
22. *F.O.R. General Committee Minutes,* 14 March 1916.
23. *Meeting for Sufferings Minutes,* April and March 1916.
24. Gilbert, *Plough My Own Furrow,* pp. 46-7.
25. N.C.F. Letter to members, 31 January 1916.
26. N.C.F. Letter to members, 6 February 1916.
27. *The Tribunal,* 8 March 1916.
28. *The Tribunal,* 23 March 1916.
29. Cole, *Webb Diaries,* pp. 59-61.
30. *The Times,* 4 April 1916; Rae, *Conscience and Politics,* pp. 108-12.
31. Murray MS, Russell to Murray 17 April 1916.
32. Marshall MS, Gore to Asquith, 11 May 1916 (Copy).
33. Marshall MS, D. Davies to Marshall, 12 May 1916 (Copy); Rae, *Conscience and Politics,* p. 154.
34. Marshall MS, Russell to Marshall, 11 April 1916.
35. Murray MS, Russell to Murray, 17 April 1916.
36. Marshall MS, Marshall to J. P. F. Fletcher, 26 May 1916 (Copy).
37. D. Hopkin, 'Domestic Censorship in the First World War', *Journal of Contemporary History,* 5, 4 1970: *The Tribunal,* 11 May 1916, Allen 'A Personal Word'; Marshall MS, Jones to Allen, 29 May 1916.
38. Marshall MS, Lord Hugh Cecil to Marshall, 2 June 1916.
39. Marshall MS, Murray to Marshall, 11 June 1916.
40. Marshall MS, G. M. Ll. Davies to Marshall, 7 April 1916.
41. Marshall MS, Report of Deputation, 27 June 1916.
42. *The Tribunal,* 27 July and 3 August 1916.
43. City of London I.L.P. MS, Allen to Bryan, 10 August 1916; Gilbert, *Plough My Own Furrow,* p. 61.
44. Marshall MS, Marshall to Gen. Childs, 31 August 1916; Harvey to Marshall, 4 December 1916.

45. B. Russell, *Justice in War Time* (London, 1916) pp. ix, 14, 27; *Portraits from Memory* (London, 1956) pp. 38-9; *Autobiography* (London, 1968) II, pp. 17ff.
46. B. Russell, 'The Ethics of War' in *Justice in War Time.* Although Russell's activities were a source of prestige to the Peace Movement, different societies tried to 'own' them. The N.C.C.L. complained that the N.C.F. was trespassing on its preserve in the matter of Russell. Miss Marshall indignantly rejected the suggestion. Marshall MS, Marshall to B. N. Langdon-Davies, 24 October 1916.
47. Russell, 'War and Non-Resistance' in *Justice in War Time; The Principles of Social Reconstruction* (London, 1916) pp. 42-3, 106-7.
48. Russell MS, Swanwick to Russell, 21 November 1915.
49. J. M. Keynes, *Two Memoirs* (London, 1949) pp. 98-9; R. Harrod, *John Maynard Keynes* (London, 1951) p. 214; Rae, *Conscience and Politics,* p. 82.
50. M. Holroyd, *Lytton Strachey* (London, 1968) II. pp. 117-18.
51. Ed. R. Gathorne-Hardy, *Ottoline, The early memoirs of Lady Ottoline Morrell* (London, 1963) p. 261.
52. Holroyd, *Strachey,* II, p. 174.
53. Trevelyan MS, 'Rex v. Russell' 5 June 1916; Marshall MS, Snowden to Russell, 12 June 1916 (Copy).
54. Trevelyan MS, Report of Russell's speech; Hansard 5 Series, LXXXVI, 539-40, Lloyd George, 19 October 1916.
55. G. H. Hardy, *Bertrand Russell and Trinity* (Cambridge 1970 edn.); Russell MS, Lowes Dickinson to Russell n.d. 1916; Morel to Russell, 9 August 1916.
56. *The Tribunal,* 28 September and 12 October 1916.
57. Marshall MS, Child to Meyer, 13 September 1916; Meyer to Marshall, 15 September 1916; Marshall to Meyer, 16 September 1916 (Copy).
58. Marshall MS, Notes on the National Committee meeting, 14 October 1916.
59. Marshall MS, Marshall to Allen, 9 December 1916.
60. *The Friend,* 14 July 1916.
61. Brockway, *Inside the Left,* pp. 54-5; A. F. Brockway, *Is Britain Blameless?* (London, 1915) pp. 3-5; A. F. Brockway, *Socialism for Pacifists* (London, 1916) p. 33.

CHAPTER FIVE

1. Cited in V. H. Rothwell, *British War Aims and Peace Diplomacy, 1914-1918,* (Oxford, 1971) p. 38.
2. *The U.D.C.,* November 1915, C. R. Buxton, 'Why not find out?'; February 1916, F. W. Pethick Lawrence, 'Why not state terms?' and H. N. Brailsford, 'A Peace by Satisfaction'.
3. C. R. Buxton MS, Buxton to Grey, March 1916.
4. U.D.C. MS, Conference on 29 February and 7 March 1916.
5. *The U.D.C.,* January 1916, E. D. Morel, 'Why not discuss?'; March 1916, E. D. Morel, 'Whither?'.
6. Russell MS, Morel to Russell n.d. 1916; Morel MS, Grubb to Morel 3 April 1916.
7. *War and Peace,* April 1916 'The Lesson of Verdun'.
8. Marshall MS, Minutes of a special meeting, 28 April 1916.
9. *The Ploughshare,* June 1916; *The Labour Leader,* 8 June 1916.
10. C. R. Buxton MS, H. Harris to Buxton, 10 March 1916.

11. *The Ploughshare*, February, March and April 1916.
12. *Whence come wars? First Report of the Committee on 'War and the Social Order'* (London, 1916) pp. 14 and 41-2; *Ploughshare*, May 1916.
13. *The Ploughshare*, June and July 1916.
14. Ed. H. Martin, *The Ministry of Reconciliation* (London, 1916) includes essays by Cadoux, Roberts, Heath and Orchard.
15. *F.O.R. General Committee Minutes*, 19 July and 11 December 1916.
16. *The Labour Leader*, 1 June 1916.
17. *The Labour Leader*, 24 February 1916.
18. Russell MS, Swanwick to Russell, 29 June 1916; Marshall MS, Swanwick to Marshall, 5 August and 23 November 1916; Royden to Marshall, 10 August 1916.
19. U.D.C. Leaflet No. 15b, *Mr. Ponsonby and Mr. Trevelyan in the House of Commons, November 11th, 1915;* Ponsonby MS, Trevelyan to Ponsonby, 12 November 1915; Graham to Ponsonby, 25 February 1916; Burns MS, Trevelyan to Burns, 11 February 1916.
20. Trevelyan MS, Ponsonby to Trevelyan, 17 April 1916.
21. City of London I.L.P. MS, Ponsonby to Bryan, 26 May 1916.
22. *U.D.C. Executive Committee Minutes*, 18 April 1916, 16 May 1916, 30 May 1916, 18 July 1916.
23. Morel MS, Morel to E. H. Driffill, 9 August 1916.
24. Trevelyan MS, Morel to Trevelyan n.d. 1916.
25. Rothwell, *British War Aims*, pp. 268-9.
26. *U.D.C. Executive Committee Minutes*, 4 January and 18 January 1916; *U.D.C. General Council*, 2 May 1916; *The U.D.C.*, April 1916, J. A. Hobson 'The Open Door'.
27. *The U.D.C.*, June 1916, Editorial; July 1916, 'Political Economy from Paris'; U.D.C. Pamphlet No. 19a *Economic War after the War*, G. L. Dickinson, pp. 16-17.
28. Trevelyan MS, Morel to Trevelyan, 12 July 1916.
29. E. D. Morel, *Truth and the War* (London, 1916), p. xvii, pp. 316-20.
30. Morel and Newbold in *The Herald*, 9 and 16 September 1916; C. P. Trevelyan in *The U.D.C.*, August 1916. Russell MS, Morel to Russell, n.d. 1916.
31. N. Angell, *America and the War* (Boston, 1915) p. 15; *War and Peace*, February 1916, N. Angell, 'The Prospect of American Intervention'; June 1916, 'Mr. Wilson's Contribution'.
32. L. W Martin, *Peace without Victory: Woodrow Wilson and the British Liberals* (New Haven, 1958).
33. Anderson, *Noel Buxton*, pp. 81-2.
34. F.O. 800/86, Spring-Rice to Drummond, 14 July 1916.
35. F.O. 800/86, Drummond to Spring-Rice, 25 July 1916.
36. G. L. Dickinson, 'The basis of a permanent peace' in ed. C. R. Buxton, *Towards a Lasting Settlement* (London, 1916) p. 36; G. L. Dickinson, *The European Anarchy* (London, 1916); G. L. Dickinson MS, Unpublished Recollections.
37. Ashbee MS, Ashbee to Grey, 30 May 1916; Bryce MS, Dickinson to Bryce, 3 May 1916.
38. Ashbee MS, Grey to Ashbee, 6 June 1916.
39. Scott MS, Dickinson to Scott, 10 June 1916.
40. Bryce MS, Bryce to House, 26 August 1916.
41. C. R. Buxton MS, A. Williams to Buxton, 13 October 1916; Bryce to Buxton, 28 October 1916.
42. *The Friend*, 22 September 1916.
43. *The Friend*, 29 September 1916.

44. *Peace Committee Minutes,* November 1916.
45. Marshall MS, Marshall to Dickinson, 23 October 1916; Dickinson to Marshall, 24 October 1916.
46. Marshall MS, Marshall to Russell, 23 October 1916; Russell to Marshall, 25 October 1916; Russell to Marshall, 26 October 1916; Russell to Marshall n.d.
47. Wallas to Samuel, 8 October 1916 cited in J. Bowle, *Viscount Samuel* (London, 1957) pp. 141-2.
48. *The U.D.C.,* October 1916, Editorial.
49. K. G. Robbins, *Sir Edward Grey* (London, 1971) p. 343.
50. C. R. Buxton MS, Runciman to Buxton, 11 October 1916.
51. CAB 42/22/14, Hankey 'General Review of the War' 31 October 1916.
52. Lord Newton, *Lord Lansdowne* (London, 1929) p. 450.
53. Rothwell, *British War Aims,* pp. 54-5; W. B. Fest, 'British War Aims and German Peace Feelers during the First World War (December 1916—November 1918)' *The Historical Journal,* xv, 2 (1972) pp. 288-9.
54. Trevelyan MS, Ponsonby to Trevelyan, 2 June 1916; Sir John Brunner, however, remained convinced that the Germans would have to rid themselves of the 'Berlin military spirit'. S. E. Koss, *Sir John Brunner, Radical Plutocrat, 1842-1919* (Cambridge, 1970) pp. 280-1.
55. F. W. Hirst, *In the Golden Days* (London, 1947); *F. W. Hirst* by his friends (Oxford, 1958); F. W. Hirst, *The Political Economy of War* (London, 1916); M. A. Hamilton, *Remembering my Good Friends* (London, 1944) pp. 79-80.
56. *Common Sense,* 7 October 1916; C. R. Buxton MS, Molteno to Buxton, 7 October 1916; Holt to Buxton, 23 October 1916.
57. C. R. Buxton MS, Morrell to Buxton, 7 October 1916.
58. F.O. 800/86, Spring-Rice to Grey, 24 November 1916.

CHAPTER SIX

1. Marshall MS, Jones to Marshall, 22 December 1916.
2. Marshall MS, Jones to Marshall, 22 December 1916; Marshall to Brailsford, 21 December 1916.
3. *The Herald,* 23 December 1916; *Common Sense,* 23 December 1916 Angell MS, Trevelyan to Angell, 22 December 1916.
4. S. Kernek, 'The British Government's Reactions to President Wilson's "Peace" Note of December 1916', *The Historical Journal,* XIII, 4 (1970).
5. Marshall MS, Brailsford to Marshall, 15 January 1917.
6. Marshall MS, Russell to Marshall, 1 January 1917.
7. Bryce to Henry, 5 April 1917 cited in Robbins 'Bryce and the First World War' 268; Snowden in *The Labour Leader,* 12 April 1917; Russell in *The Tribunal,* 19 April 1917.
8. Marshall MS, Marshall to Lord Parmoor, 22 March 1917.
9. *The U.D.C.,* February, April and May 1917.
10. Rothwell, *British War Aims,* p. 99.
11. Hansard, 5th Series, XLI, 1473-4. MacDonald had been very cautious, writing to Trevelyan of the Rossendale contest, 'We must wait'. Trevelyan MS, MacDonald to Trevelyan, 3 January 1917.
12. *The Friend,* 9 March 1917; Marshall MS, Marshall to Trevelyan, 2 March 1917; See also Marshall to Ponsonby, 22 November 1916.
13. Marshall MS, Hodgkin to Hirst, 31 January 1917.

14. F. W. Pethick Lawrence, *Fate Has Been Kind* (London, 1942) p. 115; Election Address, seen by courtesy of Miss E. Knowles; J. Paton, *Proletarian Pilgrimage* (London, 1935) pp. 270-8.
15. C. R. Buxton MS, Memorandum 30 May 1917.
16. D. Lloyd George, *War Memoirs* (London, 1938) II, pp. 1150-1; B. Pribicevic, *The Shop Stewards' Movement and Workers' Control, 1910-22* (Oxford, 1959) pp. 32-7.
17. Ed. A. J. P. Taylor, *Lloyd George, A diary by Frances Stevenson* (London, 1971) p. 159.
18. Milner to Lloyd George, 26 May 1917, cited in A. M. Gollin, *Proconsul in Politics* (London, 1964) pp. 543-6; Milner MS, Milner to I. W. Colvin, 5 June 1917; P. A. Lockwood, 'Milner's Entry into the War Cabinet, December 1916' *The Historical Journal,* VII, 1 (1964).
19. Lansbury MS, Pethick Lawrence to Lansbury, 6 June 1917; Woolf, *Beginning Again,* pp. 211-15; D. B. Montefiore, *From a Victorian to a Modern* (London, 1927) p. 194.
20. Milner to Lloyd George, 1 June 1917 cited in Swartz, *The Union of Democratic Control,* p. 175.
21. *Peace Year Book 1917* (London, 1917); *The Arbitrator,* April 1917; *Monthly Circular of the National Peace Council,* June 1917. The U.D.C. was affiliated to the N.P.C. in July 1917.
22. Russell MS, Trevelyan to Russell, 25 June 1917.
23. *Report of the Annual Conference of the Independent Labour Party held at Leeds, April 9-10, 1917* (London, 1917).
24. J. R. MacDonald, *National Defence* (London, 1917) pp. 15-17.
25. *The Herald,* 14 April 1917.
26. *The Socialist Review,* July-September 1917.
27. *The Ploughshare,* August 1917.
28. *The Tribunal,* 4 January 1917 'Alter our basis' Barratt Brown.
29. Marshall MS, Circular by Russell and Marshall 3 February 1917.
30. Marshall MS, Russell to Redfern 26 February 1917; Redfern to Russell, 3 March 1917.
31. *The Tribunal,* 22 February 1917, 'Liberty and National Service'.
32. Rae, *Conscience and Politics,* pp. 183ff.
33. Marshall MS, Memorandum 'The Position in the Home Office Camps' 3 March 1917.
34. Marshall MS, A. Rose to Marshall, 6 April 1917.
35. Marshall MS, Russell to Rose, 27 April 1917.
36. Marshall MS, Norman to Russell, 29 April 1917.
37. Marshall MS, 'Report of Miss Marshall's interview with General Childs, April 26 1917'; 'Copy Extract from Letter sent by Miss Marshall to a Government official with whom she had an interview respecting the reported reconsideration by the Government of the whole C.O. problem' 27 April 1917.
38. Marshall MS, Norman to Russell, 3 May 1917; Norman to Marshall, 5 May 1917; Russell to Marshall, 7 May 1917; Russell to Norman, 7 May 1917; Norman to Marshall, 6 May 1917; Marshall to Norman, 9 May 1917.
39. Marshall MS, Home Office Camps 'Enclosure F'; Graham to Marshall, 23 May 1917.
40. Marshall MS, Marshall to Smillie, 2 June 1917.
41. Gilbert, *Plough My Own Furrow,* pp. 78-83.
42. Marshall MS, Ammon to Marshall, 8 June 1917.
43. *The Tribunal,* 14 and 21 June 1917; Marshall MS, Russell to Marshall, 6 June 1917.

44. F.O.R. General Council Minutes, 30 March 1917.
45. Marshall MS, E. Ellis to Marshall, 8 May 1917.
46. Marshall MS, Marshall to E. E. Hunter, 27 August 1917.
47. Allen MS, Allen to Barratt Brown, August 1917.
48. Murray MS, Lowes Dickinson to Murray, 17 and 20 December 1916.
49. Bryce MS, Bryce to Lowell, 14 February 1917.
50. Bryce MS, Lowes Dickinson to Bryce, 7 March 1917.
51. H. N. Brailsford, *A League of Nations* (London, 1917); Marshall MS, Brailsford to Marshall, 15 January 1917.
52. J. A. Hobson, *Democracy after the War* (London, 1917) pp. 18, 147-8 and 207-8.
53. G. L. Dickinson, *The Choice Before Us* (London, 1917); Ashbee MS, Dickinson to Mrs. Ashbee, ? May 1917.
54. L.N.S. Pamphlets No. 2 *Report of Meeting of May 14, 1917* (London, 1917); W. K. Hancock, *Smuts, The Sanguine Years, 1870-1919* (Cambridge, 1962) pp. 463-4.
55. Bryce MS, Lowes Dickinson to Bryce, 16 May 1917; Bryce to Lowell, 20 July 1917; W. H. Dickinson to Theodore Marburg, 17 May 1917 cited in ed. J. H. Latané, *The Development of the League of Nations Idea, Documents and Correspondence of Theodore Marburg* (New York, 1932) II, p. 302.
56. L.N.S. Publications No. 16, *Proceedings of the First Annual Meeting* (London, 1917).
57. G. P. Gooch, *The Project of a League of Nations* (London, 1917); A. Williams, *The Minimum of Machinery* (London, 1917) L.N.S. No. 18; R. Unwin, *Functions of a League of Nations* (London, 1917) L.N.S. No. 19; Lord Bryce and others, *Proposals for the Prevention of Future Wars* (London, 1917); Ed. L. S. Woolf, *The Framework of a Lasting Peace* (London, 1917).
58. H. A. L. Fisher, *James Bryce* (London, 1927) II, p. 137.
59. C. M. Mason, 'British Policy on the Establishment of a League of Nations, 1914-1919' Cambridge Ph.D., 1970, pp. 75-85.
60. Mason, 'British Policy . . .' p. 95.
61. CAB 23/3: W.C. 154 (22) 5 June 1917.
62. W. H. Dickinson MS, Bryce to W. H. Dickinson, 21 April 1917.
63. *The Herald of Peace*, October 1917.
64. *Minutes of the Peace Committee*, September 1917.
65. *The Ploughshare*, March 1917; See also *The Community of Nations* (London, 1917).
66. *The Friend*, 6 April 1917.
67. MacDonald, *National Defence*, p. 60.
68. *War and Peace*, January 1917, Russell 'Two Ideals of Pacifism'; Hobson 'Social Force or Lynch Law'; Ponsonby 'The enthronement of force; practical objections'; G. L. Dickinson 'The League to Enforce Peace'.
69. *War and Peace*, June 1917, Letter from Pethick Lawrence; August 1917, Letter from Hobson.
70. Marshall MS, E. Snowden to Miss Tillard, 24 August 1917.

CHAPTER SEVEN

1. S. Roskill, *Hankey, Man of Secrets* (London, 1970) I, p. 418.
2. *The Tribunal*, 24 May 1917, Russell 'Russia and Peace'.
3. Runciman MS, Henderson to Runciman, 17 August 1917.

4. I owe this information to Dr. R. McKibbin.
5. Trevelyan MS, Ponsonby to Trevelyan, 13 August 1917.
6. Morel MS, Morel to Ponsonby, 20 July 1917; Morel to Leach, 24 July 1917.
7. MacDonald to Buckler, 17 August 1917 cited in A. Nevins, *Henry White: Thirty Years of American Diplomacy* (New York, 1930) pp. 343-5.
8. *U.D.C. Council Minutes,* 27 July 1917.
9. Russell MS, Palme Dutt to Russell 15 November 1917.
10. *The Ploughshare,* September 1917.
11. Haig to Robertson, 13 August 1917 cited in Rothwell, *British War Aims,* p. 98.
12. Bryce to T. Roosevelt, 25 October 1917, cited in Fisher, *Bryce,* II, p. 176.
13. T. Jones, *Whitehall Diary* (London, 1969) I, p. 37.
14. *The Herald,* 13 October 1917.
15. *The Labour Leader,* 27 September 1917.
16. *The Labour Leader,* 4 October 1917.
17. *The Labour Leader,* 1 November 1917.
18. *The Labour Leader,* 6 September 1917.
19. Hopkin, 'Domestic Censorship'.
20. S. Hobhouse, *Forty Years and an Epilogue* (London, 1951).
21. Mrs. H. Hobhouse, *I Appeal unto Caesar* (London, 1917) pp. 7-8.
22. Marshall MS, Meyer to Marshall, 11 September 1917.
23. A. S. Peake, *Prisoners of Hope* (London, 1918); 'North Briton', *British Freedom 1914-17;* J. S. Duckers, *Handed Over* (London, 1917); Rae, *Conscience and Politics,* pp. 208-25.
24. S. Sassoon, *Siegfried's Journey* (London, 1945); Russell MS, Russell to Swanwick, 20 July 1917.
25. Marshall MS, Miss Marshall's notes, 26 April 1917.
26. Marshall MS, Salter to Marshall, 27 November 1917.
27. Marshall MS, Ayles to Marshall, 28 February 1917.
28. Allen MS, Russell to Marshall, n.d. 1917.
29. Allen MS, Allen to Marshall, 12 November 1917.
30. Hopkin, 'Domestic Censorship'; Jones, *Whitehall Diary,* I, p. 44.
31. Swartz, *The Union of Democratic Control,* pp. 178-87.
32. *U.D.C. Executive Committee Minutes,* 11 December 1917.
33. Cited in Lord Parmoor, *A Retrospect* (London, 1936) pp. 122-3.
34. Hopkin 'Domestic Censorship'; *Commission of Enquiry into Industrial Unrest, No. 7 Division, Report of the Commissioners for Wales, including Monmouthshire.* Cd. 8668.
35. *Hansard,* 13 November 1917 col. 311.
36. Lockwood, 'Milner's Entry'.
37. Newton, *Lansdowne,* pp. 463-83; A. J. Mayer, *Political Origins of the New Diplomacy, 1917-18* (New Haven, 1959) pp. 282-5; H. Kurtz, 'The Lansdowne Letter' *History Today* XVIII/2 February 1968; Correspondence with Mr. Kurtz; *History of The Times,* IV Part 1, p. 342.
38. C. Petrie, *Life and Letters of Sir Austen Chamberlain* (London, 1940) II, pp. 96-7.
39. Rothwell, *British War Aims,* pp. 145-6.
40. *Common Sense,* 1 December 1917.
41. *Common Sense,* 15 December 1917.
42. Marshall MS, Swanwick to Marshall, 29 November 1917; Russell to Marshall, 30 November 1917.

43. Courtney MS, Lady Courtney, Diary, 2 December 1917; Ponsonby to Lady Courtney, 29 November 1917.
44. *The Socialist Review,* January-March 1918.
45. *The U.D.C.,* Editorial, January 1918. There were still many, however, like Gilbert Murray, who found the Lansdowne group 'too pacifist' and declined to associate themselves with it. Courtney MS, Murray to G. P. Gooch, 1 November 1919.
46. *Common Sense,* 12 January 1918.
47. *Common Sense,* 26 January 1918.
48. *Common Sense,* 2 February 1918; Newton, *Lansdowne,* p. 473.
49. H. N. Fieldhouse, 'Noel Buxton and A. J. P. Taylor's "The Trouble Makers"' in ed. M. Gilbert, *A Century of Conflict* (London, 1966) pp. 189-92.
50. A. Henderson, *The Aims of Labour* (London, 1918) Appendix 1.
51. M. P. Price, *My Three Revolutions* (London, 1970); F. S. Cocks, *The Secret Treaties* (London, 1918); U.D.C. Leaflets 40b, 41b and 43b. *Secret Diplomacy.*
52. *The Labour Leader,* 10 and 17 January 1918; *Common Sense,* 19 January 1918.
53. *The U.D.C.,* February 1918.
54. C. R. Buxton MS, Circular Letter, 22 January 1918.
55. Marshall MS, E. Hunter to Marshall, 4 February 1918.
56. *The Labour Leader,* 31 January 1918.
57. *The National Weekly,* 26 January 1918.
58. *The Labour Leader,* 17 January 1918.
59. *Justice,* 21 December 1917.
60. *The National Weekly,* 26 January 1918; *The U.D.C.,* February 1918.
61. *Common Sense,* 9 February 1918 and 2 March 1918.
62. Newton, *Lansdowne,* pp. 472-3.
63. *Common Sense,* 9 March 1918.
64. *The U.D.C.,* April 1918.
65. Ponsonby MS, Interview with the Prime Minister, 27 June 1918.
66. Morel MS, Morel to Cadbury, 7 April 1918.
67. *The Labour Leader,* 18 April 1918.
68. *Common Sense,* 30 March 1918.
69. Spender to Buxton, 27 February 1918 in ed. Gilbert, *Century of Conflict,* p. 195.
70. *Common Sense,* 3 August 1918; Newton, *Lansdowne,* p. 476.
71. *The Labour Leader,* 7 March 1918.
72. Russell MS, Allen to Russell, 15 January 1918.
73. Murray MS, Russell to Murray, 15 February 1918.
74. *The Tribunal,* 21 February 1918.
75. Russell MS, Dickinson to Russell, 19 April 1918; Allen to Russell, 10 April 1918.
76. *The Tribunal,* 21 March 1918.
77. *The Tribunal,* 9 May 1918.
78. Cited in Graham, *Conscription and Conscience,* pp. 302-3.
79. Russell MS, Allen to Russell, 27 June 1918.
80. Allen Diary, 1 February 1919 cited in Gilbert, *Plough My Own Furrow,* p. 129.
81. *F.O.R. General Committee Minutes,* 3 and 4 June 1918.
82. S. B. James, *The Men who dared* (London, 1917 or 1918) pp. 97-8.
83. *The Ploughshare,* October and July 1918.
84. Mayer's views in *Political Origins of the New Diplomacy,* p. 327 are criticized by Mason, 'British Policy . . .' pp. 167-9.

85. Bryce MS, Bryce to Lowell, 8 February 1918.
86. Mason, 'British Policy . . .' p. 203.
87. Jones, *Whitehall Diary* I, p. 53.
88. Jones, *Whitehall Diary* I, p. 62.
89. W. H. Dickinson MS, G. L. Dickinson to W. H. Dickinson, 4 June 1918; W. H. Dickinson to G. L. Dickinson, 5 June 1918.
90. Murray MS, Report of the meeting of 26 July 1918; D. Davies to Murray, 5 August 1918.
91. Wilson, *Origins of the League Covenant,* pp. 126-172.
92. W. H. Dickinson MS, W. H. Dickinson to Murray, 19 and 24 August 1918.
93. Lord Grey of Fallodon, *The League of Nations* (London, 1918) pp. 14-15
94. Murray MS, Minutes of the meeting between the committees of both societies, 10 October 1918.
95. Bryce MS, Bryce to Eliot, 6 November 1918.
96. *Minutes of the Meeting for Sufferings,* December 1918.
97. *The Labour Leader,* 8 August 1917 and 27 June 1917.
98. *The Tribunal,* 7 November 1918.
99. *The Labour Leader,* 24 October 1918.
100. *The U.D.C.,* November 1918.
101. A. Henderson, *The League of Nations and Labour* (London, 1918) p. 12; J. A. Hobson in *The U.D.C.,* October 1918.

CHAPTER EIGHT

1. *The Labour Leader,* 5 December 1918; Trevelyan MS, Election Address.
2. *The Labour Leader,* 2 January 1919.
3. *The Leicester Pioneer,* 20 December 1918.
4. Ponsonby MS, Trevelyan to Ponsonby, 30 December 1918; Cocks to Ponsonby, 29 December 1918; F. Ponsonby to A. Ponsonby, 4 January 1919; Snowden to Ponsonby, 2 January 1919.
5. Gilbert, *Plough My Own Furrow,* p. 127; Marshall MS, Marshall to Allen, 2 January 1919.
6. *The Labour Leader,* 13 February 1919.
7. *The Labour Leader,* 10 April 1919.
8. *The U.D.C.,* March 1918; *The Labour Leader,* 15 May 1919.
9. *The Labour Leader,* 29 May 1919.
10. N. Angell, *The Peace Treaty and the Economic Chaos of Europe* (London, 1919); J. M. Keynes, *The Economic Consequences of the Peace,* (London, 1919).
11. Murray MS, 'The Position of the League of Nations Question in the Forthcoming Peace Conference; A Memorandum prepared by the Acting Committee for H.M. Government.'
12. Murray MS, Zimmern to Murray, 21 December 1918.
13. W. H. Dickinson MS, Cecil to W. H. Dickinson, 13 April 1918.
14. Murray MS, Cecil to Murray, 20 December 1918 and 4 January 1919.
15. Cecil MS, Cecil to Lloyd George, 4 April 1919.
16. Murray MS, W. H. Dickinson to Murray, 19 February 1919; 'Observations on the Draft Covenant of the League of Nations by the Research Committee of the League of Nations Union.'
17. Bryce to Storey, 20 February 1919 cited in Fisher, *Bryce,* II, p. 212;

Murray MS, Grey to Murray, 21 March 1919; Bryce to Henry, 10 April 1919 in Fisher, *Bryce,* II, p. 216.

18. Murray in *The International Review,* March and May 1919.
19. Cecil MS, Cecil to Lloyd George, 27 May 1919.
20. Bryce MS, Drummond to Bryce, 6 June 1919; Cecil to Bryce, 2 August 1919.
21. Bryce to Storey, 27 November 1919 in Fisher, *Bryce* II, p. 232.
22. Murray MS, Cecil to Murray, 1 January 1920.
23. *The Socialist Review,* July-September 1919.
24. *The Herald of Peace,* September 1919.
25. *F.O.R. General Committee Minutes,* 2 June 1919.
26. C. Heath, *The Pacific Settlement of International Disputes* (London, 1918?) pp. 81-2; W. E. Wilson, *The Foundations of Peace* (London, 1918) pp. 92-3; *National Peace Council Monthly Circular,* August-September 1918.
27. *The Friend,* 3 January 1919.
28. *The Friend,* 31 January and 30 May 1919.
29. *Ploughshare.* February 1919.
30. *The U.D.C.,* March 1919.
31. *The Herald,* 11 January 1919.
32. *U.D.C. General Council Minutes,* 8 March 1919.
33. Cited in H. M. Swanwick, *Builders of Peace* (London, 1924) p. 122.
34. *The U.D.C.,* November 1919.
35. *The International Review,* February, April, May, July and December 1919.
36. J. King, *Political Crooks at the Peace Conference* (London, 1919); *The Labour Leader,* 27 February 1919.
37. *The Tribunal,* 20 March 1919.
38. *Common Sense,* 7 and 14 May 1919.
39. C. D. Burns, *The League and Labour* (London, 1919).
40. *Labour and the Peace Treaty* (London, 1919).

CHAPTER NINE

1. *The Herald of Peace,* October 1928.
2. Cadoux MS, Dunnico to Cadoux, 7 December 1916.
3. *F.O.R. General Committee Minutes,* 8 September 1919.
4. A. M. Royden, *The Great Adventure* (London, 1915); G. M. Ll. Davies, *Pilgrimage of Peace, with a memoir by C. E. Raven* (London, 1950); G. J. Jones, *Wales and the Quest for Peace* (Cardiff, 1969).
5. *Friends and War* (London, 1920) p. 23.
6. W. H. Ayles, *Why I worked for peace during the Great War,* n.d., pp. 13-16. I am grateful to Mrs. W. H. Ayles for a copy of this pamphlet. S. Mews, *Religion and English Society in the First World War* (Cambridge, forthcoming) will deal with the whole subject.
7. Ed. J. E. Carpenter, *Ethical and Religious Problems of the War* (London, 1916); J. Oman, *The War and its Issues* (Cambridge, 1915); Ed. G. K. A. Bell, *The War and the Kingdom of God* (London, 1916).
8. B. Sundkler, *Nathan Soderblom* (London, 1968); D. Hudson, *The Ecumenical Movement in World Affairs* (London, 1969); ed. A. Peel, *The Christian and War* (London, 1925); *Christianity and War. A report presented to C.O.P.E.C., Birmingham April 1924* (London, 1924); Ed. G. K. A. Bell, *The Stockholm Conference 1925* (London, 1926); R. E. Roberts, *H. R. L. Sheppard: Life and Letters* (London, 1942).

9. D. B. Meyer, *The Protestant Search for Political Realism, 1919-41,* (Berkeley, 1960); R. Niebuhr, *An Interpretation of Christian Ethics* (London, 1936); G. Harland, *The Thought of Reinhold Niebuhr* (New York, 1960); H. Martin, *The Christian as Soldier;* N. Micklem, *May God Defend the Right* (London, 1939); *The Theology of Politics* (London, 1941).
10. A. Ponsonby, *Democracy and Diplomacy* (London, 1915); *The Nation,* 27 December 1915.
11. Murray, *Faith, War and Policy,* pp. 100-104.
12. Morel MS, Kerr to Morel, 29 July 1915.
13. *The Labour Party Conference Report, 1919* (London, 1919).
14. E. D. Morel and H. B. Lees-Smith, *'Foreign Policy' and the People,* (London, 1921?); E. D. Morel, *The Secret History of a Great Betrayal* (London, 1923); *The Black Scourge in Europe* (London, 1920); *Foreign Affairs,* December 1920.
15. W. M. Walker, 'Dundee's Disenchantment with Churchill', *Scottish Historical Review,* vol. 49, 1970, 85-108; R. W. Lyman, 'James Ramsay MacDonald and the Leadership of the Labour Party, 1918-1922', *Journal of British Studies,* 2, 1, 1962.
16. Morel MS, Ponsonby to Morel, 23 May 1924.
17. Morel MS, Ponsonby to Morel, 30 August 1924.
18. Morel MS, MacDonald to Morel, 18 March 1924.
19. Morel MS, Ponsonby to Morel, 1 May 1924.
20. Ponsonby MS, Baldwin to Ponsonby, 16 December 1927.
21. Ponsonby MS, Swanwick to Ponsonby, 18 October 1938.
22. H. M. Swanwick, *New Wars for Old* (London, 1934); *Collective Insecurity* (London, 1937).
23. Angell, *After All,* p. 243; N. Angell, *The Fruits of Victory* (London, 1921); *Preface to Peace* (London, 1935); *The Unseen Assassins* (London, 1932); *This Have and Have Not Business* (London, 1936).
24. Hobson MS, Unpublished South Place Ethical Society Lectures, 1932, seen by courtesy of Mrs. M. J. Scott.
25. H. N. Brailsford, *After the Peace* (London, 1920) pp. 42-9.
26. H. N. Brailsford, *Olives of Endless Age* (New York, 1928) pp. 206-7.
27. Brailsford in the *New Republic,* 11 May 1932, 17 August 1932, 17 April 1935.
28. H. N. Brailsford, *Property or Peace?* (London, 1934) p. 261.
29. Brailsford in the *New Republic,* 28 July 1937.
30. Brailsford to the *New Republic,* 17 June 1940 cited in J. J. Martin, *American Liberalism in World Politics, 1931-1941* (New York, 1964) pp. 1147-48.
31. G. L. Dickinson, *The Future of the Covenant* (London, 1920); *Causes of International War* (London, 1920); *War: Its Nature, Cause and Cure* (London, 1923); *The International Anarchy* (London, 1926); Dickinson MS, Unpublished Recollections; F. H. Hinsley, *Sovereignty* (London, 1966) pp. 209-11.
32. R. Niebuhr, *The Children of Light and the Children of Darkness* (London, 1945) p. 118.
33. Hobson MS, MacDonald to Hobson, 2 May 1924.
34. Rae, *Conscience and Politics,* p. 231.
35. *The Tribunal,* 24 April 1919.
36. *The Tribunal,* 8 May 1919.
37. *The Tribunal,* 15 May 1919.
38. *The Tribunal,* 22 May 1919.

39. *The Tribunal,* 17 July 1919; Rose now described himself as 'virtually a Tolstoyan' and spoke slightingly of the 'revolutionary pseudo-C.O. who wants Russian revolution.' Allen MS, Rose to Allen, 23 February 1919.
40. *The Tribunal,* 24 July 1919.
41. Brockway, *Inside the Left,* pp. 338-40; Brockway, *Salter,* p. 237; Brockway, *Pacifism and the Left Wing* (London, 1938) p. 9.
42. Allen in ed. J. Bell, *We did not fight* (London, 1935) p. 37.
43. Ponsonby MS, Russell to Ponsonby, 31 October 1936.
44. J. D. Mabbott, *The State and the Citizen* (London, 1952) pp. 136-7.
45. Morel MS, Murray to Morel, 23 August 1919; Morel to Murray, 27 August 1919; Trevelyan MS, Morel to Trevelyan, 29 August 1919.
46. Morel, *Military Preparations for the Great War,* p. 12.
47. Murray MS, MacDonald to Murray, 9 July 1923; Hobson to Murray, 27 December 1920; Ponsonby to Murray, 25 November 1922.
48. Murray MS, Murray to Cecil, 22 August 1939.
49. Murray MS, Noel-Baker to Murray, 21 June 1927.
50. *No More War,* February 1929.
51. Murray MS, Cecil to Murray, 7 November 1922.
52. Cecil MS, Cecil to Chamberlain, 16 August 1927.
53. Cecil MS, Chamberlain to Cecil, 18 July 1934.
54. Cecil MS, Cecil to Chamberlain, 16 August 1927.
55. Ponsonby MS, Cecil to Ponsonby, 24 November 1932.

Bibliography

PRIVATE PAPERS

Allen MS. When seen, this collection was kept privately by Margery, Lady Allen of Hurtwood. The papers are now at the University of South Carolina.

Angell MS. The papers of Sir Norman Angell at Ball State University, Muncie, Indiana.

Ashbee MS. The journals and papers of C. R. Ashbee at King's College, Cambridge.

Bryce MS. The papers of Viscount Bryce of Dechmont, Bodleian Library, Oxford.

Burns MS. The papers of John Burns, The British Museum.

C. R. Buxton MS. The papers of C. R. Buxton in the possession of his daughter, Miss Eglantyne Buxton.

Cadoux MS. The papers of the Rev. Dr. C. J. Cadoux in the possession of his son, Dr. T. J. Cadoux.

Cecil of Chelwood MS. The papers of Viscount Cecil of Chelwood, The British Museum.

City of London I.L.P. MS. The London School of Economics and Political Science.

Courtney of Penwith MS. The papers of Lord Courtney of Penwith, The London School of Economics and Political Science.

G. Lowes Dickinson MS. The papers of G. Lowes Dickinson, King's College, Cambridge. The unpublished autobiographical fragment, 'Recollections', is in the possession of Sir Dennis Proctor.

W. H. Dickinson MS. The papers of Lord Willoughby of Painswick, The Bodleian Library, Oxford.

Grey of Fallodon MS. The official papers of Viscount Grey of Fallodon, Public Record Office, London. F.O.800/35-113.

Hobson MS. No correspondence survives from the period of the First World War, but his daughter, the late Mrs. M. J. Scott, had a few relevant letters relating to the inter-war period.

Lansbury MS. The papers of George Lansbury, The London School of Economics and Political Science.

Marshall MS. The papers of Miss Catherine Marshall, Cumbria Record Office, Carlisle.

Milner MS. The papers of Alfred, Viscount Milner, New College, Oxford.

Morel MS. The papers of E. D. Morel, The London School of Economics and Political Science.

Murray MS. The papers of Gilbert Murray, The Bodleian Library, Oxford.

Ponsonby MS. The papers of Lord Ponsonby of Shulbrede, The Bodleian Library, Oxford.

Runciman MS. The papers of Viscount Runciman of Doxford, The
University of Newcastle-upon-Tyne.
Russell MS. The papers of Bertrand Russell, McMaster University, Canada.
Scott MS. The papers of C. P. Scott, The British Museum, London.
Trevelyan MS. When seen, the papers were in the keeping of the family
of Sir Charles Trevelyan. They are now deposited in the library of the
University of Newcastle-upon-Tyne.
Minutes of the General Committee of the Fellowship of Reconciliation.
Minutes of the Council of the Fellowship of Reconciliation.
Minutes of the Council of the National Peace Council.
Minutes of the Peace Committee of the Society of Friends.
Minutes of the Meeting for Sufferings of the Society of Friends.
Minutes of the General Council of the Union of Democratic Control.

PRINTED SOURCES

1. NEWSPAPERS, JOURNALS, CONFERENCE REPORTS, ETC.
The Arbitrator, The Call, Common Sense, The Friend, Goodwill, The
Herald, The Herald of Peace, Justice, The Labour Leader, Monthly Circular
of the National Peace Council, The Nation, The National Weekly, The
New Witness, No More War, The Peacemaker, The Ploughshare, The
Socialist Review, The Tribunal, The U.D.C. (Foreign Affairs from July
1919), War and Peace (The International Review from January 1919).
The Independent Labour Party: Annual Conference Reports, 1914-1919.
The Labour Party: Annual Conference Report, 1919.
The International Polity Summer School Proceedings, 1914 (London, 1915).
The Official Report of the Seventeenth Universal Congress of Peace
(London, 1909).
Towards Permanent Peace. A record of the Women's International Congress
held at The Hague, April 28-May 1 1915 (London, 1915).
The Peace Year Book, 1913-1917 (London, 1913-17).
Commission of Enquiry into Industrial Unrest, No. 7 Division. Report of
the Commission for Wales, including Monmouthshire (Cd. 8668).
Report of the London Yearly Meeting of Friends, 1915 (London, 1915).
Message of the Society of Friends in the present emergency, August 1914
(London, 1914).
Whence come wars? First Report of the Committee on 'War and the Social
Order' (London, 1916); Friends and War (London, 1920).
Christianity and War. A Report presented to C.O.P.E.C. 1924 (London,
1924).
A full list of wartime U.D.C. pamphlets and leaflets is given by Dr Swartz
on pp. 231-3 of his book. Since the citations in my text are acknowledged
in the reference notes it seems unnecessary to repeat the full list here.

2. BIOGRAPHIES AND AUTOBIOGRAPHIES

Anderson, M. *Noel Buxton. a Life* (London, 1952).
Angell, N. *After All. An autobiography* (London, 1951).
Attlee, C. R. *As it Happened* (London, 1954).
Bell, J. (Ed.) *We did not fight* (London, 1935).
Blake, R. N. W. *The Unknown Prime Minister* (London, 1955).
Bowle, J. *Viscount Samuel* (London, 1957).
Brittain, V. *Pethick-Lawrence. A Portrait* (London, 1963).
Brockway, A. F. *Socialism over Sixty Years. The Life of Jowett of Bradford*
(London, 1946).

Brockway, A. F. *Inside the Left* (London, 1947).
Brockway, A. F. *Bermondsey Story. The Life of Alfred Salter* (London, 1949).
Churchill, R. S. *Lord Derby* (London, 1959).
Cocks, F. S. *E. D. Morel. The Man and his Work* (London, 1920).
Cole, M. (Ed.) *Beatrice Webb's Diaries, 1912-24* (London, 1952).
Cole, M. *The Life of G. D. H. Cole* (London, 1971).
Conwell-Evans, T. P. *Foreign Policy from a Back Bench, 1904-18. A study based on the Papers of Lord Noel-Buxton* (London, 1932).
Courtney, K. *Extracts from a Diary during the War* (Privately printed, 1927).
Davies, G. M. Ll. *Pilgrimage of Peace, with a memoir by C. E. Raven* (London, 1950).
Dudley, J. *The Life of Edward Grubb* (London, 1946).
Elton, Lord. *The Life of James Ramsay MacDonald* (London, 1939).
Evans, H. *Randal Cremer* (London, 1909).
Fisher, H. A. L. *James Bryce* (London, 1927).
Forster, E. M. *Goldsworthy Lowes Dickinson* (London, 1934).
Gilbert, M. *Plough My Own Furrow. The Life of Lord Allen of Hurtwood* (London, 1965).
Gollin, A. M. *Proconsul in Politics* (London, 1964).
Hamilton, M. A. *Arthur Henderson* (London, 1938).
Hamilton, M. A. *Remembering My Good Friends* (London, 1944).
Hammond, J. L. *C. P. Scott of the Manchester Guardian* (London, 1934).
Hancock, W. K. *Smuts: The Sanguine Years, 1870-1919* (Cambridge, 1962).
Harrod, R. F. *The Life of John Maynard Keynes* (London, 1951).
Hendrick, B. J. *The Life and Letters of W. H. Page* (New York, 1926).
Hirst, F. W. *In the Golden Days* (London, 1947).
F. W. Hirst by 'His Friends' (Oxford, 1958).
Hobhouse, S. *Forty Years and an Epilogue* (London, 1951).
Hobson, J. A. *Confessions of an Economic Heretic* (London, 1938).
Holroyd, M. *Lytton Strachey* (London, 1968).
Hughes, D. P. *The Life of Hugh Price Hughes* (London, 1904).
James, D. *Lord Roberts* (London, 1954).
Jones, T. *Whitehall Diary* I (London, 1969).
Kent, W. *John Burns. Labour's Lost Leader* (London, 1950).
Keynes, J. M. *Two Memoirs* (London, 1949).
Kirkwood, D. *My Life of Revolt* (London, 1935).
Koss, S. E. *Sir John Brunner, Radical Plutocrat, 1842-1919* (Cambridge, 1970).
Lansbury, G. *My Life* (London, 1928).
Latané, J. H. (Ed.) *The Development of the League of Nations Idea; Documents and Correspondence of Theodore Marburg* (New York, 1932).
Lloyd George, D. *War Memoirs* (London, 1938).
McAllister, G. *James Maxton. The Portrait of a Rebel* (London, 1935).
Magnus, P. *King Edward the Seventh* (London, 1964).
Marlowe, J. *The Life of Sir Arnold Wilson* (London, 1967).
Marwick, A. J. B. *Clifford Allen. The Open Conspirator* (Edinburgh, 1964).
Micklem, N. *The Box and the Puppets* (London, 1957).
Montefiore, D. B. *From a Victorian to a Modern* (London, 1927).
Morley, Viscount, *Memorandum on Resignation* (London, 1920).
Morrell, O. *Ottoline. The Early Memoirs of Lady Ottoline Morrell.* Edited by R. Gathorne-Hardy (London, 1963).
Morrison, H. *An Autobiography* (London, 1960).

Murray, G. *An Unfinished Autobiography*. Edited by J. Smith and A. Toynbee.
Nevins, A. *Henry White. Thirty Years of American Diplomacy* (New York, 1930).
Newton, Lord, *Lord Lansdowne* (London, 1929).
Noel-Baker, E. B. and P. J. J. *Allen Baker, M.P. A Memoir* (London, 1927).
Orchard, W. E. *From Faith to Faith* (London, 1933).
Oxford and Asquith, Earl of, *Memories and Reflections* (London, 1928).
Parmoor, Lord, *A Retrospect* (London, 1936).
Paton, J. *Proletarian Pilgrimage* (London, 1935).
Peel, A. and Marriott, J. A. R. *Robert Forman Horton* (London, 1937).
Pethick Lawrence, F. W. *Fate Has Been Kind* (London, 1942).
Petrie, C. *The Life and Letters of Sir Austen Chamberlain* (London, 1940).
Postgate, R. *The Life of George Lansbury* (London, 1951).
Price, M. P. *My Three Revolutions* (London, 1970).
Richards, E. R. *Private View of a Public Man. The Life of Leyton Richards* (London, 1950).
Roberts, R. E. *H. R. L. Sheppard. Life and Letters* (London, 1942).
Roskill, S. *Hankey, Man of Secrets* (London, 1970).
Royden, A. M. *A Threefold Cord* (London, 1948).
Russell, B. *Portraits from Memory* (London, 1956).
Russell, B. *Autobiography II* (London, 1968).
Sassoon, S. *Siegfried's Journey, 1916-1920* (London, 1945).
Shinwell, E. *Conflict without Malice* (London, 1955).
Simon, Viscount, *Retrospect* (London, 1952).
Snowden, Viscount, *An Autobiography* (London, 1934).
Stewart, W. J. *Keir Hardie* (London, 1921).
Sundkler, B. *Nathan Soderblom* (London, 1968).
Swanwick, H. M. *I Have Been Young* (London, 1935).
Taylor, A. J. P. (Ed.) *Lloyd George, A Diary by Frances Stevenson* (London, 1971).
Thomas, J. H. *My Story* (London, 1937).
Trevelyan, C. P. *From Liberalism to Labour* (London, 1921).
Unwin, S. *The Truth about a Publisher* (London, 1960).
Vipont, E. *Arnold Rowntree. A Life* (London, 1955).
Wall, J. F. *Andrew Carnegie* (New York, 1970).
White, H. C. *Willoughby Hyett Dickinson* (Gloucester, 1956).
Wood, A. *Bertrand Russell. The Passionate Sceptic* (London, 1957).
Wood, H. G. *H. T. Hodgkin. A Memoir* (London, 1937).
Woolf, L. S. *Beginning Again* (London, 1964).
Wrench, J. E. *Alfred, Lord Milner. The Man of no Illusions* (London, 1958).

3. Printed Sources

Angell, N. *The Great Illusion* (London, 1910).
Angell, N. *War and the Workers* (London n.d. 1913?)
Angell, N. *War and the Essential Realities* (London, 1913).
Angell, N. *Foundations of International Polity* (London, 1914).
Angell, N. *Commercial Security: Can it be obtained by armaments?* (London, 1914).
Angell, N. *America and the European War* (Boston, 1915).
Angell, N. *Why Freedom Matters* (London, 1917).
Angell, N. *War Aims; The need for a parliament of the Allies* (London, 1917).
Angell, N. *The Peace Treaty and the Economic Chaos of Europe* (London, 1919).

Angell, N. *The Fruits of Victory* (London, 1921).
Angell, N. *The Unseen Assassins* (London, 1932).
Angell, N. *Preface to Peace* (London, 1935).
Angell, N. *This Have and Have Not Business* (London, 1936).
Anon. *The Community of Nations* (London, 1917).
Ayles, W. H. *Why I worked for peace during the Great War*, n.d.
Bell, G. K. A. *The War and the Kingdom of God* (London, 1916).
Bell, G. K. A. (Ed.) *The Stockholm Conference 1925* (London, 1926).
Bennett, J. B. S. *Norman Angellism; How it concerns you* (London, 1914).
Bishop of London, Dr John Clifford and others, *Kaiser or Christ?* (London, 1914).
Brailsford, H. N. *The War of Steel and Gold* (London, 1914).
Brailsford, H. N. *A League of Nations* (London, 1917).
Brailsford, H. N. *After the Peace* (London, 1920).
Brailsford, H. N. *Olives of Endless Age* (New York, 1928).
Brailsford, H. N. *Property or Peace?* (London, 1934).
Brockway, A. F. *Is Britain Blameless?* (London and Manchester, 1915).
Brockway, A. F. *Socialism for Pacifists* (London, 1916).
Brockway, A. F. *Pacifism and the Left Wing* (London, 1938).
Bryce, Viscount and others, *Proposals for the prevention of future wars* (London, 1917).
Burns, C. D. *The League and Labour* (London, 1919).
Buxton, C. R. (Ed.) *Towards a Lasting Settlement* (London, 1916).
Buxton, C. R. *The Alternative to War* (London, 1936).
Carpenter, J. E. (Ed.) *Ethical and Religious Problems of the War* (London, 1916).
Cecil, Lord, *The Moral Basis of the League of Nations* (London, 1923).
Clifford, J. *The War and the Churches* (London, 1914).
Cocks, F. S. *The Secret Treaties* (London, 1918).
Cole, G. D. H. *Labour in War Time* (London, 1915).
Coulton, C. G. *Pacificist Illusions* (London, 1915).
Darby, W. E. *The Claims of the 'New Pacificism'* (London, 1913).
Davies, Lord, *Force and the Future* (London, 1934).
Denman, R. D. *On the Road to Peace* (London, 1915).
Dickinson, G. L. *Foundations of a League of Peace* (Boston, Mass., 1915).
Dickinson, G. L. *After the War* (London, 1915).
Dickinson, G. L. *The European Anarchy* (London, 1916).
Dickinson, G. L. *The Choice Before Us* (London, 1917).
Dickinson, G. L. *The Future of the Covenant* (London, 1920).
Dickinson, G. L. *Causes of International War* (London, 1920).
Dickinson, G. L. *War: Its Nature, Cause and Cure* (London, 1923).
Dickinson, G. L. *The International Anarchy* (London, 1926).
Duckers, J. S. (Ed.) *Handed Over* (London, 1916).
Fry, J. M. *Christ and Peace* (London, 1915).
Gooch, G. P. *The Project of a League of Nations* (London, 1917).
Graham, J. W. *War: From a Quaker point of view* (London, n.d.).
Grane, W. L. *The Passing of War* (London, 1912).
Grey, Lord. *The League of Nations* (London, 1918).
Heath, C. *The Pacific Settlement of International Disputes* (London, n.d.).
Heath, C. *Pacifism in time of war* (London, n.d.).
Henderson, A. *The League of Nations and Labour* (London, 1918).
Henderson, A. *The Aims of Labour* (London, 1918).
Hirst, F. W. *The Political Economy of War* (London, 1916).
Hobhouse, Mrs. H. *I Appeal unto Caesar* (London, 1917).
Hobhouse, L. T. *Democracy and Reaction* (London, 1904).

Q

Hobson, J. A. *The Social Problem* (London, 1901).

Hobson, J. A. *The Psychology of Jingoism* (London, 1902).

Hobson, J. A. *The Crisis of Liberalism* (London, 1909).

Hobson, J. A. *Towards International Government* (London, 1915).

Hobson, J. A. *Democracy after the War* (London, 1917).

Hobson, J. A. *Imperialism* (London, 1938 ed.).

Humphrey, A. W. *International Socialism and the War* (London, 1915).

Hunter, R. *Violence and the Labour Movement* (London, 1916).

James, S. B. *The Men who Dared* (London, 1917).

Kapp, R. O. *The Failure of Sociology* (London, 1914).

Keynes, J. M. *The Economic Consequences of the Peace* (London, 1919).

King, J. *Political Crooks at the Peace Conference* (London, 1919).

Labour and the Peace Treaty (London, 1919).

Labour and War Pamphlets. No. 2. Militarism, J. B. Glasier; *No. 3. The Peril of Conscription*, J. B. Glasier; *No. 11. Morocco and Armageddon*, E. D. Morel (London, 1915).

Lambert, R. C. *The Parliamentary History of Conscription in Great Britain* (London, 1917).

League of Nations Society, *Explanation of the Objects of the Society* (Letchworth, 1916).

League of Nations Society Publications, *No. 2. Report of the Meeting of May 14, 1917: No. 16. Proceedings of the First Annual Meeting: No. 18.* A. Williams, *The Minimum of Machinery: No. 19.* R. Unwin, *Functions of a League of Nations* (London, 1917).

Lindsay, A. D. 'The Political Theory of Mr Norman Angell', *The Political Quarterly,* December 1914.

Lindsay, A. D. *Pacifism as a Principle and Pacifism as a Dogma* (London, 1939).

Loreburn, Lord, *How the war came* (London, 1919).

MacDonald, J. R. *Labour and War* (London, 1912).

MacDonald, J. R. *National Defence* (London, 1917).

Martin, H. (Ed.) *The Ministry of Reconciliation* (London, 1916).

Martin, H. (Ed.) *The Christian as Soldier* (London, 1939).

Morel, E. D. *Morocco in Diplomacy* (London, 1912).

Morel, E. D. *Ten Years of Secret Diplomacy* (London, 1912).

Morel, E. D. *Truth and the War* (London, 1916).

Morel, E. D. and Lees-Smith, H. B. *'Foreign Policy' and the People* (London, 1921?).

Morel, E. D. *Military Preparations for the Great War* (London, 1922).

Morel, E. D. *The Secret History of a Great Betrayal* (London, 1923).

Morel, E. D. *The Black Scourge in Europe* (London, 1920).

Murray, G. *The Foreign Policy of Sir Edward Grey* (Oxford, 1915).

Murray, G. *Faith, War and Policy* (London, 1917).

Murray, G. *The League of Nations and the Democratic Idea* (Oxford, 1918).

Murray, G. *The League and its Guarantees* (London, 1920).

Murray, G. *The Problem of Foreign Policy* (London, 1921).

Newbold, J. T. Walton, *How Europe Armed for War* (London, 1916).

Newbold, J. T. Walton, *The War Trust Exposed* (London, 1916).

Newbold, J. T. Walton, *Capitalism and the War* (London, 1918).

'North Briton', *British Freedom, 1914-1917* (London, 1917).

Oman, J. *The War and its Issues* (Cambridge, 1915).

Peake, A. S. *Prisoners of Hope* (London, 1918).

Peel, A. (Ed.) *The Christian and War* (London, 1925).

Perris, G. H. *Our Foreign Policy and Sir Edward Grey's Failure* (London, 1912).

Perris, G. H. *The War Traders* (London, 1913).
Pollard, A. F. *The League of Nations: An Historical Argument* (Oxford, 1918).
Ponsonby, A. *Democracy and the control of foreign affairs* (London, 1912).
Ponsonby, A. *Democracy and Diplomacy* (London, 1915).
Robertson, J. M. and others, *Essays towards peace* (London, 1913).
Royden, A. M. *The Great Adventure* (London, 1915).
Russell, B. *Justice in War Time* (London, 1916).
Russell, B. *Principles of Social Reconstruction* (London, 1916).
Snowden, Viscount, *Dreadnoughts and Dividends* (London, 1914).
Suttner, B. von (Trans. T. Holmes), *Lay Down Your Arms* (London, 1892).
Swanwick, H. M. *New Wars for Old* (London, 1934).
Swanwick, H. M. *Collective Insecurity* (London, 1937).
Willis, I. C. *How we came out of the war* (London, 1921).
Wilson, W. E. *Christ and War* (London, 1913).
Wilson, W. E. *The Foundations of Peace* (London, 1918).
Woolf, L. S. *The Framework of a Lasting Peace* (London, 1917).

SECONDARY WORKS

SECONDARY WORKS
Aron, R. *On War* (London, 1958).
Aron, R. *Peace and War* (London, 1966).
Beales, A. C. F. *The History of Peace* (London, 1931).
Bealey, F. and Pelling, H. *Labour and Politics, 1900-06* (London, 1958).
Bisceglin, L. R. 'N. Angell and the "pacifist" muddle' *Bulletin of the Institute of Historical Research*, XLV (May, 1972).
Bosanquet, H. D. *Free Trade and Peace in the Nineteenth Century* (Oslo, 1924).
Boulton, D. *Objection Overruled* (London, 1967).
Briggs, A. and Saville, J. *Essays in Labour History II* (London, 1971).
Brittain, V. *Rebel Passion* (London, 1964).
Brock, P. *History of Pacifism* (London, 1972).
Bussey, G. and Tims, M. *The Women's International League for Peace and Freedom* (London, 1965).
Byrd, R. O. *Quaker Ways in Foreign Policy* (Toronto, 1960).
Carlton, D. *MacDonald versus Henderson, the foreign policy of the Second Labour Government* (London, 1970).
Carr, E. H. *Conditions of Peace* (London, 1944).
Carr, E. H. *The Twenty Years' Crisis* (London, 1946).
Chamberlain, W. J. *Fighting for Peace* (London, 1929).
Crosby, G. R. *Disarmament and Peace in British Politics, 1914-19* (Cambridge, Mass., 1957).
Dennis, P. *Decision by Default. Peacetime Conscription and British Defence, 1919-39* (London, 1972).
Dowse, R. E. 'The Entry of the Liberals into the Labour Party, 1910-20', *Yorkshire Bulletin of Economic and Social Research*, August 1961.
Dowse, R. E. 'The I.L.P. and Foreign Politics, 1918-23', *The International Review of Social History*, Vol. VII, 1962, Part 1.
Dowse, R. E. *Left in the Centre* (London, 1966).
Dubin, M. D. 'Toward the Concept of Collective Security: The Bryce Group's "Proposals for the Avoidance of War," 1914-1917' *International Organization* XXIV/2, Spring 1970.
Fest, W. B. 'British War Aims and German Peace Feelers during the First World War (December 1916—November 1918).' *The Historical Journal*, XV, 2 (1972).

Field, G. C. *Pacifism and Conscientious Objection* (Cambridge, 1945).
Fischer, F. *Griff nach der Weltmacht. Die Kriegszielpolitik des Kaiserlichen Deutschland, 1914-18* (Düsseldorf, 1961).
Forster, K. *The Failures of Peace* (Washington, 1941).
Fry, A. R. *A Quaker Adventure* (London, 1926).
Gilbert, M. (Ed.) *A Century of Conflict, 1850-1950, Essays for A. J. P Taylor* (London, 1966).
Gottlieb, W. W. *Studies in Secret Diplomacy during the First World War* (London, 1957).
Graham, J. W. *Conscription and Conscience* (London, 1922).
Graubard, S. R. *British Labour and the Russian Revolution, 1917-24* (London, 1956).
Halévy, E. *Imperialism and the Rise of Labour* (London, 1951).
Hanak, H. 'The Union of Democratic Control during the First World War' *Bulletin of the Institute of Historical Research,* November, 1963.
Hancock, W. K. *Four Studies of War and Peace in this Century* (Cambridge, 1961).
Hardy, G. H. *Bertrand Russell and Trinity* (Cambridge, 1970 edn.).
Harland, G. *The Thought of Reinhold Niebuhr* (New York, 1960).
Haupt, G. *Socialism and the Great War* (London, 1972).
Hayes, D. *Conscription Conflict* (London, 1949).
Hazlehurst, C. *Politicians at War* (London, 1971).
Hinsley, F. H. *Power and the Pursuit of Peace* (Cambridge, 1963).
Hinsley, F. H. *Sovereignty* (London, 1966).
Hirst, M. E. *The Quakers in Peace and War* (London, 1923).
Hopkin, D. 'Domestic Censorship in the first world war' *Journal of Contemporary History,* Vol. 5, 4, 1970.
Hudson, D. *The Ecumenical Movement in World Affairs* (London, 1969).
Ingram, K. *Fifty Years of the National Peace Council* (London, 1958).
Johnstone, J. K. *The Bloomsbury Group* (London, 1954).
Jones, A. R. *The Life and Opinions of T. E. Hulme* (London, 1960).
Jones, G. J. *Wales and the Quest for Peace* (Cardiff, 1969).
Jones, R. T. *Congregationalism in England, 1662-1962* (London, 1962).
Kendall, W. *The Revolutionary Movement in Britain, 1900-1921* (London, 1969).
Kernek, S. J. 'The British Government's Reactions to Woodrow Wilson on Questions of Peace, December 1916-November 1918' Cambridge Ph.D. Thesis 1971.
Kernek, S. J. 'The British Government's Reactions to President Wilson's "Peace" Note in December 1916' *The Historical Journal,* XIII, 4 (1970).
Kuehl, W. F. *Seeking World Order, The United States and International Organization to 1920* (Nashville, 1969).
Kurtz, H. 'The Lansdowne Letter', *History Today,* XVIII/2, February 1968.
Lockwood, P. A. 'Milner's Entry into the War Cabinet, December 1916', *The Historical Journal,* VII, 1 (1964).
Louis, W. R. and Stengers, J. E. D. *Morel's History of the Congo Reform Movement* (Oxford, 1968).
Lyman, R. W. 'James Ramsay MacDonald and the Leadership of the Labour Party, 1918-22' *Journal of British Studies,* November 1962.
Lyons, F. S. L. *Internationalism in Europe, 1815-1914* (Leyden, 1963).
Mabbott, J. D. *The State and the Citizen* (London, 1952).
McBriar, A. M. *Fabian Socialism and British Politics, 1884-1918* (Cambridge, 1962).
McCallum, R. B. *Public Opinion and the Last Peace* (London, 1944).

McKibbin, R. I. 'The Evolution of a National Party: Labour's Political Organization, 1910-1924' Oxford D.Phil. Thesis.

Martin, D. A. *Pacifism: an historical and sociological study* (London, 1965).

Martin, J. J. *American Liberalism in World Politics, 1931-1941* (New York, 1964).

Martin, L. W. *Peace without Victory: Woodrow Wilson and the British Liberals* (New Haven, 1958).

Marwick, A. J. B. 'The Independent Labour Party, 1918-32' Oxford B.Litt. Thesis 1960.

Marwick, A. J. B. *The Deluge: British Society and the First World War* (London, 1965).

Mason, C. M. 'British Policy on the Establishment of a League of Nations, 1914-1919' Cambridge Ph.D. Thesis 1970.

Mayer, A. J. *Political Origins of the New Diplomacy, 1917-1918* (New Haven, 1959).

Meyer, D. B. *The Protestant Search for Political Realism, 1919-41* (Berkeley, 1960).

Mews, S. *Religion and English Society in the First World War* (Cambridge, forthcoming).

Miller, D. H. *The Drafting of the Covenant* (New York, 1928).

Mitchell, D. *Women on the Warpath* (London, 1966).

Monger, G. W. *The End of Isolation* (London, 1963).

Morgan, K. O. *Wales in British Politics, 1868-1922* (Cardiff, 1963).

Naylor, J. F. *Labour's International Policy* (London, 1969).

Nef, J. U. *War and Human Progress* (London, 1950).

Nelson, H. I. *Land and Power* (London, 1963).

Newsome, D. *Godliness and Good Learning* (London, 1961).

Niebuhr, R. *An interpretation of Christian Ethics* (London, 1936).

Niebuhr, R. *The Children of Light and the Children of Darkness* (London, 1945).

Nuttall, G. *Christian Pacifism in History* (Oxford, 1958).

Pelling, H. *America and the British Left* (London, 1956).

Pelling, H. *Popular Politics and Society in Late Victorian Britain* (London, 1968).

Peterson, H. C. and Fite, G. C. *Opponents of War, 1917-18* (Wisconsin, 1957).

Playne, C. E. *Society at War 1914-1916* (London, 1931).

Playne, C. E. *Britain Holds On, 1917-1918* (London, 1933).

Pollard, S. *A History of Labour in Sheffield* (Liverpool, 1959).

Pribicevic, B. *The Shop Steward's Movement and Worker's Control, 1910-22* (Oxford, 1959).

Price, R. *An Imperial War and the British Working Class* (London, 1972).

Robbins, K. G. 'Lord Bryce and the First World War', *The Historical Journal*, X, 2 (1967).

Robbins, K. G. 'British Diplomacy and Bulgaria, 1914-1915' *Slavonic and East European Review*, October 1971.

Robbins, K. G. *Sir Edward Grey* (London, 1971).

Robbins, L. *The Economic Causes of War* (London, 1939).

Rodman, B-S. 'Britain Debates Justice: an Analysis of the Reparations Issue of 1918' *Journal of British Studies*, November 1968.

Ropp, T. 'Conscription in Great Britain, 1900-1914: A Failure in Civil-Military Communications? *Military Affairs*, 20, 1956.

Rothwell, V. H. *British War Aims and Peace Diplomacy, 1914-1918* (Oxford, 1971).

Scott, J. D. *Vickers: A History* (London, 1962).

Soffer, R. N. 'New Elitism: Social Psychology in Pre-war England' *Journal of British Studies*, May 1969.

Springhall, J. O. 'The Boy Scouts, Class and Militarism in relation to British Youth Movements, 1908-1930', *International Review of Social History*, Vol. XVI, 1971 Pt. 2.

Stansky, P. *The Left and War* (London, 1969).

Steiner, Z. S. *The Foreign Office and Foreign Policy, 1898-1914* (Cambridge, 1969).

Swanwick, H. M. *Builders of Peace* (London, 1924).

Swartz, M. *The Union of Democratic Control in British Politics during the First World War* (Oxford, 1971).

Taylor, A. J. P. *The Troublemakers: Dissent over Foreign Policy, 1792-1939* (London, 1957).

Taylor, A. J. P. 'Politics in the First World War' *Proceedings of the British Academy* Vol. XLV.

Thornton, A. P. *The Imperial Idea and its enemies* (London, 1959).

Trebilcock, C. 'Legends of the British Armaments Industry, 1890-1914: A Revision', *Journal of Contemporary History*, 5, 4 (1970).

Trevelyan, C. P. *The Union of Democratic Control, its history and its policy* (London, 1919).

Ullman, R. *Intervention and the War* (Princeton, 1961).

Vagts, A. *A History of Militarism* (London, 1959).

Van der Slice, A. *International Labor, Diplomacy and War, 1914-19* (Philadelphia, 1941).

Walker, W. M. 'Dundee's Disenchantment with Churchill' *Scottish Historical Review*, Vol. 49, 1970.

Walters, F. P. *A History of the League of Nations* (London, 1960)

Weinroth, H. 'The British Radicals and the Balance of Power, 1902-14' *The Historical Journal*, XIII, 4, 1970.

Wiener, M. J. *Between Two Worlds: The Political Thought of Graham Wallas* (Oxford, 1971).

Wilson, F. M. *The Origins of the League Covenant* (London, 1928).

Wilson, T. (Ed.) *The Political Diaries of C. P. Scott* (London, 1970).

Winkler, H. R. *The League of Nations Movement in Great Britain, 1914-19* (New Brunswick, N.J., 1952).

Woodward, E. L. *Great Britain and the German Navy* (Oxford, 1935).

Zeman, Z. A. B. *A Diplomatic History of the First World War* (London, 1971).

Abbreviations

B.S.P.	British Socialist Party
F.O.R.	Fellowship of Reconciliation
F.S.C.	Friends Service Committee
I.L.P.	Independent Labour Party
L.F.N.A.	League of Free Nations Association
L.N.S.	League of Nations Society
L.N.U.	League of Nations Union
N.C.A.C.	National Council against Conscription
N.C.C.L.	National Council for Civil Liberties
N.M.W.M.	No More War Movement
N.P.C.	National Peace Council
P.N.C.	Peace Negotiations Committee
P.P.U.	Peace Pledge Union
T.U.C.	Trades Union Congress
U.D.C.	Union of Democratic Control
W.I.L.	Women's International League for Peace and Freedom

Index